Make Us D

The Story of Liverpool's 2013/14 Season

Make Us Dream

The Story of Liverpool's 2013/14 Season

Neil Atkinson and John Gibbons

deCoubertin
B O O K S

Published by deCoubertin Books Ltd in 2014.
deCoubertin Books, 145-157 St John Street, London, EC1V 4PY
www.decoubertin.co.uk

First edition.

ISBN: 978-1-909245-21-1

A CIP catalogue record for this book is available from the British Library.

Designed in Liverpool.

Cover design by David Williams.
Printed and bound by CPI Group (UK) Ltd, Croydon, CR0 4YY

FOREWORD

by Ben Smith

WHERE DO YOU START? How do you begin to sum up a season of a thousand dazzling images and a dozen 'I was there' moments with words and words alone?

This was no ordinary football season. This was the season when everything changed. The season when the status quo, at least to some degree, went out of the window and the pre-season predictions were being torn up by November. This was the season that blew through the English game like a breath of fresh air. The season when daring, adventurous football made an audacious comeback and the season when everyone associated with Liverpool Football Club found hope, and with it power and effectiveness and purpose and direction. And I am not talking about the incredible results or the records that tumbled relentlessly, nor am I talking about the statistics or the style and swagger with which the team played. I'm talking about something much more important than that, something that returned to Anfield this season, something that you won't see on a league table, or read in a newspaper. It was something I felt every time I went to Anfield to write or broadcast this incredible story, in fact, it was something I felt every time I was in the city. You could see it in people's faces, hear it in their laughter.

That same feeling came flooding back to me when I read the vivid and vibrant writing in this wonderful, passionate book. Because what leaps off the pages and what Neil Atkinson, John Gibbons and all their many esteemed contributors capture so brilliantly in what you are about to read is the feeling of reclamation, the feeling of a city and a football club finding harmony. The feeling that for the first time in a long time, Liverpool felt like a club at peace once again, a club buoyed by belief not burdened by fear or pressure. The defeats of Arsenal, Manchester City and Spurs were, of course, significant moments. But what comes through in this book is that it was the defeat of the darkness and back-biting which has engulfed the club over the past decade that may ultimately prove the most important one of all. Liverpool burned away that darkness and let in the light with the way they played, with the enjoyment they brought back to Anfield.

Neil and John lived and breathed every moment of it. They talked about it, fought about it, they wrote about it and ranted about it (as listeners to *The Anfield Wrap* podcast will testify). They were there when it mattered and when it didn't. As a result, the story they have chronicled with such contagious passion is as compelling as it is instructive. It tells the story of a season that will stand the test of time, in such a way that ensures this book will stand with it. From a memorable pre-season which culminated at the mythical MCG in Melbourne to explosive and exhilarating victories at Anfield, the story of the season is told in a way that the mainstream media simply couldn't match. The depth, the insight, the love, the stories, the humour. This is a book that gives words to the memories, it is a bible of what really happened, how people really felt, what the fans said to each other in the pub, what it meant to go to the game, to enjoy and endure it. You'll know what I mean when you read Neil's review of Liverpool's trip to Craven Cottage. It touches on every key moment, on and off the pitch, in a way that is utterly comprehensive and forensic.

This book has been written with heart and head. There is insight, there are brilliant and witty observations, there are love letters, there are moments of despair and disappointment. There is wide-eyed awe at Luis Suárez's exhilarating blend of grace and devastation – the magician from Montevideo, with feet as sensitive as a pick-pocket's hands. And delight at the way Liverpool poured forward time after time, scattering opposition shirts like laundry torn from a washing line. There are tears too, tears of pain, tears that the dream was snatched away and tears of pride. History weighs heavy at Anfield, it always has and always will – the present cannot exist without the past. But this was the season that Brendan Rodgers took Liverpool back to the future and created a feeling that this is now a football club ready to create new history. It no longer feels that Liverpool's past is holding it back.

After the final match of the season against Newcastle at Anfield, Rodgers walked back to his office to be with his family. He was asked when he had known the title had gone. Was it Steven Gerrard's slip against Chelsea? 'No, no,' he said. 'I knew when Jordan got sent off against Man City. I knew I couldn't replace him. But it's gone now. All that matters to me is that we made them dream.'

These pages carry those hopes and dreams. What a title race. What a season.

Ben Smith, June 2014

MELBOURNE VICTORY 0 LIVERPOOL 2

24 July 2013.
Goals: Gerrard 32', Aspas 90'

HITCH YOUR STAR TO THIS WAGON

THE SCORELINE ISN'T THE RELEVANT FIGURE. It never is in pre-season friendlies anyway. But on this day it is especially irrelevant. Ninety-five thousand people is relevant; 95,446 to be exact. That many went to the MCG to watch Liverpool play Melbourne Victory.

It's a lot of people.

It is a mind-boggling number of people.

Australia boggled the mind. Not because of anything particularly Australian. Indeed, I was struck by exactly how unstereotypically Australian they were in both Melbourne and Sydney, which is patently ridiculous and probably insulting. People have a habit of being people everywhere. I presented three shows there and each was so warmly received. In front of every crowd I was struck by how overwhelmingly happy people were to have us. How welcome they made us. How much they wanted to hear about football.

Australia boggled the mind because of the people getting involved. Involved in football. Involved in the culture around it. Ninety-five thousand people singing 'You'll Never Walk Alone'. What felt like the whole of Melbourne wearing red.

Nine hundred and fifty came to our show the night before 95,000 descended on the MCG. They threw themselves in. They'd thrown themselves in before we even got there. They were drenched in Liverpool football and Liverpool culture. They wanted more and more of it.

What's interesting about the intensity of Liverpool's popularity is that for four years we hadn't been very good. And for the time that came before that we had been very good only sporadically. I think the cultural aspect is part of what has helped sustain Liverpool in the collective imagination the world over. Liverpool means things that Arsenal, Chelsea, Manchester City and the rest just don't. Perhaps can't. Cities are strange things, the ones that grab people, even if they have never been there, and the ones that don't. New York City means more to the world than Los Angeles despite the latter controlling and producing the bulk of American culture consumed in the 21st century. Barcelona is more romantic than Madrid. Venice destroys Milan. St Petersburg overshadows Moscow.

We get to play at being that cultural aspect. We get to bring bands, tell jokes, talk about a city. Make football as large and inclusive and bold as it can be. We get to do all that because people, these unstereotypical and real Australians, have created the space for it in their own heads. We get there and they are teaching us their songs, the songs they have created about the football team and the city they love. They are so excited. So excitable. It's their football club. It's their city. Liverpool Football Club doesn't exist to win trophies. It doesn't even have to be very good. It exists to represent the city and those who wish to hitch their star to its wagon.

Ninety-five thousand people in Melbourne wanted to hitch their star to its wagon.

Craig Johnston helps. Being the first Australian to really make his name in football and to do so at Liverpool during the club's most golden era helps all the more. Craig Johnston, charisma and curls. And quality.

It helped us that Craig Johnston was involved in all three shows. And all Craig Johnston wanted to talk about was Luis Suárez. How much he loved Luis Suárez. The oceans he'd cross for Luis Suárez. What Luis Suárez represented. All the winning. Craig Johnston's wagon was well and truly hitched.

The following night at the MCG Steven Gerrard genuinely celebrated his opening goal. I wonder how much it mattered to him. It looked like it mattered. The biggest crowd he has ever played in front of and he scored. He celebrated it. This is important. In my mind, very important. Correlation isn't causation.

I was in awe. I wanted to hitch my star to their wagon. I looked at the MCG, at the thousands, virtually one hundred thousand. I thought about Liverpool's friendly in Indonesia with its remarkable Iron Lady banner created in memory of Anne Williams. I thought about Liverpool's friendly in Thailand to come. A city come to claim its own half way around the world and I was in awe. What a thing to be part of.

We go and do those things, the talking aloud, and people don't come to see us. They come for something much bigger than that. They'd rather be in Anfield every week. They want to be close to the team, they want to be close to that shrine behind the Kop goal. They want that sense of belonging. Liverpool let anyone in. Liverpool should let anyone in. All we can ask is the love of team and city. It's a simple thing. There's a purity to it.

I think about the Indonesia leg of the tour just gone and I think about Thailand leg to come and I think about the 950 who came the night before, the 95,000 who were there on the night and my heart soars.

I recognise that this isn't the smooth opening article a book like this demands. I recognise that. But when the mind boggles it doesn't unboggle. It doesn't undo itself and then make coherent sense again. Everything started here in a sense. I thought about all these people with their 4 a.m. kick-off times and their supporters' clubs all season. All season I thought about the magic they were getting. All season I thought they'd played their part. Started something in some way. Correlation isn't causation, of course it isn't, but these people reminded Liverpool FC of something, I think. They reminded Liverpool FC of something it looked to have forgotten.

You are a big noise. You are the most romantic club in world football. You are the business.

You are serious. It is here and it is now and you are serious.

We came back. We spread the word. It's bananas in Australia, mate. Those lads and girls know what they are about. We get to go every week and they get up at 4 a.m. and think we're the business.

We'd best be it then.

No backward steps.

Neil Atkinson

CELTIC 1 LIVERPOOL 0

10 August 2013.
Goals: Baldé 12'

ANOTHER CRAZY WIN

WE'D BEEN TO IRELAND BEFORE. In the February just past we said we were doing a live *Anfield Wrap* show in Dublin and then announced it was in Bray. Every Liverpool fan in Ireland tweeted us saying Bray wasn't in Dublin. Like the cocky so-and-so's we are we did our first talking out loud in a 500-capacity venue (in a place no one wanted to go to). As someone who has played in bands most of my adult life I did try and explain how hard it was to sell out even a 100-capacity venue. No one seemed interested, although we did take Guillem Balague, Tony Evans and The Tea Street Band with us just in case. It sold out. It was a wonderful, improbable night. We made loads of new mates.

So I was less concerned when we decided we would go back to Ireland, to Dublin proper this time, to coincide with the Liverpool vs Celtic friendly at the Aviva Stadium. We went over on the Friday and got hammered. Saturday morning we got up and played the almost traditional (does twice count as a tradition?) game of football against the Irish Reds. We got beat again, although it was closer this time. We're better at the talking.

Then we went to the venue of the show. It quickly became apparent that this

11

was a very different space to the last occasion. Bray was a conference room, all seated, which meant slightly organised chaos. This was a night club, all standing and loads of pillars, which meant potential bedlam. I was concerned again. I worry. Others told me not to worry. I started drinking. Most of the group went the game. Myself and Neil stayed behind to make sure everything was OK for the bands, although we did watch the game upstairs. I can't remember much of the match, to be honest. I remember we were rubbish, and I remember we couldn't live with Baldé. Oh well, at least that was the last time that season we struggled to cope with a physical centre forward.

We then went to a bar round the corner to put the finishing touches to the show. I'm not going to tell you any more about the place, because, frankly, I don't want you all to ruin it. It's an improbably good bar so close to the nonsense that is Temple Bar on one of the busiest streets in Ireland. The music, the people, the beer were all perfect. It was so good we almost forgot what we were there for. I just hope it's still there in all its all glory when we go back.

The show itself was mad, a mixture of *Anfield Wrap* fans who wanted tactical analysis of the game and lads who had been drinking all day and just wanted to party. It was tough to work out who outnumbered who. I tried to bridge the gap by singing Philippe Coutinho songs. Everyone joined in. Tony Evans was great talking about 1983/84 for those who could hear with the struggling sound. Dion Fanning played the part of glass-half-empty pessimist with vigour. Kevin Sampson showed drunken disdain for the concept of a microphone. Neil managed to keep us all on the runaway mine train long enough to reach the end.

After certain things had been added (me acting out famous goal celebrations) and others had been abandoned (half the agenda) we finished and the bands came on. The Hummingbirds came on and loads of attractive girls appeared. Where were they for Rob Gutmann on Jordan Henderson? Ian Prowse came on and serenaded us with Celtic songs of love and war. The Tea Street Band came on and smashed everyone's head off. Then I played music until I was aggressively told to pack it in by the owner.

What I find interesting about looking back at these events is that they remind me of where we were at that time and the belief, or otherwise, of the fan base. The first trip came just after the January transfer window we were yet to know the full benefit of. The questions and conversations I remember that night were all, not unreasonably, of whether Brendan Rodgers had the experience to lead a side like Liverpool, and whether he was the right man to undertake the mammoth job in hand. By the summer I remember those I spoke to being more positive, but there was still debate over how much the team had genuinely progressed since Dalglish had been replaced, and whether the Champions League was a realistic target.

In the end I think we just about finished up that night. It wasn't a one-sided victory by any stretch of the imagination. By away-performance standards it was more Cardiff 3 Liverpool 6 than Tottenham Hotspur 0 Liverpool 5. But we're in the results business at the end of the day, and we left with more tales than hangovers. Another crazy win.   **John Gibbons**

LUIS SUÁREZ TELLS THE WORLD HE WANTS TO LEAVE LIVERPOOL...

... AND IT MAKES NO ODDS.

I understand why people think Suárez saying publicly he wants to leave matters. I understand the recourse to emotion. That's the aim.

When he ran on against Olympiakos in Gerrard's testimonial at Anfield, Suárez may have been surprised by the warmth of the response. I suspect his agent was. I suspect it made him think, we've got to do something about this. We need these people to barrack him. We need to do an interview which separates him from them. This is the next step. It is the only step. We need to do something to bring this move about.

Let's go all the way. He wants to go. The problem is ...

It makes no odds.

It's a manipulative move. By player, by agent. But it is merely saying publicly what has been said privately to the club. It is the explicit articulation of a number of implicit leaked nuggets to newspapermen. You knew Luis Suárez wanted to go. You know he really wants to go. He wants to play at the highest level and currently Liverpool cannot offer that.

It makes no odds.

The crux of it isn't unreasonable. This is where we are. We end this forthcoming season four years and six months on from our last Champions League fixture. Luis Suárez is, in my view, the best attacking footballer in the world who doesn't currently play for Barcelona or Real Madrid. He ought to have the opportunity to play at that level. His talent isn't wasted at Liverpool – it's appreciated like nothing on earth. It's a glorious, marvellous, rambunctious thing which we have loved for two and a half seasons now. It should be showcased in European Cup finals as Zidane's and Messi's, Dalglish's and Di Stéfano's has been.

It makes no odds.

The player is under contract at Liverpool. Now presuming that the clause doesn't oblige Liverpool to accept anything (and this had better be the case or Liverpool's competence question is only going to go nuclear), the reality is that Liverpool choose whether he stays or goes. Liverpool choose what to do with an offer of £40m plus one pound. Liverpool choose.

Liverpool have chosen.

The situation is that Liverpool's challenge for a finish fourth or higher is easier if Luis Suárez doesn't play for anyone this season than if he plays for Arsenal and Liverpool have £50m to spend. This is the reality. This is where we are as well. What stuns me is that Arsenal haven't offered 60 or 70 million for the player. Because any amount he is worth to Liverpool he is worth that plus 10 million to Arsenal. He is the player who would cement them in the top four barring catastrophe. He is the player who would make them genuine contenders.

But it would make no odds.

A sale to Arsenal is suicide for a Liverpool that has spent four years dangerously close to coma, though finally showing serious signs of fight. This is a serious sign of fight, the second half of last season, a serious sign of fight. Selling Suárez would be switching the life-support machine off. A sale to Madrid slightly less so, but still gives Liverpool a huge question as to how they effectively spend any money. How effectively they can spend the money. Without being able to offer …

… and on we go.

I love the expression 'it makes no odds'. What exactly does it mean? It doesn't make that much sense in theory but your mouth has a symmetry as it says it. It's what not being impressed sounds like. It's your mouth shrugging.

It's the response. The only response to this tantrum.

Garments shouldn't be rent, hair should remain in the scalp, tears shouldn't be shed and shirts should remain uncharred.

Let's not give anyone what they want. No heat. No light. No shouting. Just a collective 'It makes no odds, lad'.

Neil Atkinson

LIVERPOOL 1 STOKE CITY 0

17 August 2013.
Goals: Daniel Sturridge 37'

CHAMPIONS ELECT

OPENING DAY IS THE BEST. Anything could happen from here. I always get ridiculously optimistic, but why not? In theory every team has an equal chance before a ball is kicked, no one has lost yet, everyone has the same points. Of course, in practice, some are more equal than others, but for now it's all to play for. Maybe Hull will win the first five. Maybe Chelsea will get relegated. Maybe we will win EVERY game. It's unlikely, but it's still possible. That's the beauty of opening day.

Of course, in recent years Liverpool have had a habit of quickly crushing this pre-season positivity. We had only won one of our previous ten opening-day fixtures. You'd go into the ground dreaming of league titles and walk out wondering if you could hibernate until next August and start again with loads of new lads you could pin your hopes on. We're already behind them lot, and we'll never catch them now.

Two of those last ten opening games particularly stick in my mind for providing a journey from optimism to depression in 90 minutes flat. The first is Sheffield United away in 2006/07. The season before, we had finished the league campaign with 82 points and won the FA Cup. It was logical to expect that the next step for Benítez's gang of achievers was a genuine title charge. But when the team came through at Bramall Lane, we suddenly didn't look particularly strong, and we needed a disputed penalty to draw the game.

The second is Sunderland at home in 2011/12. Liverpool had been brilliant in the second half of the season before under Dalglish, showing genuine top-four form and scoring a tonne of goals in the process. We'd spent heavily in the summer and it felt to everyone that we were set for a new adventure, under new owners and with the most popular man in the club's history at the helm. Sunderland at home seemed a perfect game to get the season off to a flier, but after starting well Liverpool could only draw again. Same old Liverpool.

You might argue that the opening fixture shouldn't be the be-all and end-all. There are 37 games left to turn it round, and plenty of teams have won things after shaky starts, or started brightly and gone down. But not really Liverpool, in the Premier League era at least. Both of the opening games I have discussed were ominous signs of the season to come. The 2006/07 team struggled all season away from home, losing the next away fixture 3–0 to Everton and only winning once in the league away from Anfield before the beginning of December. In contrast the Sunderland result at the start of 2011/12 was the first of nine league draws at Anfield that season, as the team became specialists in dominating for long periods of play, missing chances, and allowing the opposition back in the game once heads had gone down and Charlie Adam couldn't run.

But the last time we won an opening fixture, this time away at Sunderland in 2008/09, was the last time we mounted a significant title challenge, so maybe the omens are with us this time. Yes, we only won 1–0, and we weren't particularly great, but we won 1–0 without playing that well at Sunderland too. That time Torres, this time Sturridge. New heroes, new hope.

You don't need to be that great opening week. It's about the win. It's about not being behind the leaders already. It's about keeping that daft pre-season optimism going for another week. No one has beaten us yet. Maybe no one will. Maybe we'll win the lot. You can't tell me it definitely won't happen. We're gonna win the league.

John Gibbons

A P E N A L T Y S A V E

ONE OF THE KEY THEMES in David Peace's brilliant, bewildering novel *Red or Dead* is monotony.

Through Bill Shankly, Peace explores the essential sameness of football, the relentless, inevitable, intense orderliness enshrined in the game's very structure.

You do the same things, in the same ways, at roughly the same cities and towns. You could be doing them for the rest of your life. This is your life.

At least managers and players are getting paid.

The means by which football takes over their lives, our lives, and much of our national life is the league. Until the Football League, it was Old Etonians and Royal Engineers and Everton messing about in the FA Cup or playing in loosely-structured local competitions.

We didn't even bother forming till the league was four years old, having given it a decent chance to bed in. In their first season in the first Division, Liverpool played Aston Villa, Sunderland and West Brom. They also played Stoke.

Stoke have become the living embodiment of the league and what it does to you. You accept Stoke. You get Stoked. You bow your head, write it off as a bad job, explain away dropped points because it's Stoke. Since they came back up it's always been Stoke.

In July, when the pattern of your life until the following May is roughly laid out for you, you see Stoke and you dread Stoke. You worry for your new signings, you panic about what forwards who score roughly once every six games will do against the fragile hothouse flowers who suddenly seem to make up your central defence.

And this season, it's Stoke first. Not buried somewhere in November when we've already drifted out of contention, but straight away, in the daytime, at lunchtime, before anyone else kicks a ball.

Stoke have a new manager, are aiming to be different, sick of the sight even of themselves. But we know they'll still be Stoke, and they are. They compete. They go long. They understand refereeing better than any official yet born, better than the chip in the ball, better than a team of Hawkeyes. They get in our heads.

We worry for Iago Aspas, his slight frame seemingly at odds with the challenge we face. But he plays his part in the number 10 role, drifting between the liniest lines in the league.

The other concern is Simon Mignolet. Our new goalkeeper looks nervy. His kicking in the first half is poor, an anxious Kop at his back feeding off his discomfort.

Nobody feels secure. Nobody expected to - we're playing Stoke. Daniel Sturridge settles an argument from 20 yards with a beautifully pure strike, but we're still unmistakeably playing Stoke.

Peter Crouch is a worry. Kolo Toure looks imperious against a side with little pace to hurt him. Mignolet makes a fine diving save. Liverpool pass away the minutes, retaining possession and appearing composed. Then Daniel Agger handles in the box. This will be a draw. The house always wins.

And yet this time, this year, it doesn't. The house doesn't win, the league doesn't win, monotony does not win. Mignolet saves the penalty, and saves the follow-up. He immediately gets on with organising his defence for the resulting corner.

We have three points. Stoke have none. It took a Sturridge shot and a Mignolet save. In however many moments you get in 90 minutes, we had the best two, the two that mattered.

Walking back to town, the routine rhythm of the season interrupted already, tables are checked and pictures are tweeted. As everybody else kicks off, Liverpool are top of the league. Isn't it funny? By a quirk of scheduling, we're top of the league. Hahaha. Enjoy it while you can, lads. Enjoy it while you can.

We can.

Gareth Roberts

THE BUZZ

PAUL COPE SAID TO ME: 'Listened to your Melbourne podcast. And I just thought, yeah. We should enjoy it. It should be great. It used to be. We get to go and do this and all we do is act like it ruins our day whereas people around the world would kill to do this every week. Well, let's start fucking enjoying it. I'm going to have a great season.'

Rob Gutmann said to me: 'I'll take the scrappiest 1–0 from Stoke. The scrappiest.'

I said to him: 'I think we need a statement-of-intent display. A performance. Houllier or Benítez seasons can start scrappy but this Liverpool side did its best stuff in style last season.'

Against Stoke, we got scrappy. We got a statement of intent. We got both.

Liverpool were terrific at times. Fluid and intelligent. Lucas and Gerrard held court in centre mid. Coutinho shining like a national guitar. Aspas lithe. Sturridge splendid then brave. Kolo Touré became a man we'd follow to the very jaws of hell. Then they tired without the second they deserved. They had to fight. The side was painfully let down by the vice-captain before Mignolet got us all out of jail.

Mirror football journalist John Cross was channelling Emmylou Harris on Twitter. He described the Liverpool collective as 'The city of forgiveness where everyone bar the unfaithful lover is to blame'. John, you need to get up here. We aren't anywhere near as romantic as that these days. We spend our time fighting the darkness that hacks at our heels every year and being tainted by that fight. But at our best these days there's a noisy, gnarled defiance that I love. Nothing says Liverpool like a communal 'fuck off, you'. Loud, while through gritted teeth. Watch the last 20 minutes of Chelsea at home in 2005 again. Spurs home 2010. City in the 2012 League Cup semi. Just fuck off, you.

The sheer fuckoffed-ness in the aftermath of Mignolet's penalty save was glorious. Liverpool's day was saved. Our day was saved. It was the sound of 40,000 days saved. The sound of 40,000 days saved times 19. Times 38. How many days can one save save? The darkness of Martin Skrtel against City, combined with the Dempsey cock-up and the Arsenal debacle, all that darkness let in last season wasn't being let through the door against Stoke.

The darkness that was Hodgson, Hodgson endless Hodgson, that was Skrtel and Carragher breaking each other's face, that was Charlie Adam running round in centre mid shattered and apologetic after 60, wasn't darkening these parts. Just fuck off. Fuck off with that. We don't want that taint. Not this year. We won't have it again. It's taken too much of a toll. We won't stand for it. We were roaring because it was kept at bay and because we need to keep it at bay. Liv-er-pool belted out by all quarters because that is who we are, for better or worse. Liv-er-pool, fuck-off, you.

And so we were all out. We all had a great day. A great Saturday with laughs and shrugs and songs and drinks and jokes. We were buzzing. So let's keep buzzing. Let's all come together to build some massive defences against the darkness that dogs us. We aren't good enough to assume it won't grab at us. But we all have to work at it. We are good enough to keep shaking it off. We owe it to each other around the world not to acquiesce to it any more. We need to keep buzzing. While we are buzzing we can see the darkness off. We can block it out with laughs and shrugs and songs and drinks and jokes.

Saw Cope. He said someone started moaning near him after three minutes. He felt a bit sorry for him. That bloke needs to get with it. Look at them. They suddenly could be a red gang again. Not yet a squad but a gang. I want to be one of Kolo's Heroes. I want Steven's lime green boots. I want Lucas to stick up for me against a million grocks.

Saturday sits on my shoulder. I want it today and tomorrow and a week on Wednesday. I want it 37 more times. People'd kill to do this every week.

Neil Atkinson

ASTON VILLA 0 LIVERPOOL 1

24 August 2013.
Goals: Sturridge 21'

DANIEL STURRIDGE

DANIEL STURRIDGE FINISHED THE 2012/13 SEASON with 11 goals in 16 games, or 10 in 14 league games, a start to his Liverpool career which compared favourably with any of the renowned strikers to have played for the club. There were some complaints at the time that such an explosive start didn't get the recognition it deserved, but I think it was reasonably understandable. Nationally the press aren't going to pay much attention to a Sturridge-led surge from tenth (when he signed) to seventh – even when some of the football was so easy on the eye – when there are far more noteworthy things happening at either end of the table.

Even for Liverpool supporters there wasn't much of a clamour to laud the achievement, for the simple reason that even relatively young fans have experienced seasons with success, seasons with trophies, seasons that ultimately mattered. In football all goals are equal, but some are more equal than others. Stan Collymore scored 35 goals for Liverpool and I can remember about three of them (and one of those was a freak bobble). Luis Garcia scored 30 and I reckon I can have a good go at naming the lot.

Through no fault of his own, Sturridge came to us at a time that was more

21

Collymore's era than Garcia's, and it's the goals in big seasons that really mean something to fans. For all the nonsense reasons given for why Sturridge wasn't as instantly loved by the Kop as he might have been, it was rarely acknowledged that we've seen tonnes of great players during far better times. Most Liverpool fans were largely willing to accept 2012/13 as a transition season, but it was hard to get particularly excited about anything going on within it when it ends in finishing seventh. It's all a bit 'and what?'

Saying all that, I do wonder what Daniel Sturridge must have been thinking in the summer of 2013 when the Suárez circus was in full steam. When Liverpool's season seemed to hinge on Suárez staying or leaving he must have felt like saying, 'Don't worry, lads, I'm really good at the scoring.' Even when Suárez decided to stay, all the talk was of how they would cope in the first six games without him, everyone seemingly ignoring again the lad who was really good at the scoring.

But if Sturridge was annoyed, he let his feet do the talking. Any frustration he might have had was leathered into the winner at Stoke. If his first of the season was a sledgehammer, his second was a sculpture. After a lovely dummy from Coutinho, the type that never usually come off but lead to a lot of thumbs up afterwards, it was all Sturridge's magic feet. Later in the season he spoke to *The Anfield Wrap* about how, when he plays at his instinctive best, he has to watch his goals back to see what he actually did. He would have enjoyed seeing what he did against Villa, dancing round defenders and firing into the roof of the net with Guzan helpless.

I think it was that game when Sturridge went from top player to match winner in many eyes. Or maybe it was just in mine. The season was two games old and, notwithstanding other good performances, he had won both on his own and it wouldn't be long before he was doing it again. Maybe we wouldn't miss Suárez as much as we thought we would those first six games. Although I reckon Danny would have told you that all along.

John Gibbons

BENTEKE EVERYWHERE

Liverpool 1 Aston Villa 3 – 15 December 2012. Liverpool crumbled to a defeat under an aerial bombardment. Christian Benteke bossed Liverpool into submission. He wasn't the first to do this. Far from it.

Benteke, and the Bentekes, are terrifying. Physical centre forwards change football matches. It isn't as simple as winning a few headers. It's the pace, the disruption, the aggression. But also the touch. Everyone used to laugh about Crouch being described as having a good touch for a big man. The reality is that footballers playing centre forward at this level tend to have an excellent touch. You don't get this far without it.

Benteke, and the Bentekes, have always been kryptonite to Liverpool defences I've watched with the exception of those helmed by Sami Hyypia. Hyypia wasn't impervious to good footballers putting themselves about – no one can be. But he improved Liverpool markedly overnight, and progressively for years.

Aston Villa 1 Liverpool 2 – 31 March 2013. Liverpool got battered first half. Benteke was everywhere. Second half they came out and played. They played and played and Villa couldn't cope. They got themselves ahead and Villa came with a late bombardment against us but we held out.

Aston Villa 0 Liverpool 1 – 24 August 2013. And nothing. Liverpool dominated the first half against Villa, Sturridge did marvellous things. And at the other end – one chance for Benteke. One half-shout for a penalty. No panic. No battering. No disturbance. Yes, Liverpool sat deep second half but they never felt anywhere near as stressed and stretched.

Kolo Touré.

Kolo had turned up, told the world and the dressing room they could win the league. Told everyone how magnificent they were. Told them they were leaders and men and footballers. They seemed to have more fun. Gerrard in brightly coloured boots and with a beard. He gave the club the boost a two-time league-winning player can give. He wasn't jaded, he was genuinely pleased to be here. Liverpool was a privilege, not a chore. These players weren't limited, they were limitless. Kolo was the first to say in one sense, 'We are Liverpool. Tra-la-la-la-la.'

And then he played against Stoke.

Kolo against Stoke was magnificent. Crouch couldn't get near the football match, Liverpool were well marshalled and tight. And then Kolo attacked. A red streak charging forward in a straight line. The move broke down. Kolo charged back. A red streak charging backwards in a straight line. Stoke punted the ball upfield. Kolo headed it clear. The Kop cheered, sang his name, and Kolo clapped back.

Benteke was beaten back by the Liverpool led by Touré. If Touré didn't win the first ball, he pressed the second. He wasn't interested in being dominated. Benteke's only a fella, he seemed to be saying. He's only one guy. We can deal with this. After the game he got a special ovation from the away contingent. They loved him and he loved them, giving the impression every weekend he had spent not playing for them had been a weekend wasted.

He came, he played, he was larger than life. He was prepared to be larger than life.

There's a simplicity to his impact. He never hit the heights of these two league games again. But on and off the pitch he talked. Some stories need big characters to introduce them. The start of our tale is glorified by Sturridge. The start of our tale is antagonised by Suárez. But the start of our tale is defined not by a heroic goalkeeper, nor an inspirational captain, but by an Ivorian who knew what the business was about and spread, through word and deed, the idea that the business could be done.

Neil Atkinson

LIVERPOOL 4 NOTTS COUNTY 2

27 August 2013.
Goals: Sterling 4', Sturridge 29', 105', Henderson 110'; Arquin 62', Coombes 84'

THE EXUBERANCE OF YOUTH

I ENJOY THE MUCH-MALIGNED LEAGUE CUP. It's cheap for a start, which will always appeal to my frugal nature. The dearest ticket for this game was £20 and kids could get in for a fiver. These prices mean you get a lot of younger fans at the game, which makes a nice change from old fellas moaning down your ear, although I'm sure having to repeatedly get up because a young lad needs the toilet/wants a hot dog/both would wear pretty thin eventually too. The away fans are miles better, selling out whole ends and actually acting like they are enjoying themselves. It had been over 20 years since we'd played league games against Notts County, so many of their fans would have been visiting for the first time, with a spring in their step, at least until they saw the dreadful view you get from the back of the Anfield Road. Excitement to be at football can be sniffed out by the 'too cool for school', seen it all before crowd, but I'll take it over miserable class traitors from other Northern towns singing 'Sign On' at you any day of the week.

Mostly though I look forward to watching the emerging talent at our club. I've never understood those who demand a full-strength team for the early rounds of the cup. I watch them lads every week. But I'm not quite enough of an anorak to go to under-21 games yet, and my girlfriend has firmly decided we watch 'quite enough of that football' in the house for me to get away with 90 minutes of Norwich under-21s away, so this is it for me. A chance to either be baffled why someone isn't getting more of a go in the league, or slowly realise why they weren't even making the bench. Either way, we'd have fun finding out.

Team-wise it was the first chance to have a proper look at Alberto and Cissokho, although the latter would last only ten minutes before getting injured. I was also looking forward to seeing Wisdom at centre half, although due to the make-up of the bench that only lasted ten minutes too before he was shifted to full back for Daniel Agger. But perhaps the most intriguing starters were the wide duo of Raheem Sterling and Jordan Ibe. It's almost impossible to imagine at the time of writing, as the season draws to its close, but at that point some were suggesting Ibe might have moved ahead of Sterling in the pecking order, after a terrific cameo last game of the season against Queens Park Rangers and some very assured performances in pre-season. Even if this wasn't quite the case, it still made for an intriguing battle between the two.

If this was a straight shoot-out for the title of most likely to emerge, Raheem Sterling fired first, scoring after four minutes. It was the type of goal he'd scored many times on his way through the age groups, moving past players at will and finding space for a shot, but had not managed up to then for the first team. With the goal coming so early it is hard to know if this changed the way the wide players played, but they certainly seemed to decide the direct approach was the way forward after that.

Another reason to favour young players in games like this is that they just try harder. Keen to impress or excited to play in front of a big crowd, they will run harder than an older pro who has one eye on the weekend league fixture and is slightly concerned by the enthusiasm of the opposition tackling. However, young players can often try too hard, and that is what seemed to happen to Sterling and Ibe in this game. In their determination to recreate Sterling's early goal that had seemed all too easy, they were frequently on the ball a touch too long, trying to take on one extra man, rather than looking to shift it quickly. It was frustrating given how easily we carved open their defence for the second goal that such flowing football wasn't attempted more often. It must have been very frustrating for Daniel Sturridge, who found more open space than ball.

But these can be tough games for inexperienced players, who often seem to struggle to work out the level they are playing at. They know they are better than other players their age, they know Premier League football is a massive step up from that, but whereabouts do Notts County sit on that scale? Sterling's early goal seemed to convince him and Ibe this was similar to what they were used to, but their defenders were much more streetwise, and wouldn't be fooled again, despite multiple attempts.

In the end it was a more experienced young player, Jordan Henderson, who came off the bench to seal the game for Liverpool with a schoolyard goal of his own. The difference was he recognised when the move was on, extra time bringing tired legs to defenders who had given their all. The fact that it went to extra time could be seen as ammunition for the 'play the best team' brigade, but I disagree. A good mix allows young players to experience genuine first-team situations, and they will have benefited from the experience. But what of Alberto? I just remember him looking perplexed by the whole thing. Perhaps, of this type of football, he had much more learning to do.

John Gibbons

TWELVE-NIL

'I'D RATHER WIN A LEAGUE GAME 12–0 than win the League Cup this season.'

Tony Evans is furious. He's spluttering with rage. Rory Smith is laughing. Refereeing. 'Don't interrupt, Tony, you had your say.'

'And I'll have it again. The youth of today.'

We're at the christening of Francesca Heaton, in an Ormskirk pub. The congregation are an eclectic bunch and Andy Heaton (who produces loads of our material and will be a recurring character through this book) has told me emphatically there must be no shop talk. I'm with Steve Graves and Kate Forrester, Rory and his partner Kate, Brockle and Tony. All there is is shop talk. It's a room of people obsessed with shop. It's a room full of people who do nothing but talk.

Evans: 'You get to show London who's boss.'

It fascinates me, this. I know what Tony's referring to. A late-70s, 80s feeling of going down to London, acting, looking, being cock of the walk. Cream of the crop. Staying over, having a great night, an adventure. Saying to them, we are this wonderful, beautiful, brightly coloured thing that you can never be.

But currently there are two issues with this:

1.   We aren't cream of the crop.
2.   I don't care what London thinks of us. I really, really don't.

The first of these is more straightforward. So let's talk about the second first. Sitting here with these erstwhile gentlemen of the press, The Times of London no less, it occurs to me, though I don't say it, that showing off in front of London leaves me cold. The game's global now, not national, not European. Global. And while the League Cup might have a global audience, while Liverpool will always have a global element, the London aspect does nothing for me. I'd rather go mad in the city of Liverpool after we've scored twelve than mooch round whatever disconnected borough of the capital we end up in in London, always thinking the party is better somewhere else. I don't care about impressing those there or rubbing it in their faces. I'd rather the cup finals weren't played in a fraudulent, Pharisaic capital. Our football isn't their business. We don't even need to be defiant; we're self-confident enough in Liverpool now not to need to impress.

I don't hate London, though I do hate what it does to this country, I just don't care about it. It is theirs. It is other. They have their things – gross inequality and Nick Robinson, for instance – and we have ours. Come to ours. Come. We have shop. We have talk. An endless supply. You'll have much more fun.

On the first issue what I try to explain to the spluttering Evans, still lamenting the standard of Liverpudlian education, is that a 12–0 home win leads us to a world where we are cream of the crop. Putting 12 past a side at home leads to fear and to intimidation. It helps the goal difference. Finishing in the Champions League places leads to adventures and staying over and great nights. In front of the world. You get all this wonderfulness. They'll be watching in London too.

You also get a bigger squad with more good players in. You put yourself in a better position to get the results you need across a host of competitions. You put yourself in a position where League Cups can be continually challenged for.

What I want to say to him, though I can't, is that more than anything in the world I want a world where they bow down, where they all submit. Give in. I want that world. Tony had that world and that world had baubles like League Cups to go with the constant submission. To be part of that world. What a world it must have been. We've had League Cups since then and there isn't one I'd give back but now, more than ever, I want the 12–0, that record, I want what comes with it. Being a side that can score 12 goals in a league match. I want the good players, the Champions League adventure, I want the journey towards the top and then, when there, when the world knows it, when Europe knows it, when Britain knows it, we saunter down Wembley way like angelic demons or demonic angels, bright red peacocks that want to be stroked, flattered or fought.

Come and adore them.
They're the Kings of Europe.

Then we'll win the League Cup. On the way to a glorious treble.

I want to say all that. But the talk moves on. It always moves on. Now we're on where is or isn't Wool. Everyone's laughing, Tony's effervescent, Brockle pointing out the colour of her bins versus those in Pimlico, Rory and Steve explaining the concept of Wool and the importance of bin colour to Kate. Talk, talk, talk. Always the talk. Right or wrong, always the talk.

12–0.

Neil Atkinson

LIVERPOOL 1 MANCHESTER UNITED 0

1 September 2013.
Goals: Sturridge 4'

RAW DEFIANCE

I COULDN'T REMEMBER a Manchester United game this early. In the season that is. Manchester United games kicking off early in the day were now regular occurrences, with police seemingly of the opinion that if we're all still half-asleep we will forget we hate each other. It doesn't seem to particularly work – you just get used to it and adjust your drinking times accordingly.

But the biggest home game of the season (apologies to The Ev) taking place on 1 September was a strange sensation, especially as we were still very unsure about what each team had to offer. Liverpool had won their first three games, but hadn't been completely convincing as yet and had been given a slight shock and a couple of injuries in the week against Notts County. Manchester United were an even more unknown quantity. They'd got an impressive result on the opening day away at Swansea followed by a respectable point at home to Chelsea, but the full extent of the Ferguson, or Moyes, factor on the club remained uncertain.

The team news brought mixed blessings. Wayne Rooney being missing was undoubtedly a boost, but Kolo Touré hadn't recovered from his injury picked up in the week. It's remarkable, looking back, how much this worried people and a sign of both how well Touré had started the season and how Martin Skrtel's reputation had fallen. Even those left who maintained belief in the Slovak's ability would have been concerned with his rustiness, having lost his place the previous campaign to Jamie Carragher and not getting much of a look-in since. But Skrtel was excellent that day, and didn't look back all year.

The feeling in the air at a United game is almost impossible to describe. An animosity that needs no words, although gets plenty of them just to make sure. A tension, almost on the point of explosion, that used to terrify me as a ten-year-old boy. Seriously: a film with a pair of boobs in gets a '15' certificate, but you can take a child to this horror show? I used to be far less frightened of Freddy Krueger than I was of what the presence of 3,000 men from Manchester was doing to the fellas around me.

Liverpool score after four minutes. It goes off. Sturridge again. Liverpool seem unsure what to do next, perhaps not expecting to have broken through so early. Later in the season they'd have scored four more before half-time, but a team without a measure of either their own abilities or the opposition's was uncertain. They played out the game like a boxer fending off a dangerous opponent with a long-armed jab and a secure defence.

The fans bought in to it. If football supporters can see the plan, believe in the plan, they will back you to the hilt. Despite the early victories, much of the support still retained a feeling of 'get as many points as we can before Suárez comes back and then take it from there', and besides, a win against any Manchester United side will always be deemed a good result. So we roared and we screamed and we questioned the referee's parentage for having the audacity to give decisions against us. We played our part like you feel home crowds against Manchester United, against runaway league champions, have to.

When everyone is together sheer defiance can sometimes be enough. Sheer defiance from a much-maligned centre half determined to keep his place. Sheer defiance from a keeper who clearly thought this was all mad. Sheer defiance from gifted attackers who abandon what they enjoy doing most and concentrate on harrying, pressing and harassing. Sheer defiance from a crowd who had decided that Liverpool were going to win, no matter what, as they had done before and will do again. It must be easy for any opposition player to concede defeat in the face of it. The Manchester United players certainly didn't seem to have a solution to defiance that afternoon.

We'd seen togetherness already from the squad that season – with Mignolet after his saved penalty, with players and crowd after Aston Villa – but this was the strongest display yet, a group togetherness and determination led by a captain maybe starting to suspect that this set of players were stronger than they had let on. Full-time whistle. A bigger noise still. Fans and players defiant. Liverpool, top of the league. Liverpool, Liverpool, top of the league. **John Gibbons**

WHEN DOES OURS START AND THEIRS FINISH AGAIN?

IT WAS A MATCH AGAINST MANCHESTER UNITED but also a celebration; the Anfield fixture closest to the 100th birthday of the late, great Bill Shankly.

When such a man is being revered so publicly, it's hard not to allow your thoughts to drift; to consider just how important great managers are in shaping everything a football club does – from the stands to the pitch to the boardroom.

For Liverpool, perhaps, it's more important than at other clubs. Such is our passion, as fans, for the club. Such is the way we live and breathe football in this city. We need a figurehead. We need a man who can inspire. We need a leader.

We've seen it both ways – the brilliant butterfly effect of the right manager, and the dire consequences of the wrong one. Against United at Anfield, it felt like we saw both at the same time in the opposing dugouts.

At times, it's felt like Manchester United's relentless gut-wrenching habit of winning would never end. Ah, but it comes in cycles, people would say. We've had our time, this is theirs, others added. We'll come back, they'll have a dip. It's the way it goes: cycles, eras, periods of dominance … Er, sound. So when does ours start and theirs finish again?

The previous season, United didn't look great yet they still won the title with ease – another trophy in the cabinet despite the Glazers. The Mancs still lording the dance even with the devil on their back.

But Ferguson couldn't go on forever and when it happened, when he finally quit, I don't mind admitting that I actually punched the air. Punched it hard. This was big. It was massive. A huge chance for them to get it all very wrong. Ferguson was old-school, a ruler, a figurehead – a man with a statue and a stand named after him, for fuck's sake.

He'd been holding that place up, dragging United over the line, doing what he does with officials and playing the media like a fiddle. His mere presence was worth points to United: from the favourable calls from officials to the extra per cent put in from players keen to avoid a bollocking.

Whoever came next had a huge job on their hands to fill his shoes. And when it was announced it was David Moyes? Well, there I was again. Punching the air. They had their pick of managers the world over. They were Manchester United, a trophy-winning machine, a club with money to spend and a team competing in the Champions League.

And they went for Moyes, a manager Phil Coutinho admitted before this game he had never even heard of.

I've never understood the fuss about Moyes. I suppose he did OK at Everton, but he won nothing and seemed to bottle it when it really mattered, which included every time he came to Anfield and in the FA Cup semi-final. Thanks, David.

His greatest achievement was coining the 'People's Club' phrase. Evertonians love that, don't they? But the truth is, even when Everton were in form, and arguably had a better side than us, it was the same old Moyes when it came to taking on Liverpool: safety first, don't get beat, stop the opposition first and try to nick one second.

Quite why he was considered for a job at a club that expects to win every week is anyone's guess. But that's their problem. Or it was until the inevitable happened and they got shut of him. Even without him, though, it means more uncertainty and instability. It's great.

This was a relatively easy win for a game against Manchester United, a result that added to the growing stock of our manager, while also shining a light on the weaknesses of Moyes, and of United.

This was a side that for years would run through walls for its manager. It had all the traits of the man we loved to hate – a winning mentality, a belligerent attitude, a belief that a game was never over.

More often than not, it found a way. And if you weren't out of sight come 80-odd minutes, you knew you were in for an onslaught. That was down to Ferguson and it was horrible. The waves of attacks were as frequent as the waves of nausea. And too often down the years his sides would deliver the ultimate sickener before the last whistle blew.

This side, though? This manager? More whimpers than warrior spirit. What was clear here was that Moyes was making his mark. Unfortunately for the Mancs, it was the all-too-familiar skid mark of worry from a manager that fears failure above all else – ironically, a trait that leads him to lose too many games.

The Sturridge-inspired win for the Reds (we're the Reds, they're the Red Devils, and anyone who says anything different needs telling) meant it was 13 visits to Anfield for Moyes without a victory. But this time the tired old excuses were not an option for the Scot. Manchester United are not Liverpool's poor relation. There's no money moan that will stand up to scrutiny. Even the playing resources offered few straws to clutch at – when the game wasn't going his way Moyes was able to bring on Hernández, Nani and Valencia. Brendan Rodgers, meanwhile, turned to Alberto, Sterling and Wisdom.

With excuses at a premium, Moyes clearly felt in something of a corner. Had it been Ferguson in the same situation, he would have either swerved the press conference or created a shitstorm out of an incident in the game or the standard of refereeing. The art of deflection.

Moyes instead claimed it was 'probably the best we've played this season', a quote remarkably similar to Roy Hodgson's 'Utopia' speech after defeat at Goodison Park. Just as we didn't want to hear the manager of Liverpool talking about good performances after losing to Everton, you can be certain the United support didn't want that from Moyes after surrendering at Anfield.

For us, though, it was great. Moyes will never ever be a Bill Shankly. He hasn't got the bottle. Brendan Rodgers, though? Well, who knows, but his balls are growing by the day.

Gareth Roberts

ONE-NIL

IT ALWAYS SCARES ME how weird time is. I think someone has messed about with it. It passes by so quickly I sometimes have to pause to work out exactly how many long, lonely months it's been since Dirk Kuyt left us, or whether I'm already dead or not.

True to form, our 1–0 victory over Manchester United, on 1 September 2013, seems barely two weeks ago in my poor, addled mind. But simultaneously, it seems like a lifetime ago, because things are so different now. A glance back through the match reports uncovers lots of talk of Brendan Rodgers showing great promise, and how he'll surely settle for fourth place this year, and how it's looking good so far, but you never know, do you? There's a certain amount of enjoyable needle to be got from reading them back. Or maybe that's just me.

I had a seat by myself in the Kop and I was childishly pleased, because it meant I got to hold up a bit of the Shankly centenary mosaic. (It was the most pointless bit as well – I was right at the bottom and in the corner – but leave me alone and let me have my fun.)

I don't think we quite knew it for certain then, or wanted to say the words aloud, but we were already dangerous. Meetings among the top sides in the league had been tight, with United being held to a draw at Old Trafford by Chelsea only days before their Anfield visit. That win was massively important – from a sentimental point of view, because we so desperately wanted it to honour the 100th birthday of our legendary Scot – but also in terms of belief, of showing what could be done.

Deep down, I think we expected to win the game, even then, a couple of weeks into the new season. More than 90 minutes of football were played after Sturridge's winning header and it may have been just me, it may be that it's paled into insignificance given the stress and emotion we all experienced during the latter part of our league campaign, but the tension wasn't as high as it could have been. We were fast, we were tight, and United didn't look like getting one past us.

They were frustrated and angry. We weren't arsed. We were better than them. Even then, we were better than them. Even with the still-banned Luis Suárez out, and Iago Aspas instead of Raheem Sterling in the starting line-up. David Moyes doesn't beat us at Anfield.

Such was the level of nonchalance among us in the second half, a goodly portion of the Kop end got badly distracted when someone thought they saw Kolo Touré sitting in the Main. Whispers spread round very quickly. Loads of people squinting and craning necks. I spotted Neil. He looked excited, as did everyone else. I still have no idea if Kolo was there or not, but the expectation and the excitement definitely was. It's great to have the benefit of hindsight and all that, but I think that narrow win, that early success, told us all something of much better things to come. We were just getting started.

Kate Forrester

TRANSFER DEADLINE DAY #1

2 September 2013.

BUYING YOUNG DEFENDERS

FOR THE FIRST TIME, we did a live broadcast around the closing of the transfer window on 2 September 2013. It was an act of disguise. The theory is that a broadcast based around the closing of the transfer window should focus on the transfers of footballers themselves. What we did instead was use the opportunity to talk to supporters of other teams about how they saw the season coming. However, circumstances exploded around us and Everton looked like they were going to sell Fellaini and buy no one, United had lawyers crawling around after Herrera in Spain, and so we had to talk about actual transfers. This is rarely a good thing.

We didn't need to bother with Liverpool. This window Liverpool had everything sewn up on the morning of the second; by English football standards, this is swot behaviour, coursework handed in on the morning it is due. Haven't you got a life? The rest of us are still in the library trying to make it happen. By European standards, this is a bit last-minute, but what do they know, with their organisation and planning and sanity and Michael Robinson. They could have Jim White resplendently surrounded by yellow.

(Jim White fact – Andy Heaton rang Jim and asked if he'd come on our show for a laugh. He said Jim was lovely on the phone, was chatting to him for over an hour, is well aware of the vaudeville of the enterprise and, though contractually he obviously and rightly couldn't come on, when Andy said, 'Any advice to pass on to the lads?' he replied, 'Just enjoy it.' I want a pint with Jim White.)

The business Liverpool had done that morning involved the signing of Mamadou Sakho – then aged 23 – and Tiago Ilori – then aged 20. Both were central defenders. There is three years' difference in their ages, but Sakho had made 151 senior appearances for Paris Saint-Germain whereas Ilori had made 12 for Sporting. Sakho cost Liverpool £15m, Ilori reportedly around half that, though his fee has never been confirmed.

Without getting into the merits of Sakho, he was clearly a signing for the first team. He was ready for the first team. You could point at those games for PSG, the fact he had worn the captain's armband, the fact that he had French caps under his belt, and you could say that this player was a first-team defender. And, should he be a success, at his age Liverpool have eight to ten years of him at the centre of their defence.

Ilori, on the other hand, was a gamble. He wasn't a signing for the first team. By the end of the campaign he had made no first-team appearances for Liverpool and had gone out on loan to Granada in Spain, where he played fewer than ten games.

Three years' difference in their ages, huge differences in their profiles, significant but not definitive differences in their price tags.

My problem, though, isn't the money paid for Ilori. He really could turn out to be very good. My problem is this:

When does he get his game?

He arrives at Anfield, 2 September, with Skrtel, Agger, Touré and the newly bought Sakho all ahead of him. You can make an argument that Andre Wisdom is ahead of him too; he started at centre back against Notts County. Some would love to say Martin Kelly is as well. When do you play him?

This is nothing new. A list of names:

Frode Kippe
Carl Medjani
Miki Roqué
Jack Hobbs
Godwin Antwi
Gabriel Paletta

Daniel Ayala
Danny Wilson
Sebastián Coates

These are all young centre backs Liverpool have bought in the last 20 years. Some for small fees, some for large fees. The point remains the same – none could establish themselves in the first team. Some were clearly good players. Some have gone on to be very good players – Paletta is now an Italian international (Roqué's opportunity to reach his potential was tragically cut short after he died of pelvic cancer in 2012). All this is before we look at prospects that have come through Liverpool's youth ranks.

None could get into Liverpool's first team and stay there. Some – Sebastián Coates for example – are just unlucky or badly managed. He should have started as many games as possible at the end of Kenny Dalglish's final season when Liverpool could no longer plausibly finish fourth. He should have kept his place after Manchester City at home in 2012 under Brendan Rodgers. That he didn't is suggestive of why these players struggle to establish themselves. Managers, at the highest level, are under a pressure to succeed that precludes giving young centre backs extended chances. (See also Alex Ferguson and Phil Jones.)

Young players are exciting. They give life to a team, give zest. They'll go through a brick wall, as Brendan Rodgers often says. We love watching young players. They make football a joy.

If they are attackers.

Attackers can try things. A young attacking player can try ten things and if three of them come off, he looks inordinately exciting. One could lead to a goal. Imagine what he'll be like in five years, we can say, just imagine. Bring him on, he plays without fear. Give him the last 20, he'll go at them.

Do you want a defender who plays without fear? Who tries things? A young defender plays and if he does ten things and gets nine of them right, you remember the thing he got wrong; it could have led to a goal. It'll almost certainly have led to a goalscoring opportunity. And now he's worried, he's concerned and 45,000 people have just gone bananas. Because while a footballer or football team might try and play without fear, part of supporting a football team is the fear of conceding.

Footballers need to play to develop. For defenders to develop they need to play against the best and the best make everyone look daft. But they also need to make mistakes against those who aren't the best. And if you are at Liverpool, where the aim is to win every game, where one mistake can mean the difference between first and second, fourth and fifth, silverware or empty cabinets, then it becomes harder again.

Tiago Ilori merely joins this list at this stage; perhaps he'll buck the trend. But it appears to me that the only way we know is if he plays. And to play he has to elbow very good players out of the way, keep his place in the team and manage all this while occasionally not being very good and settling in a new country. Sakho makes sense as a signing. His youthful follies have been on Paris Saint-Germain's time. I'm reluctant to have anyone's on ours. Because I want to win.

Neil Atkinson

SWANSEA CITY 2 LIVERPOOL 2

16 September 2013.
Goals: Shelvey 2', Michu 64'; Sturridge 4', Moses 36'

THE MAGIC OF JONJO SHELVEY

'For me, you're going to be a big player, all right. But...'
Brendan Rodgers to Jonjo Shelvey, summer 2012

BEFORE KICK-OFF IT IS SEVEN HOURS. Four hundred and eighteen minutes, to be precise.

That's how long it's been since Liverpool have conceded a goal in the league.

Watch *The Deer Hunter* twice and then stand on your head for 52 minutes afterwards. That's 418 minutes. Imagine loads of professional footballers from last season to this not being able to score a goal past us during that time. Actually, you don't need to imagine it. That's what's happened.

The last player to score against us was Dimitar Berbatov. No one has been mad enough or nonchalant enough, or just goddamned Berbatov enough, to be able to do it since.

Impenetrable. Resolute. No Paserán.

We are Liverpool. We only kick off once a game.

These Impenetrable Reds are off to Swansea, a near foreign land, on a

Monday night. Better men than these have tried to breach us and failed. This will be no problem.

Eighty-seven seconds. Swansea 1 Liverpool 0.

The scorer – Jonjo Shelvey.

We hadn't found anyone mad enough to score against us since Berbatov. We have now. Jonjo Shelvey, the maddest player I've ever seen.

The issue with footballing madness is its occasional brilliance, the transient ability to conjure magic from normality. It's a beguiling trait, highly seductive. So much so that when Liverpool sold Shelvey in the summer, we all knew that he would occasionally make us regret it. In games we weren't watching for 90 minutes we would see clips of the Shelvey brilliance – the long shots, the raking passes. Vines, Vines, Vines. Vine was made for Jonjo Shelvey. Six seconds maximum. Repeat. Jonjo Shelvey, the star of Vine of the Day.

This goal he scores tonight is typical of Jonjo. A one-man chaos theory that blusters his way through the Liverpool defence. Assist – Shelvey. Goal – Shelvey. He's best left to his own devices – other people get in the way.

The other issue with madness of course is, well, its inherent madness. Just two minutes after scoring Shelvey passes to Sturridge in the penalty box and Sturridge equalises for Liverpool. Daniel Sturridge and Jonjo Shelvey aren't on the same side.

After that he passes to Moses who then puts Liverpool ahead with his first goal for the club. Victor Moses and Jonjo Shelvey aren't on the same side.

Three assists for Shelvey already. One for Swansea, two for Liverpool. What was I saying about other people getting in the way? These other 21 players on the pitch are just a blur. Teammates, opposition, all rolled into one. Just give me the ball and let me do my own thing. Sometimes I do brilliant things, just watch me.

In the second half he does one of those brilliant things. He picks the ball up in the centre of the pitch, lays it off, makes a 20-yard run that no one tracks and then cushions a header perfectly for Michu to equalise. It's one of those fleeting moments when Shelvey 'gets' football and everyone that has ever backed him says, 'See, see, he's got real quality. Told you, told you, told you – blah blah blah.'

One person that stopped backing him, though, was Rodgers. Rodgers isn't seduced by madness. To him, a flawed genius is exactly that – flawed.

Shelvey represents a type of player that we've seen too many of at Liverpool since we were winning leagues. Flickering talents, given incredible latitude by successive managers who hope they will turn the corner and start to do the brilliant things they occasionally do more often. In many respects these are the hardest players to sell. It's the flashes of magic that we all cling on to.

And this is why Rodgers' gamble with Shelvey is so significant. He knows a player like Jonjo doesn't get anywhere near the first team for United, City, Arsenal or Chelsea. In that sense, selling him is a sign of Rodgers' ambition, a sign of what he's not prepared to settle for.

As for Jonjo? Well, one day they'll invent a game that involves kicking a ball that he'll be brilliant at.

It will be a game of isolated incidents, football reduced to a moment, a bat of an eyelid. Tactics, concentration, teammates, opposition, formations, game intelligence, the laws of the game – all of this will be stripped back to what came first, just you and the ball in a state of childlike wonderment. And with that ball, Jonjo Shelvey will do something absolutely astonishing.

And so will Ryan Babel.

And so will Titi Camara.

And so will Charlie Adam.

And so will Joe Cole.

Martin Fitzgerald

LIVERPOOL 0 SOUTHAMPTON 1

21 September 2013.
Goals: Lovren 53'

THE DARKNESS

THE DARKNESS SNAPS BACK.

Everything hangs by a thread. That's the worst part of this. Southampton turn up and shut Liverpool down and your brain feels like it could fall out of your head. No ideas, no hope of any ideas. No light anywhere. Southampton score and for all the world it looks like a 1–0.

Football hurts.

Three league wins wherein you weren't that impressed with anything but the winning. One frustrating draw defined by an ex-Liverpool player. And then this.

Your hopes betrayed.

Being hopeless is the worst. Just when you'd been convincing one another that something was brewing and possible here, hopelessness clatters into you, closes you down, harries you all over the pitch.

We'd grown used to hopelessness. Welcome the darkness back, sitting on your shoulder, poking you in the ear. Twisting its finger, rubbing the dry earwax into your brain. Sandpapering your cerebellum. This is all you are. All you can be. Hopelessness won't give you a minute, nagging at you like a migraine that never quite comes.

Four centre backs in a line. Touré at right back, Sakho at left back and Agger and Skrtel at centre back. Four centre backs in a line, getting pressed and never getting going, unconvincing beyond halfway and oddly porous behind it.

Full back is probably now the toughest position to play on the pitch. Practically everyone dislikes their full backs. They think they're either not good enough on the ball or not good enough in the tackle. He can get up and down, but his touch isn't good enough. He puts a great ball in but he doesn't stop enough crosses. Where is he on the overlap? Where is he on the cover? We expect full backs to be omnipresent and omnipotent.

This isn't a job for a central defender, something we can see by virtue of the fact neither of the starting centre backs finished the game for Liverpool. Both those who started wide found themselves in their more natural positions. But it was too late.

In fairness, it looked too late from the first whistle.

Liverpool ran around a bit, mostly hopelessly. Sturridge couldn't find a way in to the football match. Aspas could barely get near the ball. Henderson looked blunted. Moses occasionally showed something early on but Southampton soon put a stop to that. They knew exactly how to deal with this Liverpool side, and deserved their victory.

This is what we didn't want this season. After Australia and Dublin and three 1–0s and all the intent and talk of easier opening games, a home defeat where nothing works is the essence of what we did not want.

My head throbs with how much I didn't want this. I can't take this again, I can't watch another season lapse into a chase for a fourth place that always seems out of reach and which will never be the adventure we crave. It's a harsh place, Anfield, when things are hopeless. Its people are so hard on what they watch, hard on each other. We bicker. We vent. There's cant everywhere: in your hair, your mouth, your belly button. I don't want to turn up to this every week. I don't want to think about Benítez or Dalglish. I don't want to look back, I want to look in awe. I want to feel renewed. I did feel renewed. Insecure, but renewed. Watching the last ten minutes I feel jaded. Transported back into black-and-white.

The final whistle goes. 'Fucking hopeless Liverpool.' Trudge out into the evening. Congregate and try to wash the cant off yourself, try to make sense of the hopelessness and turn it into coherent discussion. Then someone says it: 'Suárez is back next week.'

A chink of light, bright light, strikes through the gloom. Suárez is back next week.

Suárez is back next week.

Suárez.

Neil Atkinson

MANCHESTER UNITED 1 LIVERPOOL 0

25 September 2013.
Goals: Hernández 46'

THREE AT THE BACK

THERE WAS DEBATE ALL SEASON on whether Liverpool's frequent formation changes were due to necessity, flexibility, pragmatism or indecision, with respective conclusions reached showing the varying degrees of confidence in the manager as much as anything else. For all those who believed he was trying to find effective solutions to an imbalanced squad, there were others who claimed he was chopping and changing until he stumbled on a winning formula.

This would be our first look at three at the back, a formation that had widely gone out of fashion and was associated at Anfield with the ultimately frustrating Roy Evans era. However, in theory it seemed to be a good way of dealing with key selection decisions, most notably up front and at centre half.

Possibly the best selection headache possible for a manager to have was the return of Luis Suárez from his ten-game ban. Sturridge had been playing as the focal point of the attack, so where to fit Suárez in? It seemed unfair to move Sturridge out wide or deeper considering how well he had started the season, while asking Suárez to play more withdrawn after making such a song and dance out of keeping him seemed unwise too. A 3–4–1–2 allowed both to play as out-and-out strikers with Victor Moses behind, linking midfield and attack.

In defence Rodgers may have felt under pressure to get expensive new signing Mamadou Sakho in his favoured role of centre half, after a less than impressive showing at left back the previous game. Kolo Touré had performed slightly better at right back the same match, but was still clearly a centre half, while it seemed unfair for Martin Skrtel to miss out after impressing so much since his return. This formation allowed all three to play closer to their preferred position, and let us play three players where we were well stocked to compensate for other areas where we weren't.

Both first-choice full backs should have relished a higher starting position, with Glen Johnson always keen to attack and Joe Enrique surprising everyone with his left-wing cameos the previous season. Unfortunately Johnson wasn't available so the right side was occupied by Jordan Henderson, who certainly had the energy to cope with the demands of the position and whose dead-ball delivery promised a decent level of crosses into the box. In the middle Gerrard and Lucas, having been somewhat overrun in midfield against Southampton, should have been able to find life slightly easier with three centre halves behind them and Moses able to drop in.

All sounds good, doesn't it? So did it work? Well, ultimately decisions are evaluated on results, and Liverpool lost the game, but there was enough in the performance to encourage the manager to continue with the formation a little longer. Up front, Suárez looked understandably rusty but showed willing to link up with Sturridge, with plenty of thumbs up all round. At the back Liverpool conceded from another set piece, but the defence looked solid enough otherwise, with Mignolet rarely troubled, while a higher level of possession suggests a reasonable control of midfield. However, Henderson didn't take to the right wing back role as well as hoped before being shifted inside for Kelly, who looked even more ill-suited to a mildly attacking role. Moses, while playing reasonably well and being unlucky not to score, also struggled with where to position himself on the pitch, and looked much happier when able to drift wide.

Interestingly, Liverpool's league record with the 3–4–1–2 formation (three wins, one draw, one defeat) was exactly the same as the five league games which came before, perhaps suggesting it had been neither success nor failure. Just like the Southampton game, it was the next loss that would prompt another change, with a return to four at the back. But all season the themes remained: the balancing act between defensive solidity, midfield control and harnessing the brilliance of Suárez and Sturridge. With Brendan Rodgers expertly tinkering until we were at our most formidable. Or trying everything until something came off. Depending on which side of the fence you sat.

John Gibbons

SUNDERLAND 1 LIVERPOOL 3

29 September 2013.
Goals: Giaccherini 52'; Sturridge 28', Suárez 36', 89'

YOU MOSTLY GET WHAT YOU DESERVE

SUNDERLAND FEELS TO ME like a ground we haven't got a great record at, even though when I look through the results now we have won more times there than I thought. Maybe it's just the losses that stick in your head. In particular I remember going there in 2002 when an absolutely dreadful Sunderland team beat us 2–1 with Michael Proctor (who a friend of mine claimed looked below average when he used to watch him at York City) scoring the winner. Igor Biscan played centre half that day. Christ.

But for most others Sunderland away has become synonymous with the 'beach ball' goal, largely because of the injustice of it all. How could the referee have let it stand? It bounced off a bloody beach ball and into the goal! I found Steve Bruce's reaction after the game rather odd. Of the goal, he said, 'If anybody knew that rule – that it is supposed to be a dropped ball – then you are a saddo.' Bruce there, seemingly ignoring the fact that referees ARE saddos and are employed, now professionally, to know all the rules of the game, even the obscure ones.

But I didn't criticise the referee too much, even at the time. Partly because I have had a go at refereeing once and it was the worst experience of my life. A few

47

years ago I was having a spell in goal for a mate's university team, largely because they couldn't find anyone else. One week I turned up with a rotten hangover and managed to injure my wrist during the warm-up. Any hope that I might be able to go home and lie on the sofa were quickly dashed when it became apparent that the referee hadn't turned up. Everyone slowly turned round and looked at me.

It turned out our opposition were, for want of a better phrase, a gang of bell-ends. Disputing every decision against them like I'd slept with their mother and spat in their face, showing venom rarely seen outside Goodison Park on a derby day. I think everyone who watches football should referee a proper game at least once. You'll have a new-found respect for officials when you've stood in the rain getting screamed at by poxy students with an increasingly swelling and purple wrist (me, not them).

However, the main reason I didn't have a go at the referee too much is I thought we were dreadful. Lacklustre, unimaginative, lacking any quality, and that was just Jay Spearing. We didn't look like scoring all day and got beat. It might not be as exciting a headline as 'Beach Ball Costs Liverpool', but that is essentially what happened that day.

Much was made this season of the fact that Liverpool were working with Dr Steve Peters on their mental approach to the game. Not much is known about what he is doing specifically with the players, but one thing he has mentioned is that he is a big believer in trying to control the things you can and not worrying about the things you can't. Admittedly he probably hasn't seen a goal deflection off a beach ball too many times in sport, but I am sure his convictions would remain, and you would hope they are shared by top-level football managers as well. They may talk about luck and referees in post-match press conferences, but I am sure in private they would admit that their players just hadn't done enough in games they had lost. This is why I don't truly believe José Mourinho when he complains about the 'ghost goal' in 2005. I am sure deep down he wonders why a team who had shown superior quality to Liverpool all season took 185 minutes to create a decent chance.

So fast-forward to 2013 and Sunderland vs Liverpool again. As is often the case when a club changes manager, Sunderland started brightly and threatened just as much as Liverpool in the early stages. But the game changed on a goal, and the goal was a Liverpool one. Steven Gerrard took a corner, Daniel Sturridge made a bit of a mess of the header, but it went in anyway. Liverpool countered brilliantly for the rest of the game and won 3–1.

So that's the story, right? Liverpool reaffirm top-four credentials with tough away win, while Sunderland show enough spirit to encourage fans to believe they could battle the drop. Except instead, at half-time and after the game, we are subjected to endless replays of the opening goal, which suggest that it hit the top of Sturridge's arm before going in. This is what is offered up as 'analysis' by the television: incident-led drama rather than any attempt to understand the game itself.

The newspapers, while not as bad, still seemed keen to reflect it as a key part of the narrative. The Guardian stated that 'it seemed to serve as a microcosm of Sunderland's wretched luck of late', with no reference whatsoever to the fact that Daniel Sturridge was completely unmarked, or that Seb Larsson, supposedly on a post, displayed the most pathetic attempt to get in the way of a shot since the whole Liverpool team in the 1996 FA Cup final.

Television presenters and journalists can talk about what they like, of course, but the problem is it has an effect on everyone else. Contentious decisions are now shown to managers and players on big screens in post-match interviews in the hope of getting a juicy instant reaction. But instead it just gives them an easy cop-out. We didn't lose because our defenders can't run, or our strikers can't score. We lost because of THAT.

I understand why managers and players want to do it. It's much better to be seen as unlucky than useless. But we shouldn't let them off the hook so easily. People often say the luck 'evens itself out' over the season, but the fact is you normally get what you deserve in each game, and for every mistake a referee makes, there is normally a player who has made ten more. It might not be as noticeable, and it might not be as newsworthy, but they are much easier for a team to resolve than things they can't control.

John Gibbons

BARMOUTH

WE WENT TO BARMOUTH the weekend of this game. Steve and Kate. Me and Brockle. John and Laura. We all went to Barmouth. It's difficult, the tyranny of football. It makes simple things like a weekend away tough to negotiate. You have to time it right.

We timed it right. A Sunday where we are away and on the television. Manchester United had lost to West Bromwich Albion, a defeat we only discovered on *Match Of The Day.*

The following day we walked across Barmouth to find a screen with the game on in a caravan park. This is what you have to do. I drank too much. Much too much. The whole weekend much too much too much too much. When we go we take a lot of wine and I took there being any left on the Sunday night after the match as a personal affront. I remember: The goals. Celebrating the goals. Going mad about Davey Provan saying foul throws didn't matter. A lot. The kit. Victor Moses running with the ball. An Italian meal after the game. Barmouth's finest. It was excellent. Being overwhelmed on the final whistle. It felt huge...

I asked Steve afterwards what he remembered from the day. He emailed me a long set of recollections and they are italicized:

I don't know what I was drinking. A sort of a bitter. The brand is unknown to me but sounded Midlands provincial. This was not craft beer.

I wasn't sure what I was watching. Liverpool were on game six of this season and a routine trip to Sunderland was, suddenly and from nowhere, oddly pivotal.

There had been three wins. Then a draw and a defeat. Then Old Trafford, in the League Cup. Another defeat. Lose this and it's a downturn. Lose this and we're off whatever pace we're supposed to be on.

This is why I felt overwhelmed upon the final whistle. Overwhelmed and exhausted. The goal that killed the game came late and so it was a second half on dreadful bitter and nerves.

We were upbeat. We were at the seaside. You can't be depressed at the seaside, unless you're in most British resorts. But this is Barmouth - For Mountain, Sand and Sea as they used to say. The people reading the book have probably never been and tell them I don't want them to go, because Barmouth is as unspoilt as a place can be while still featuring waltzers.

Stand on the beach (on one of the beaches) and you can see the mountains and the broad sweep of the river Mawddach, a name which sounds impossibly dramatic when said properly.

By kick off we had optimism. It might have been the sea air and session ale talking. All we talked about was Luis Suarez; back for his first league game since biting (actually biting!) Branislav Ivanovic. And there's the third kit. Ridiculous from top to toe, it might be the worst kit ever designed. On paper.

But on footballers, and it looked magnificent. We looked magnificent. Daniel Sturridge wore it best, a robotic Greek god intent on subjugating all in his path. In Ancient Rome Tyrian purple was reserved for the emperor. The Elizabethans, with their sumptuary laws, let the royal family and a few dukes and marquesses have a go. And now the mighty Liverpool.

Suarez was back. Sturridge was serious. We were at the seaside. I was going to drink all the wine I could get my hands on. It was huge.

And we were second – second - in the league. What a weekend.

Neil Atkinson

LIVERPOOL 3 CRYSTAL PALACE 1

5 October 2013.
Goals: Suárez 13', Sturridge 17', Gerrard (pen) 38'; Gayle 76'

A DISAPPOINTING 3 – 1

22 December 2012, Anfield – 4–0 Fulham
19 January 2013, Anfield – 5–0 Norwich
17 February 2013, Anfield – 5–0 Swansea
2 March 2013, DW Stadium – 4–0 Wigan
27 April 2013, St James' Park – 6–0 Newcastle

CRYSTAL PALACE VISITED ANFIELD and Brendan Rodgers' Liverpool hadn't battered anybody yet this season. They had looked irresistible at times against Sunderland. Sturridge and Suárez were back in tandem. Crystal Palace, managed by Ian Holloway, looked the worst team in the league.

Manage your expectations accordingly.

Mine were through the roof and first half they were not disappointed: Suárez scoring from the floor, Sturridge from an impossible angle. Gerrard from the penalty spot. Liverpool were irresistible, attacking from all angles in a 4–4–2 imposed by Lucas's suspension, with Henderson and Gerrard in centre midfield.

And then nothing. Loads and loads of nothing. Yes, Palace did well and kept battling but Liverpool were disappointingly leaden. Crystal Palace overloaded Liverpool in midfield, found space and kept the ball away from them.

How odd this is. To turn up, watch your side put the game to bed first half and walk away disappointed. It's a vagary of football. One of those instances where being good is an issue. I want Liverpool to be good. I want Liverpool to be quick out of the blocks. But put these halves the other way round – Crystal Palace frustrate Liverpool, open the scoring, get through to half-time. Manager gives a team talk and second half Liverpool blow Palace away, scoring three goals with endless movement and verve – and I walk away the happiest of men. We float back into town. Look how good they are, we say. They overcame adversity. We go bananas.

But sidestep adversity by virtue of sheer superiority and I spend the second half contemplating how on earth I'm going to get a night out going, considering the lack of momentum Liverpool have just offered me. Get to the pub. All right that. Suárez is good. Sturridge is good. Went a bit flat. What are you having? How's work?

How's work!? Low ebb.

Manage your expectations accordingly. Being good at football makes things more complicated than you might like.

Postscript Written the Day of the Return of This Fixture (5 May 2014)

I ACTUALLY EXPECT more games like this next season. More games where sides turn up to Anfield so aware of their own wretchedness and impending defeat Liverpool can barely summon the energy to properly put them to the sword. We'll have midweek games with the Champions League on the horizon. We'll start turning up expecting four or five, getting three and feeling a bit flat off the back of it. It'll be professional and it'll be impressive but perhaps that bit less fun. A smidgeon less brio about the enterprise.

I don't know where I stand on this impending sanity. I'm worried about it. Nothing might ever be as much fun as this again. I couldn't sleep last night for my excitement. I can't concentrate today. If Liverpool become great and 3–1 becomes routine then nothing might ever feel like this again. I am stunned at how much I've fallen in love with football this season, the sheer barefaced cheek of it all.

I hate football and boyfriend/girlfriend metaphors. But let's do one and let's fully commit to it: This season has been like meeting, 14 years on, the girl you thought was the girl of your dreams when you were both 19, and she's now a woman and she's well better than your dreams. Well, well, well better. The best. She's blown your head off. Everyone's looking at you agog. You've obviously got to go out with her for a bit, see how it goes, but what if that sheen wears off? You can't stop thinking it. What if that sheen wears off?

Please God, don't let the sheen wear off. Don't let that sheen ever wear off.

Please.

Please.

Neil Atkinson

NEWCASTLE UNITED 2 LIVERPOOL 2

19 October 2013.
Goals: Cabaye 23', Dummett 56'; Gerrard (pen) 42', Sturridge 72'

FOLLOWING IT EVERYWHERE

THIS MORNING I'm on my way to Manchester airport, flying to Texas (via New York) for a week of work with my day job. It means I'll be in the air when Liverpool face Newcastle in the day's early kick-off.

I don't mind my job; it brings its own rewards and a week in the Texas sunshine sounds glamorous.

It isn't really, and it's compounded by not being able to see the match and worse still having to digest the final score in one (potentially unpalatable) gulp when I get off that plane. I know I'll get a series of texts off mates and family appearing on my phone in reverse chronological order, and will have to make sense of the events and result when my mobile kicks into gear on the other side of the Atlantic.

I try to avoid these situations whenever possible. I plan and direct these overseas work dates around the fixture list; preferably my trips coincide with the international weekends or, if that isn't feasible, to avoid missing the home games, so in that sense today could be worse – I probably wouldn't have travelled to the North East and would have settled for watching the game at home on Sky.

As much as I admire my own efforts in engineering work commitments to suit my enduring passion for the Reds, I'm pretty crap at it. Last season I missed the home wins over Reading and Swansea, not to mention the raucous Europa League near-miss against Zenit St Petersburg. A few years ago I was at 30,000 feet when Dirk Kuyt's solitary goal was enough to deny Everton at Anfield. Reading the texts that day felt like a mini-death; the first thing I computed from the briefest of messages was that we were down to ten men with Kyrgiakos sent off. My heart missed about four or five beats before I saw a text from my sister which read, with emphatic relief – 'We won 1–0'. Not the best way to experience a derby match – crystallised into about 20 ravaging seconds.

Today, I take some consolation that I was also away with work, but watching live in a bar in Abu Dhabi, for the 6–0 win over the Geordies in the same fixture last season. And of course, this year we've carried on that form and after the home win over Palace last week we go into the game top of the league. Although I have no influence over proceedings at St James' Park, no way of influencing the score by shouting at the telly, I'm confident we'll get the three points. The downside to this unexpected early-season surge to the Premier League summit is that every game matters. At the age of 46, this lifetime obsession, nay affliction, is more acute than ever. Bloody hell; as if I haven't got enough to worry about what with checking about 50 times I've still got my passport, haven't brought a bomb with me, neglected to lose my laptop, praying for an aisle seat and hoping US customs don't give me the usual grilling about what the fuck I'm even thinking of doing on their turf again.

The flight to JFK leaves at 9.30 a.m., about three hours before the Reds launch themselves at Newcastle. My reading matter consists of the fine fanzine *When Saturday Comes* and the overly abundant sections of the Saturday *Guardian*. After the in-flight meal and a much-needed snooze I find myself reading the match preview after the game has kicked off, which in itself is bloody ridiculous. Even more stupid is that after looking at the predicted line-ups, match odds, and form lines I get those pre-match butterflies for a game I can't see. 'Come on, Reds,' I utter to myself, without the faintest clue what's going on.

Anyway, it's time to get off this plane! While other passengers are busily gathering assorted shite from the overhead bins, I'm frantically waiting and searching for a signal from AT&T or T-Mobile or some other merciful signal provider. Nothing. The match will have to wait until the customs hall. I turn off my phone again – I don't want half-baked information buzzing through while I'm whizzing along an airport conveyor belt.

Once I'm stationary in the vast queue at immigration, I turn on the phone. A 3G signal appears, and the texts start flying in. I half-close my eyes and scroll to the top so I can at least digest a flavour of events before the finality of the result. In order, they read as follows – with a varying degree of thanks to Chris Maguire, Chris Hannaway, Phil Allan, Gillian Nevin and Ursula Nevin:

'Fucks Sake'
'Shite this'
'Where's Gerrard?'
'They're just running through us 'ere'
'Looks dead windy'
'Mignolet there?'
'Fuck off, it bent away from him massively'
'Where are you watching it, Ally?'
'At home'
'Thank fuck for that, ten men as well now'
'Get in'
'Yes'
'What the fuck are we playing at here?'
'Get Moses off'
'Yeah, he's shite'
'Fucking hell'
'Need to get our shit together here'
'Ah well, not too bad, babe. Text me when you arrive x'

Needless to say, I'm in state of flux and still don't know the score, although the last text, from my wife, while stopping short of a giving me a much-needed scoreline, hints at a draw. I finally get an internet signal strong enough to source (and endure) Jeff Stelling's smarmy face on the Sky Sports footy app. The first thing I see is that with all the three o'clock games now finished, we've dropped to third. A rapid flick to 'fixtures' confirms that we've drawn 2–2, despite playing against ten men for an hour. Gerrard has scored his 100th league goal from the spot, equalising Cabaye's opener. Their lad's been sent off for hauling down Suárez. We've conceded a daft second from a set piece and Sturridge has salvaged a point late on. We haven't played well, it seems.

I watch it later on my laptop via a link to Match of the Day in my hotel in Texas. From the highlights it looks like we could and should have won it towards the end. Suárez has clipped the bar at the death. I'm always resolved that a point away from home is never a bad result, but this is becoming less and less true in the unbalanced modern Premier League. Almost certainly two points dropped, and an awful way to follow the game.

We need to beat West Brom at home next Saturday. And guess where I'm going to be? Yes, back at 30,000 fucking feet. **Mike Nevin**

WHAT IS A GOOD POINT?

I WAS HOSTING THE ANFIELD WRAP after Liverpool drew 2–2 with Newcastle United and our most regular contributor Rob Gutmann said something on it like, 'At the end of the season, a point at Newcastle will be seen as a good point.' It's the same point Mike Nevin above thinks is a bad point.

It stayed with me at the time because it felt like a big shout after a frustrating result.

In their next home league game Newcastle United beat Chelsea 2–0. The following week they go to Spurs and win. Not long after that, they win at Old Trafford. They win three of the next four at home, drawing the other, and batter Stoke City 5–1. Rob seems correct.

However they lose at home to Arsenal in their last game of 2013 and then lose to Manchester City midway through January 2014. They get embarrassed at home 4–0 by Spurs, 3–0 by Everton and 4–0 by Manchester United before the season draws to a close.

At the end of the season, a point at Newcastle will be seen as a good point.

I'm writing this at the end of the season. And I still don't entirely know. The concept of the football season – and I know this is basic but stay with me – is that you play 19 other teams home and away and then you can rank everyone in terms of how good they are. Everyone plays to their level, more often than not, and everyone finds their level in comparison to one another.

In a sense, we can end the season saying the table doesn't lie. Newcastle finish ninth. They have probably been the ninth-best side this season. Even when they were trying to be good, they were probably the ninth-best side.

And yet, had Liverpool played them at home in October and away in March, they probably would have taken six points. Fixture lists are odd and have a greater impact than people think at the best of times, but their idiosyncrasies are further underlined when a side effectively stops playing. Newcastle declared in January and have been pootling along ever since, settling for an inevitable mid-table position.

If this annoys you, imagine what it does to Newcastle supporters. I always think of the Woody Allen quote from Annie Hall for football clubs. To paraphrase: 'Football clubs are like sharks. They have to keep moving forward or they die. And what we have on our hands here, is a dead shark.'

Newcastle United: a dead shark. They've ended up having a season that is thoroughly maddening. And ended up finishing top half. Had they been less maddening would they be any more successful? They end the season on 49 points. What difference would 62 points have made? One or two places? Still no European football.

The only real way 62 points would have made a difference is to make Gutmann irrefutably correct. It would have been a good point. I wonder if sides like Newcastle at the moment, Everton under Moyes, Southampton, Stoke, I wonder if these sides and their supporters are happy with that, the idea that anyone who comes to their ground has to have a scrap to get a point and three is a significant achievement. If so, I understand. You want your home to be as much of a fortress as possible because it can always be a springboard to future achievement.

Declaring stops that: choosing not to have European football, choosing not to contest a cup because you don't want European football kills everything that football should be about. Not being good enough to get 62 points is one thing – deciding not to strive for achievement any more is another entirely. Hope should never be bled out of football clubs. You can be terrible but hopeful. Next week should be different, be better, because everyone at this thing I go to wants that. Football clubs are repositories for hope.

The people who run Newcastle have broken that relationship between supporters and hope and that's the worst thing you can do. Up and down the country, up and down the leagues, people watch poorer sides than Newcastle. They watch sides in greater trouble than Newcastle. Sides more wretched, in poorer facilities. Few of them, though, are having less fun. Because they always have tomorrow, whereas Newcastle have abolished it.

There's even more to this conversation about a single sentence though.

At the end of the season, a point at Newcastle will be seen as a good point.

This is what Rob said. And he makes a good point about the good point. The reason why this is a good point is that it is a debatable one. Too often people who speak on record about football get their words thrown back at them when they can be shown to be wrong. The reason we love football is because it makes you be wrong, makes you reassess, shifts and turns and trips you up and makes you fall on your face. Someone who is always right is someone who plays it safe, desperate to be a pub bore, telling you they told you so when they were right about the inevitable and pointing out you were wrong when you took a flyer.

So all this, all the above, every word in this book can be absolute broken biscuits. Football exists as the world's most popular sport because people love to talk about football. Being right is great – making a shout which stays with someone for eight months, and then makes them write a thousand words, is ultimately better.

Neil Atkinson

LIVERPOOL 4 WEST BROM 1

26 October 2013.
Goals: Suárez 12', 17', 55', Sturridge 77'; Morrison (pen) 66'

THE BRILLIANCE OF SUÁREZ

ONE OF MY FAVOURITE PIECES OF FOOTBALL WRITING this season was an interview with Paolo Suárez in FourFourTwo magazine. It's lovely because it's a reminder of the background Luis has come from and what he has had to overcome to get where he is, all told by a big brother who couldn't be prouder. You should definitely read it if you haven't already. Paolo, a professional footballer himself, clearly thinks his little brother is ace. He should have come to Liverpool vs West Brom in October. He would have been in good company that day.

I often say that if Liverpool decided not to enter any competitions next season I'd happily pay my season ticket to just watch him, on his own, run round Anfield with a ball, scoring into an empty net and shouting at himself. He's been terrific right from the start of his Liverpool career, but there are certain games when there might as well not be anyone else on the pitch, as all eyes in the crowd are on him and what he's going to do next. This was one of them.

The first goal would be ridiculous from any other human, but becoming standard for Luis. When he runs at defenders they often just freeze, knowing he's about to make them look stupid, but not quite sure how he's going to do it. On this occasion it was through his legs, and the shot was away before the keeper knew what was going on. The second was ridiculous, even by his standards. A diving header from the edge of the box from a clipped Cissokho cross with impossible levels of power and precision. It felt almost retro to me, the kind of goal your dad used to tell you Ian St John would score, and you wouldn't believe him. He looked like he was laughing his head off. The third was an example of an underrated skill Suárez has, although it is understandable that among so many talents, some get forgotten. On those in-swinging free kicks it's usually Suárez rather than the much taller players who Gerrard looks for, with his uncanny ability to get to the front post first like a speed skater battling for the first corner.

Aside from that he hit the bar with an overhead kick no one apart from him saw coming and was just a general nuisance to the opposition all day. I think he nutmegged an unused substitute at one point. If I was a Premier League defender I would have two big marks on my calendar for the Liverpool games that I would stare at for weeks leading up to them and happily cross out with a marker. Thank Christ for that, I can go back to playing normal fellas who try and run round me but not through me or at me. Who don't try and score every second of the game. Who sometimes just jog or walk for a few minutes. Who don't treat me having the ball as an insult to some Uruguayan god.

At the start of the season I put a bet on Daniel Sturridge to be the Premier League top scorer at a very long-looking 20–1. After Sturridge scored a gorgeous lob of his own that day Steve Graves commented to Mike Girling next to him that my bet was looking good and Mike replied, 'Nah, Suárez will catch him.' He was, of course, right. Suárez had missed the first five games of the season, and already looked like catching an on-fire Sturridge after playing just four.

What's funny is that I'd almost forgotten about this game until I watched it back, after a season of so many ridiculous performances and stunning goals. We should never forget how lucky we are to watch Luis Suárez play for Liverpool every week. I'm going to bore my kids to death about him. West Brom had Victor Anichebe up front that day. Imagine that.

John Gibbons

ARSENAL 2 LIVERPOOL 0

2 November 2013. Goals: Cazorla 19', Ramsey 59'

HJC LONDON ROCKS

WE ARE GETTING GOOD at the talking aloud in front of a crowd business. I think. The next stop on our worldwide tour of bluster and nonsense was as part of the HJC London Rocks event in London. The event had started the previous year, with nearly 500 turning up to the William Blake pub on Old Street and raising over £14,000 for the Hillsborough Justice Campaign. This year's event was held a stone's throw away from the Emirates, allowing people to attend before, during and after the game.

The beer was cheap, although not as cheap as we had advertised (oops), and the music started straight away with rock band Contra blowing away cobwebs and hangovers (although that might have just been me). After that a few of us bounded onstage for what we in the business call 'messing about'. We talked about what to expect and waited for team news and tried to gauge the mood of the room and JON FLANAGAN IS PLAYING! Wow, I don't think even his dad was expecting that. 'Insight and opinion' turned into about ten minutes of lads with microphones going 'Flanno? Really? REALLY?' Then those who had tickets went to the match and those who didn't stayed and watched it on big screens.

It's always a big two hours or so that, for those who go the game and those who don't. I've come back from the match and found my mates who haven't gone in a terrible state and wondered how on earth it had happened in what had seemed like a short space of time. On this occasion the shoe was on the other foot, and I'd coped with Liverpool slipping to a defeat by drinking at a rampant pace and found myself rather worse for wear before the rest of the lads came back and I realised I had to stand up and talk in front of people. I had the length of a John Power set to sort myself out. I didn't. I carried on drinking and sang Cast songs dead loud while hugging strangers.

But stand up and talk in front of people we eventually did. Journalist and Arsenal fan Natasha Henry joined us and was gracious but chuffed in victory. Writer and Southend fan Iain Macintosh told us we were doing great in his lovely reassuring voice. I think what I said was that we should remember how good it was just to be part of big games again. If I did I stand by it. I had got sick of watching games between the top four the previous few years and thinking how much better at football than Liverpool both teams were. No more. Arsenal were the deserved winners that day, but we were on top for periods and it looked every inch a top-of-the-table clash. Sometimes defeats can make you realise you are right where you belong, just as much as victories.

Myself and Neil then did an auction, with many people being generous in the prizes they donated and the amounts they bid. Special thanks have to go to Martin Fitzgerald from See Tickets who threw in a pair of VIP tickets to Glastonbury at the last, last minute, not only because it was a great gesture, but also because it distracted my friends' plot to make me auction off my leather jacket. I would have been bloody freezing on the rainy walk home without it. Then The Tea Street Band came on and blew everyone's head off.

The main driving force behind the night is Kristian, a South African living in London. One thing that has always staggered me from watching the Reds abroad, and that I think is unique to Liverpool Football Club, is how much our supporters all over the world buy in to everything to do with the club. Fans who should be happy to decorate their walls with pictures of their favourite players search for a much deeper connection with the team and the city, and nothing symbolises that more than Hillsborough. I know, because they have gone on record saying it, that organisations like the HJC are truly grateful for the support they have received from all corners of the globe. So far that night has raised more than £11,000 with some money still to come in. Plus we all had a laugh.

I tell you what, though, next time I'm staying over. The less said about the coach home at midnight the better.   **John Gibbons**

YOU MIGHT AS WELL COME FIRST AS COME FOURTH

ARSENAL HAVE BEATEN US. Significantly better on the day. Arteta dictating the game, Liverpool unable to get near him; Ramsey all pace and urgency; Giroud holding it up brilliantly, his movement terrific. The three at the back looked all at sea as Arsenal played in the spaces between and in front of them, leaving Liverpool outnumbered everywhere to all intents and purposes. Defeat tasted again.

It's a defeat that feels OK though – it's a big game and there look to be a lot more of them on the way.

Because look:

Ten games in. Ten games and Arsenal have 25 points on the board. They lead by five. Lead Liverpool by five points. Lead Chelsea and Tottenham Hotspur by five points. Lead Manchester City, Southampton and Everton by six. Lead Manchester United by eight.

Ten games in and behind Arsenal, you can throw a blanket over them.

Chelsea are going at a two points a game average. As are we, as are Spurs. City and Everton likewise. United a little off.

In the last 19 games of the previous season Liverpool had picked up 36 points. Just shy of two points a game. Chelsea had picked up 37. Similarly shy. Arsenal 40. Had Liverpool retained their two-goal lead at the Emirates in the second half of last season, each side would have had 38, precisely two points a game.

United led the pace with 43 over that period.

Minus Ferguson, you can throw a blanket over them.

After the penalty save against Stoke, after soaking that up, Steve Graves looks urgently into my eyes and tells me we can win the league. He tells me that we can go at two points a game. That we can go a little quicker. That we have the best strike force in the league. He tells me, no one is that good. He looks me in the eye and like a prophet filled with the light of truth he tells me we can win the league and no one is that good.

No one is that good.

This is liberating. No one is that good. No one is. Arsenal are going as fast as they can and despite pulling Liverpool all about the place at the Emirates, they don't seem like champions. City have no rhythm to them yet. Chelsea haven't set a thing alight. United can't get going.

No one is that good.

It's problematic really. What Steve Graves was saying is that we are post things. Post-Abramovich. Post-Ferguson. Post-Mansour in a sense. All these initial capital explosions ebbing slightly away and coping mechanisms being put in place through the rest of the league. In the previous decade Arsenal had literally been unbeatable. Then Chelsea were rock solid. Inevitable. Then United returned with Ronaldo, Tevez and Rooney and they were irresistible. All these sides looked like 90-point units. Now?

No-one is that good.

But everyone is good.

Spurs have a host of good players. Everton look stronger than ever. Southampton are an X factor. Arsenal, City, Chelsea and United aren't brilliant, but they all have squads capable of posting around 80 points.

So what do you say? What do you think? Where can you finish?

Fourth place has become fetishised within English football and even more so in Liverpool FC circles. Come fourth. Get fourth. Fourth becomes a jumping-off point into the Champions League and from there we grow.

But what gets you fourth? Last season Arsenal clinched it with 73 points. Just shy of two points a game. And if everyone can get that, but no one looks capable of that much more then, well, what if you can throw a blanket over them? The blanket could be from second to sixth, from first to fourth. From third to seventh.

You might as well come first as come fourth.

It's a wider philosophical point. Look to come first, fail, and you'll most likely come top four. Look to come fourth and fall short?

It goes wider again. What about the adventure? What about the drama? What about doing something, building something, aiming for something tangible? You aim for top four then your players who are good enough to come top four always know they'll get a move to a top-four club if they want one. They'll have a choice of four. Only one side can come first. And in a decade like this one, you don't know who that side will be in England. What's your move when no one is absolutely brilliant?

Language like 'project', 'philosophy', 'idea' is much maligned currently. I understand why; no one wants football to sound like a business retreat. But you need something for your young, upwardly, endlessly mobile and multimillion-pound per annum-earning footballers to buy into. You need to sell them an idea. They want to test themselves against the best, but they also want to be the best. That's the ultimate journey. The definitive project. And if it fails? It falls short? You have a hell of a consolation prize and we all start again in August, back on the definitive project.

So turn it into a mantra. Never, ever let it go. You might as well come first as come fourth.

Neil Atkinson

LIVERPOOL 4 FULHAM 0

9 November 2013.
Goals: Amorebieta (o.g.) 23', Skrtel 26', Suárez 36', 54'

BRENDAN RODGERS' LIVERPOOL DO NOT LOSE CONSECUTIVE LEAGUE GAMES

'Insanity is doing the same thing over and over again and expecting different results'
Albert Einstein

LIVERPOOL HAD, UNFORTUNATELY, lost plenty of league games last season, but never two in a row. Some say this is because Brendan Rodgers is a man who learns from his mistakes. I would say it's because Brendan Rodgers is a good football manager.

The previous game against Arsenal saw him abandon three at the back at half-time, giving the team much more attacking purpose as a result, but still no points. It was, however, enough to persuade Rodgers to move away from the system, for now at least, and towards something closer to a 4–4–2, with Henderson wide right supporting his central midfielders whenever possible and Coutinho wide left, given much more freedom to move forward. For Henderson it was a similar role to the one he had played when he first signed under Dalglish, with comparisons made to Ray Houghton tucking in during the 1987/88 season. This, of course, would make Philippe Coutinho John Barnes, a tough act to follow at this stage in his career, until you remember the last player to have a go at 'The Barnes role' was Stewart Downing. Only one of the centre halves from the Arsenal game survived, with Agger chosen to partner Skrtel in a more familiar pairing and Sakho dropping to the bench.

Changes and tweaks to the system and approach following defeats had characterised Rodgers' time as manager. As mentioned earlier, the move to a three-man defence had come about from a home defeat to Southampton. The previous season a home defeat to Arsenal resulted in drastic changes to central midfield, with Gerrard moved back and Nuri Şahin rarely given a deep-lying role again. Defeat at Tottenham was the end for the Downing at left back experience, while despite five league starts in a row, JonJo Shelvey didn't start another league game until May after a poor defeat at Stoke in December.

So where does this leave Brendan Rodgers' much-heralded 'philosophy'? If he changes his approach every time something goes wrong then does he truly have one? Wouldn't he be better deciding on how he wanted the team to play and sticking with it, through thick and thin, until the players learned what was expected of them like we have seen from other managers?

I would imagine he would argue that formations and philosophies shouldn't be confused. That how he sets the team up, and who he picks to play there, doesn't alter what he wants his teams to do and what he has asked from his players from the start; to look to attack, to pass the football on the floor, to be brave in possession at all times, to show collective desire for the ball when we don't have it. While it still might not have been clear what an ideal Brendan Rodgers formation was, either to us or even to him, we were certainly learning a lot more about what a Brendan Rodgers footballer looked like.

Truth be told, Liverpool could have played any formation that day and beaten a lacklustre Fulham destined for the drop. Some gorgeous Berbatov touches aside, they didn't offer anything going forward, and little resistance at the back, with Liverpool four up inside 55 minutes. Plenty of the Brendan Rodgers philosophy was on display; relentless work from Suárez up front setting the tone for the whole team, dominating possession, not letting up until the game was won. We even saw some lesser-spotted 'resting on the ball' in the last 30 minutes, with the manager and many of the players seemingly conscious of a busy international schedule over the next couple of weeks.

This wouldn't be the last Rodgers tweak of the season, and players would also rotate with form and injuries, but the manager was learning more about his players with each defeat. Although we were all hoping not to see too many more of those.

John Gibbons

EVERTON 3 LIVERPOOL 3

23 November 2013.
Goals: Mirallas 8', Lukaku 72', 82'; Coutinho 5', Suárez 19', Sturridge 89'

BLOODY HELL,
HOW GOOD WERE THEY?

I'VE GOT 'DERBY BELLY'. As usual, I've been suffering these incurable stomach collywobbles all week. Mercifully, I'm in our end today thanks to a late offer of a ticket from the ever-miraculous Andy Heaton. I've endured the last few derbies from the home section of the Upper Bullens courtesy of my Bluenose brother-in-law. The last few have worked out all right; 85 minutes sat on my hands, knees knocking like billy-o, listening to quite remarkable bitterness and fume from the natives directed at our lads, followed by a clenched-fist salute at the end of a nerve-shredding victory. Am I tempting fate today by being among my own people?

There is drink everywhere. At 11am Andy is already on the wine – it is 11am I've forced down a decent breakfast and feel sufficiently strong to down two rapid bottles of Becks to soothe the nerves. We order a taxi to take us towards Goodison; me, Andy and his friend who I have just met, Giulio. I'm intrigued and impressed by the eclectic variety of liquor in Giulio's carrier bag – a strong cider (which ends up in my hands as we speed over the Seaforth flyover), a couple of different lagers and a can of gin and tonic. Classy.

We meet Rob Gutmann and his son Danny (earphones in, no doubt listening to Joy Division) by the Everton Souvenir Shop opposite the imposing Dixie Dean statue. Contempt for all things Red fills the Walton air. We head for friendlier surroundings in the throng outside the away end and see Jamie Carragher and Daniel Sturridge's family in the same queue.

Inside the ground, I'm next to Andy. We don't say much to other; we are consumed with apprehension. It's a great view – across the Park End penalty area and unrestricted by the plethora of pillars that support the roof of the stand. I hate Everton but love Goodison Park; scene of some ugly moments, in particular those mid-90s maulings at the hands of Joe Royle's Dogs of War, but this lovely old football ground has given me more good days than bad. As usual on derby day the place is rocking. 'Ton, ton, ton,' abbreviate the Blue hordes stamping their angry feet on the old wooden boards. Our end does its best but is drowned out by a passionate, expectant home crowd. 'We don't care what the Redshite say'? For once, they seem focused on their own team's abilities to put one over on us.

Their new man – the hard to dislike, urbane, cavalier young Spaniard, christened 'Bobby' Martinez by these Roundheaded, very English Evertonians – has got them playing some lovely stuff. They're tucked right in behind us, making serious waves at a potential top-four finish. The rigour, tempo and aggression of David Moyes' team, which gave little to aesthetics and even less to tangible success, has been usurped by a passing style unimaginable from the core of Moyes' former players, augmented by the cerebral Gareth Barry, quicksilver Gerard Deulofeu and the exponential progress of the gifted Ross Barkley. They have a new focal point in another loanee, Romelu Lukaku.

For us, Sturridge is on the bench after a week in which Brendan Rodgers has cast doubt on the quality of his training. Jon Flanagan, withdrawn at half-time at Arsenal a fortnight ago, is back in – at left back. Most of us wonder at the wisdom of this selection.

The game starts and we score early. From a corner at the far end, Coutinho controls and volleys home. At a distance, it's one of those where there's a delayed reaction before we realise it's gone in. We go mental and Heaton and I are brothers in arms.

As ever, being in front makes me feel worse. This precious lead is something to cherish, so don't be fucking taking it away from me. Everton respond well and win a free kick 40 yards out. We back off, Agger looks like he's got sucked too close to the keeper and Mirallas stabs home a sickening equaliser. Andy's all over the role of Mignolet, anchored to his line, in this; but then Heaton the goalie always is. The nerves dissipate a little as parity is restored. Everton, with Barkley now running the show with his surges through the middle, are all over us. They look bloody good. For us, Gerrard's having a 'mare, Joe Allen is doing OK, and it's the unsung Flanagan who seems the most composed of our shaky back line.

Against the run of play, we win a free kick 25 yards from goal. Suárez, who has been away with Uruguay and has probably had about ten hours' kip all week, bends in a beauty past Howard's flailing left hand. Here we go again; back to shitting myself. Cheers, Luis. It's no pleasure this, none whatsoever. Why do we do this? The whistle goes and we muscle our way to a much-needed, soothing half-time pint from the prehistoric Bullens Stand concourse.

For most of the second half they absolutely batter us. Fluid interchange of relentless passes sees them one-on-one four or five times and only Mignolet keeps us in it. At the other end Joe Allen, looking a mile off but actually onside, misses an open goal after Suárez trickery. We stand there, open-mouthed.

Everton resume their attacks and the pressure eventually tells. Mignolet makes a brilliant parry but we fail to clear, Everton recycle cleverly and Lukaku side-foots home in front of a rabid Gwladys Street. Somehow, we get off the floor and Suárez is denied by Howard's reaction at the far post from Gerrard's brilliant volleyed cross. But Everton come again and as the clock ticks down there's a crushing inevitability about this, and soon after Lukaku nets again, unmarked from a corner. Goodison is bouncing and it makes me feel physically sick; Andy and I exchange rueful glances that admit they've been the better team.

I draw strength from this peculiar feeling of inferiority and urge us on to one last effort; more animated now that we're behind than when we were ahead. Liverpool also show some balls and win a free kick out on the right with a couple of minutes left. Steven Gerrard whips it through a vicious arc and Sturridge, on for Lucas, deflects it home with the deftest nod of the head. The sight of that Park End net bulging is gorgeous. Salvation! Christ, it's only a point but we go off our heads. Crestfallen Evertonians point and fume; point and fume, and head for the exits. Ha-ha-ha! Boss!

What a bloody game! Three-all. I'm done in, emotionally wrought, and it's only half past two. While the dust settles and the media acclaim this 'game of the season', we slope off into town and the infamous Yankee bar for a few bevies. We drink away the afternoon and conclude that it's more than a point. This Liverpool team has resolve to go with some of the early-season performances; and it's looking like we'll need all of that resolve to fend off this resurgent Everton in the battle for the Champions League places.

Long live the Goodison Derby.   **Mike Nevin**

GREAT THINGS COME IN THREES

GOALS. TITLES. POINTS.

1. Release From The Yoke Of Moyes; 2. The Value Of Three Points Over One; 3. The Similarities Between Martinez And Rodgers.

3–3.

Three flaming three.

I'm walking up Hardman Street. Radio City call. You OK to do post-match reaction? OK is interesting in this regard. Am I OK? I've had about nine pints. I'm shaking. I'm oddly euphoric. Yeah, I conclude. I'm OK.

And I get on the phone. I'm good. I am actually good. I am bouncing. I channel the euphoric. I talk about that amazing football match, the quality of Everton's play, the explosiveness of Liverpool's brilliance. I talk and talk and talk about what an advertisement that is for what is actually going on in this city.

So what is actually going on?

The Similarities between Martinez and Rodgers

These two men have turned up to this city at around the same time. Both have come through the English league system and have taken opportunities as they have come up; both want to play progressive football; both appear to care about their players' welfare as people, not as cattle; both have made efforts to think and speak about the city as a whole.

They appear to be managers who focus on development – of their football teams and footballers – rather than on weekend results.

It's easy to create false dichotomies in football. I'm certain managers such as José Mourinho and David Moyes want to develop their footballers. I am certain managers such as Martinez and Rodgers want to win every week. However, I think the latter see that development as paramount and as a by-product there will be more wins, more trophies. The former aim to win, and as part of that the footballers need to improve. They need to get better at x, y or z. Because it means winning is more likely.

There are no right answers. It's important, though, for a manager to be about something. And to keep being about it. Martinez and Rodgers have walked into Everton and Liverpool and said, 'This is what I do. This is what we do now. This is what we are about.' Which leads us to ...

The Value of Three Points over One

What we are about now is winning. A point at Goodison is always a good point. A point after being behind twice against your local rivals is a good point. But neither side settled for that point.

If you are trying to tell your players you are about something then there is an admirable simplicity in 'always be winning'. Never settle. Always keep playing and keep looking to win. The most striking and memorable part of the football match was the five minutes that followed Sturridge's equaliser. Both sides pushed on, looking for a decisive fourth. Liverpool created a chance, had a penalty shout, Everton went right back up the other end.

There's a logic to this. At this stage of the season, league football is primarily about accumulation of points. So why get one when you can have three? If you want to be around two points a game, if you want to better two points a game, then looking to force the three is the only option open to you.

It's also the pure option. How to get a group of young players to be bold, to come on board, to give everything? Winning. That's how. Always be about winning. Experienced teams can do complex decisions. We'll just do the winning.

Which leads to …

Release from the Yoke of Moyes

Martinez's stamp was already on this Everton side. And it was getting on to the Everton faithful as well. He arrived making big promises and, again, they needed to be backed up. In the same way a manager says something to a dressing room, he says something to a support. This is who we are now. Martinez came in and began redefining Everton as Everton, not as not-Liverpool. Moyes looked to define Everton as 'not-Liverpool' the moment he arrived and his tenure tapped into too much about the Evertonian mentality which is unpleasant.

Martinez has embarked on a slow process but a necessary one. Everton are a great club. They sit, just there, across the park, being great, being historic. But their greatness needn't be entirely historic. This book is as much about the city of Liverpool as the team, the impact a team can have on a city. Martinez has had a hugely positive impact on the city of Liverpool. Everton enjoy their football a lot more. I'd argue they enjoy being Everton a lot more – School of Science, not People's Club.

To try to change everything is admirable. I hope they never win a tombola, let alone a cup. But I will also be quietly pleased for their back-bending manager if they do.

Neil Atkinson

EVERTONIANS TEND NOT TO LIKE JOKES

EVERTONIANS TEND TO TAKE FOOTBALL very seriously. It's in their heart, it's in their soul. I'm not sure if it's always been the case, but it very much seems to be now. We apparently aren't meant to look at any aspect of the thing we do in our spare time and spend all our money on in a light-hearted way. There is no laughter in the corridors of the School of Science. Headmaster's rules.

On our radio show we occasionally like to speculate on what Tony Hibbert has had for his dinner. *It's in his egg, it's in his chips.* The Blues don't like it, they say we're disrespectful. I'm not sure what a 'disrespectful' dinner would be exactly, but we are suggesting them apparently. Like Tony Hibbert is really going to be listening to City Talk while out fishing, crying into his bait because we said he doesn't like flavoured crisps. I also got into trouble once for remarking at the high number of pubs in one area of Liverpool that have a picture of Brian Labone in. By all accounts I was making fun of his 'well-known' battle with the drink. Yeah, the tabloids were full of it. I presume the same people are furious with their own club that the Everton 'Brian Labone package' includes a glass of champagne on arrival.

You can't make fun of their manager for never winning anything. Until he leaves after ten years to a guard of honour before they realise they suddenly hate him too. You definitely can't make jokes about their close relationship with Manchester United. They can stand in the Anfield Road end singing songs celebrating Manchester United's success as much as they like, but bring it up and you won't have seen fury like it. They can tweet Manchester United fans who they know in glee at a Liverpool slip-up, but tease them over it and you'll get short shrift. For none of this is meant to be fun. Hating your rivals is a very serious business.

They can't even have fun when abusing our players. Other teams make fun of Steven Gerrard for not winning the league, making high-profile mistakes or slapping DJs. Evertonians have decided his children don't belong to him and want the world to know. Other fans made fun of Andy Carroll's hair. Evertonians accused Robbie Fowler of being on heroin. Come on, lads, has it ever occurred to you that some of our players might be all right?

I personally hope that lovely Roberto Martinez can rub off on them and they can all relax a bit. They haven't run onto the pitch during the game and tried to swap shirts with any of their players for a while, so that's something I suppose. For I have a dream, that one day right there in Stanley Park little red boys and red girls will be able to join hands with little blue boys and blue girls and just argue over which one is magic and which one is tragic with smiles on their faces. Surely that's not too much to ask.

John Gibbons

HULL CITY 3 LIVERPOOL 1

1 December 2013.
Goals: Livermore 20', Meyler 72', Skrtel (o.g.) 87'; Gerrard 27'

N A D I R

IT'S HALF-TIME AT HULL and I'm sitting here in the house fuming. Such is my rage that I've actually just backed Hull to the tune of £30 at 6–1 to win the game from 1–1 at the break.

Thankfully there's no one in, as I've spent the last 45 minutes effing and blinding at the telly. I decided not to go out and watch it as I didn't fancy a drink at 2 p.m. – and I can make some use of this extortionate Sky subscription – but I've still had to go the fridge and pour myself a drink.

All week, I've buzzed off that point last week at Goodison that left us in third place and reasoned a win today and four points out of six from consecutive away games keeps us in the hunt. Such is the cramping at the top of the division, the pursuit of a top-four place goes hand in hand with a realistic aim to contest this title race. And yet, in a game we ought to see as vital in both regards, we've just put in a lifeless, error-strewn half.

We started as flat as a fluke, bordering on complacent. Slow, laboured build-up, without purpose or drive in the first 20 minutes concluded with Hull going in front through a deflected shot from Jake Livermore; looping off Skrtel, over

Mignolet. As if to underline our complacency, we then sprang to life and Gerrard's free kick bent around the Hull wall – after Henderson was fouled – has brought us back into it. Instead of upping the pace thereafter, we've dallied on the ball, done little else and allowed Hull to go in at the halfway point with refreshed belief. I'm not sure the line-up has helped. Kolo Touré is back in for Agger (scapegoat for last week's penalty-box troubles at Goodison), which has shifted Skrtel to the left. The defence looks wonky.

Coutinho wasn't fit enough to start and Sturridge has done his ankle ligaments in training, which is likely to keep him out for eight weeks. Raheem Sterling has come back in and, though I'm a big fan, he's been shocking. What has happened to the lad? He seems bereft of confidence, in stark contrast to the breath of fresh air that helped Suárez carry us through those testing opening months under Rodgers last season. Victor Moses, after some initial autumn promise, is beginning to look like a mercenary – a disinterested nuisance seriously lacking commitment. His brainless squandering of possession led to Hull's goal in the first half.

The hopeful fan inside me says Rodgers will volley them all round the dressing room and we'll come out second half and put this one to bed. The cold-headed gambler, that has me logging on to my Paddy Power account, tells me it will be difficult to shake this lethargy. I've seen these vapid displays from the modern Liverpool before, from Rafa's last year, to Hodgson times ten, through Kenny's final months and Brendan's embryonic games; performances that exhibit an abominable assortment of careless passing, kamikaze play for the sake of possession across the backline with an eventual hoof from the keeper, and forwards being endlessly dispossessed by the most innocuous tackles. It's been a collective no-show and, Gerrard's goal apart, there has been nothing to suggest we can raise our game.

As the teams come back on, I tell myself that it's too obvious to expect the second half to follow the same pattern; that Rodgers' new resurgent Liverpool are better than this. It does, though. It bloody does.

We begin, all half-arsed, passing it round, but without intent, as though there's about three hours left to get a winning goal. Hull, once again, pick up on Liverpool's anaemia and establish a bridgehead of possession as the half wears on. Their fans, angered by the owner Assem Allam's plans to rebrand the club as Hull Tigers, are up for a fight. The acrimony inside the stadium lends itself to an energy in the crowd, blasting itself out of my surround-sound, and Hull City respond. However, against the general run of play Liverpool do finally create a clear opening when Coutinho – on for the thoroughly blunted Sterling – and Suárez fashion a chance for Moses to slide home. He manages to hit the keeper from six yards out. I lash the remote in the general direction of the telly.

You can see it coming. And sure enough, in the wake of Moses' miss, Hull retake the lead when Touré passes up the chance to clear from a melee in our box and presents the ball to Meyler to score at the second attempt. As chaotic as the performance is, and amid a fierce atmosphere, there's still time to get something from this horror show but Suárez just fails to convert a sweeping free kick. Liverpool continue to be as ragged as we've seen them for months into the dying minutes and Sagbo should score a third; but soon after, on 88 minutes, Skrtel manages to deflect a tame Huddlestone effort, sending Mignolet the wrong way for another own goal. At this point I've had enough. I've got ringing in my ears – a house of pain in my head – and I spend the remaining minutes sitting on the toilet with my head in my hands. The commentary downstairs is still just about audible from behind the locked door. I've ended up where this Liverpool performance belongs – in the bog.

After I while, I surface having reassessed the season with my kecks off. We need to draw a line under this. Like Shankly's analogy of a cut finger, this defeat is going to be very sore tomorrow, still painful come Tuesday, but much better on Wednesday when, just by chance, we've got Norwich at home.

The Mrs and kids are back home; they wisely give me a wide berth. They know what I'm like, although I put on a brave face and try my best not to ruin a nice family Sunday dinner. Later in the evening, I go on my phone to stick a wager on the Spanish footy.

There's 180 quid, courtesy of Steve Bruce and Hull, in my account. It's the most limited consolation, and tinged with Catholic guilt. **Mike Nevin**

STEVE BRUCE IS A GOOD MANAGER

THERE WILL BE THOSE WHO DISAGREE with the following assertion. And many of them will be from Sunderland. But here goes:

Steve Bruce is a good football manager.

He certainly seems to be against Liverpool. Against some of our best sides of the last ten years he has got results with Wigan, Birmingham, Sunderland and now Hull City. You don't do that if you aren't good at what you do.

I feel a bit sorry for Steve Bruce because he'll never find out how good a football manager he could be. He'll never get the big job. Instead he'll continue to organise sets of players impressively. He'll continue to mostly buy well (though do cross-reference Sunderland) and find ways for those players to achieve what he needs them to achieve. He'll go about his business being good but never being tipped for greatness. And because he'll never be tipped for it, he'll never get to achieve it, and while he isn't being tipped he'll often end up having to stay at clubs that one season too long.

Against Liverpool, he set his Hull side up beautifully, the first manager to successfully pack a defence against this Liverpool side and drain it of hope, exhaust its endless creativity. Liverpool have been their own undoing this season. And they've been harried and hassled and outplayed by both Southampton and Arsenal. But Hull simply neutered them.

This is one of the reasons he won't get the big job and one of the reasons football is fundamentally unfair. Neutering is the very opposite of sexy and yet there aren't a million miles between what Steve Bruce has repeatedly achieved against Liverpool with Wigan, Birmingham, Sunderland and Hull and how Alex Ferguson has defeated Liverpool over the same period. Stop them, frustrate them, make them turn inward, watch them beat themselves and then beat them. But Bruce did it with far inferior players.

However, Alex Ferguson was Alex Ferguson. He had won all this silverware. His sides were normally sparkling. And he managed Manchester United. When Manchester United win games, it's because they've done x, y or z well. Should Hull beat Liverpool or Manchester United, it's because Liverpool or United have done x, y and z badly.

Oh, and you have to give credit to Hull, obviously. Always an afterthought, never a talking point.

How do you change that, if you are Steve Bruce? Is it too far gone? It probably is. He's now at his fourth Premier League club. There's little chance of any plausible reinvention. He'll be taking sides to something that feels twelfth-ish. That's his niche and someone has to do it.

Steve Bruce also has the added hurdle of being so intensely Steve Bruce. No airs. No graces. Just a man who clearly understands football and footballers. Smart enough to never risk sounding stupid. He's uncomplicated and unadorned. He's a terrific homespun Lake District B&B of a football manager. He's comfy rooms and a simple yet delicious cooked breakfast.

The weekend spa that was Michael Laudrup seemed terrific at first but then there was that exposé about the state of the kitchens in the papers. No one could be bothered to clean. The metronomic Express by Holiday Inn which was David Moyes had been pleasantly surprising for years but when it was upgraded to a Crowne Plaza it only went and emphasised how unadaptable that space was. But the Steve Bruce B&B is going nowhere. The breakfasts are going down beautifully. The man can really fry an egg. Far fewer people than you think actually can.

Neil Atkinson

LIVERPOOL 5 NORWICH CITY 1

4 December 2013.
Goals: Suárez 15', 29', 35', 74', Sterling 88'; Johnson 83'

LUIS SUÁREZ'S THIRD GOAL AND WHAT IT TELLS US ABOUT EVERYTHING

IT'S EASY TO TAKE GOING TO THE MATCH FOR GRANTED when you do it all the time. Do anything hundreds of times, no matter what it is or how good it is, and your feelings about it will change. You think you've seen it all before; that you need something new or different to really pique your interest.

It's why the atmosphere at Anfield can be subdued at times. It's a relatively old crowd. Too often we wait to be entertained. And it doesn't really help that we've been shite for a while, does it?

But being able to go the match all the time *should* be seen as a privilege these days, I know that. I mean, how many Liverpool supporters are there in the world? Hundreds of thousands? Millions? And how many can afford it these days?

I don't know the answers to those questions. And I don't know how anyone who claims to know the answers knows the answers. But what I do know is that despite being one of the privileged 25,000 or so to hold a season ticket at Anfield – and it took me 15 years to get one in my own name – there are still times when I get a bit blasé about it. It's human nature, I suppose.

A December midweek game against Norwich City was one of those times. I got stuck in a load of traffic driving in to Liverpool from work in Manchester and by the time I reached Newsham Park, where I stick the car for the game, I was knackered, pissed off and worrying about missing the kick-off.

No pre-match pint to liven things up. No natter with the lads to take my mind off the office bullshit. Just a sweaty power-walk to the ground trying to wolf down a bag of chips and a rubbery sausage (steady now) along the way. Visions of a warm living room, a glass of single malt and the match on the box drifted through my mind as I bounded up the steps to the top of the Kop. After all, it was only Norwich (sorry, lads).

But I made it. Just. 'You'll Never Walk Alone' was in full flow and the teams were on the pitch ready to go. I still couldn't get properly up for it. Not really. It was just one of those days.

That was until Luis Suárez decided I was having a good night whether I liked it or not. A very good night, as it happens.

It's hard to say something new about our impish number seven but he's never boring. That said, there are good Luis Suárez games and there are great ones. This was a great one. This made the most miserable of Victor Meldrew wannabes crack a smile. This ensured that thousands of people said just three words and smiled as they filed out of Anfield that night: 'Luis Suárez, though …'

That's the beauty of football. Even when you're pissed off, feeling down, tired, can't be arsed, take your pick; this game can be like the bolt of adrenaline delivered to the heart in *Pulp Fiction*. Tonight it was Suárez holding the hypodermic. Goal number three – BANG.

If I wasn't awake before, I certainly am now; wide-eyed and wondrous. That's goal of the season, right there. Look at the technique to pull off that half-volley. *LOOK. AT. IT.*

Why isn't everyone still talking about it now? They should be. It should be on the telly every day, that goal. There should be T-shirts about it. It was better than Gazza's in Euro 96; he just had a more interesting celebration lined up. And before you say it, only against Norwich? Only in a run-of-the-mill Premier League game at Anfield? Gazza's was against Scotland!

Suárez's 40-yarder, his first of the night, was a belter, don't get me wrong, but you've seen players do that before. In fact, you've seen Suárez do that before. Against Norwich. And against that keeper. John Ruddy must hate him. In a way, he's maybe glad they've gone down because he doesn't have to play against Suárez next season. Soz, John.

Suárez's second was a poacher's Ian Rush-type hooked finish but the third. My word, the third. Look it up, watch it again. I guarantee it's better than how you remember it. No one – not one single person inside Anfield – was thinking 'goal' when it was laid in to the Uruguayan not too far from the centre circle.

No one except Luis Suárez.

The 40-yarder wasn't on this time, so instead Suárez headed for the Kop with a swarm of Norwich players around him. How can he get through there? How can he manufacture a goal from this?

Because he's Luis Suárez and he just can't get enough.

He controls it on his knee, he pulls the ball in to his foot, tight, flicks it over Leroy Fer, lets it bounce when everyone thought he'd hit it, and then shapes his body and hits an arrow-like half-volley when everybody thought he would take a touch. Ruddy no chance.

It was genius, absolute genius. A lovely goal. A real peach.

Cold, bored, pissed off? Not a fucking bit of it. The 37-year-old grump had got off home for a Horlicks and the ten-year-old me was grinning like it was Christmas Day, spinning around, hugging people and jumping up and down with smiles wide and eyebrows raised. Is that what a grown man should be doing? Is it befitting behaviour for a father of two? Who cares?

What. A. Fucking. Goal.

How much was my season ticket, Liverpool? Here, have some more money. It was all worth it.

Look at Suárez. Look at his face. He's overwhelmed by his own brilliance. Even he thought, 'Fucking hell, that was a bit special.' He clutches his face like he doesn't know what to do; like a kid shoved on to stage to deliver his lines in his first-ever nativity. He looks to the sky as though to say, 'Thank you, big fella.' But Suárez doesn't need to thank anyone. Not even God. It's all down to him. He's special. He's one of, if not THE, best player to pull on the red shirt. That's no exaggeration. We're privileged to watch this, to see the master at work in the flesh, in front of us, in our ground, on a shitty Wednesday night after work and a traffic jam.

That warm living room, the glass of single malt and the match on the box? That can fuck right off. There's time for all that later in life. Much later.

This was the place to be. This was a goal to savour. And it was just another part of a season that awoke my true passion for the Reds. Thanks, Luis. Same again next season?

Gareth Roberts

THE OTHER THREE GOALS LUIS SUÁREZ SCORED

I OFTEN WONDER about what kind of relationship Norwich fans have with Luis Suárez after everything they have seen him do. Do they secretly like watching him play? Do they openly like watching him play? Even if they can't admit it now, I hope in the future when they are talking about football with friends and family they can say how amazing it was to see such a talented player in full flow, like my dad does when he's talking about Eric Cantona or Denis Law. Most will probably still call him a dirty cheat. It's a shame, that. Everyone should get to marvel at exceptional footballers.

Liverpool started this game badly, you know. It wasn't happening for anyone. I remember being worried. I think that is partly why Suárez shoots from so far out for the first goal. For the first few months of Rodgers' management, Suárez was often playing central with the inexperienced duo of Sterling and Suso either side of him. Sometimes you could sense him looking around and thinking, 'Well, they're not going to do anything, so I'll do it on my own.' Luckily by this stage he seemed to trust those around him much more, but I sense his thought process on the first goal was something along the lines of 'Well, the passing business isn't working today, so I think I'll just kick it in the goal.' It's a sentiment Bob Paisley would have agreed with.

The second is a tougher finish that it looks, I think. At least that's what I say when I blast them over the bar in five-a-side. From Coutinho's corner, he can't be sure what touch, if any, Gerrard will get and has to adjust his body fairly late accordingly. It is interesting to note both that Gerrard was winning the headers off corners and not taking them. For a while Liverpool fans have debated whether it would be better to have Gerrard on corners or trying to head them in. This season we've had the best of both worlds, with Gerrard taking many fantastic set pieces, but also occasionally leaving them to others and using his height and physique in the box. Mixing it up worked well for Liverpool over the season, with defences never really sure what was coming.

The third is ridiculous and it has had its own article. All I will add is that Suárez's first goal was considered goal of the season at the official end-of-season Liverpool FC awards, as voted for by supporters. They were wrong. It's fantastic technique, don't get me wrong, but you will occasionally see wonderful strikes from distance in the lower leagues. That level of player can only dream of scoring a goal like his third. At *The Anfield Wrap* end-of-season awards, our listeners and readers voted Suárez's third higher, proving once and for all our following to be of better stock than your average fan. And definitely more attractive to the opposite sex.

I also like how he a) got a terrible pass in the first instance, b) laughed his head off after.

The fourth is a free kick, the type he makes look easy. Often on free kicks this season Gerrard has stood with him, to put some doubt in the goalkeeper's mind on who is going to take it. Sometimes Gerrard has even caught the keeper out by taking, and scoring, himself. This time Danny Agger was stood over the ball too for a left-foot option. I admire the players for going through usual procedure, but I would imagine John Ruddy knew who was going to take the kick. The fella who has scored a hundred goals past him, and was just about to make it a hundred and one. He still has time to set up another for Sterling. It's a nice finish by Sterling actually, and is quite possibly significant in terms of his season. But we're not here to talk about Sterling, are we, as I'm sure he'd understand. We're talking yet again about the player from whom you think you have seen it all, and then he staggers you again. The Magician from Montevideo. I'm going to bore my kids to death about him. Hang on, I've already said that, haven't I? I'm boring them already.

John Gibbons

LIVERPOOL 4 WEST HAM UNITED 1

7 December 2013.
Goals: Demel (o.g.) 42, Sakho 47', Suárez 81' & 84'; Skrtel (o.g.) 66'

THE PALPABLE GROWTH OF BELIEF

THERE WAS A LOT OF 'you can't really think …' during this season. It was understandable. These lads had been abject at Hull just days before for one thing. Utterly abject. But, well, no backward steps. Not a twitch. They were, aberrations aside, continuing to improve. It was around this stage I started to sketch out the Rule of Five. The Rule of Five is this:

You take any five-game run under Brendan Rodgers and pick any subsequent batch of five games and Liverpool's results and performances will be better.

This held firm until 27 April 2014.

We were all working this out around the time we played West Ham United at home. With every passing game, certainly in our own ground, we just seemed more assured. Everything went up a notch. This game the notch that increased was convention. Liverpool struggled to break West Ham United down in the first half but they worked at it, finally getting the breakthrough they deserved just before the break. There was nothing unhinged or unbridled about this Liverpool performance, there was just a lot of inevitable about it.

There was little stress in the ground, even when West Ham pulled one back.

Or rather when Skrtel got his name on the scoresheet. It's a good job this is a nice book, or there might be a thousand words on a thousand own goals. The stress in the ground was the interesting thing. There was an assured hush about the place, not an anxious hush. You'd rather not have hush, obviously, but this was a much better brand.

West Ham huffed and puffed but Liverpool impressed even after Gerrard went off injured. There was a wobble but they came back to finish the game off with an assertive flourish. Lucas looked very good indeed and he and Allen were able to take time out of the game before Suárez put the tin hat on it. It obviously helped that Kevin Nolan got himself sent off.

This win put Liverpool second on goal difference and this was becoming something harder to ignore. As was the value of the attacking football. What was also growing clearer was the mortality of our rivals – this weekend Chelsea were defeated at Stoke and Manchester City were held by Southampton. What happened at Hull was dreadful but we were not alone in having that in us.

There was less talk of 'you can't really think ...' afterwards and a lot more 'do you really think ...' It was another challenge overcome. Allardyce wanted to kill the game stone dead, but we'd stopped that one from working too. Win your home games. That will always give you a springboard. It sounds beyond basic but it needs reiterating. A reason to believe then and to believe now, whenever the now you read this is, is that Liverpool under Brendan Rodgers will almost certainly be good at home. This is the value of the attacking football. Liverpool were to end the campaign having won 16 of their 19 homes. The side that finished ahead won 17. The side that finished directly below won 15. And the sides that finished in fourth and fifth won 13 apiece.

You win your games by having players who stick it in the back of the net and it is worth pointing out you play more poor sides than good these days. Empower those players. Give them that belief. You can see it grow on the pitch due to the inevitable nature of Liverpool's football. And that resonates off it too. For a game with more of a hush around it than many this season, it seems odd to say, but the team and crowd were very much in harness for West Ham. We loved the loud flourishes but we feasted on the quiet certainty. Liverpool were making more and more sense.

Neil Atkinson

GOING CORPORATE

I NORMALLY SIT WITH MY DAD AT HOME GAMES. He bought two season tickets in the Upper Centenary Stand when it first opened and we've had them in my family ever since. I still remember when he told me and my sister he'd bought them; they were the most exciting books of paper I'd ever seen. I was ten years old, and I think I'd only been to three or four games up to then, and now in front of my eyes I had a whole season of watching the Reds. Well, half a season at least – they were to share, after all – so I quickly began plotting how to trick my sister out of all the big games. This didn't work, incidentally. Some games I certainly remember missing over the next few seasons were Liverpool 3 Manchester United 3 and the classic Liverpool 4 Newcastle United 3 (although I was at the poorer imitation a year later).

At some point my sister's interest waned, possibly when my dad started asking for money, and it started being just me and him. I like where we sit in the ground. The seats were slightly better at first, before they moved us back seven rows to put in more corporate season tickets with comfy cushions on them, but I still like them. I like the people around us too, and it's nice to see some of the same faces every year. We did, however, usually try and buy tickets in different parts of the ground for home cup games as it was nice to get a different perspective, but when the Automated Ticket Scheme came in it was much easier to just tick a couple of boxes at the start of each season and not have to worry about ringing up when you were meant to be in work. This did mean you have the same view every game though. The reason I am telling you all this is so you know that a different viewing perspective was the SOLE REASON for my accepting an executive box for the West Ham home game.

The box we were in belongs to Red Touch Media, who are the main sponsor of *The Anfield Wrap*. Normally they fill it with people far more important than us, but around Christmas fewer people were around so there was a chance for a few of us to get in and see how the other half live. I didn't realise until I went that all executive boxes were customised by the owners; I thought they would be all the same. Red Touch have got theirs like I dreamed my house would be when I was younger: all cool sofas and arty pictures of Liverpool Football Club and people bringing you beer.

Jokes aside, the view is fantastic. It's almost like they have put them there on purpose, close enough to the action to hear the players and appreciate their touches, but far enough away to get perspective. The days of watching behind a screen are also long gone. They have high chairs outside the box for you to sit on so you feel part of the action. As a result, for all the lovely food you get before and during the game, and all the attentive service, the actual match itself is just watching a game of footy with all your mates in great seats. Perfect.

A couple of other things worth mentioning are that you have a screen in the box showing the action. This was great for three reasons:

1.	Being able to turn round and watch replays of any big moments during the game.
2.	Being able to watch Manchester United get beat by Newcastle in the early kick-off while tucking into food and drink.
3.	Laughing our heads off when we saw Assaidi had scored the winner against Chelsea.

You also get a slightly different betting experience in that a nice lady comes and puts your bets on for you and you get paid out on the day. For some reason we all decided to throw a fiver each on Sakho at 33–1. After a bit of confusion over who had been given the first we found out this had come in. Not a life-changing amount of money for each of us but as a wedge it looked ridiculous. Now I am aware of the irony of a group of lads who see themselves as 'proper' football fans messing about with a big pile of money in an executive box, but it was still a lot of fun.

Because of this I may have got a bit carried away at this point. More beer, more food, more wine! I think we had to get asked to leave by the staff in the end because they were closing up. So we went to town for yet more beer, more wine and, for God knows what reason, even more food. After an Italian meal we went to a rooftop bar of a hotel a friend was staying at for an unnecessary nightcap where I tried to talk to two nurses on a Christmas night out about Jordan Henderson.

The next day I felt dreadful, punished for excess and gluttony. This is why I'm not allowed nice things. Back to the Centenary Stand next game, where I belong. Although I can't have been that bad. They did invite me back eventually.

John Gibbons

HALF TIME

GENEROSITY OF WORLDWIDE SPIRIT?

I WAS ASKED TO SPEAK AT A SYMPOSIUM about 'generosity' around this stage of the season. I remember because I spoke to a lot of people around this time about it. I asked John and Steve. I spoke to Wayne Scholes from Red Touch Media about his impressions of corporatism within football and whether or not Liverpool do it well.

I chatted to everyone I could find. I'd never done a symposium before and this was taking place at Homebaked, Anfield's community bakery. I was doing it with a guy from FC United called Phil Frampton. He was very much Against Modern Football when modern football wasn't that modern.

Sometimes people are tempted to say things like 'If you don't like it so much, go and set your own club up,' when people like Phil speak. Problem is, Phil has. He didn't like it. So he did something about it.

I'm ambivalent about this. I can see the value in that approach and I can only respect it, but I also think you can carve out your own space. I suppose Phil could say they needed to carve out a bigger space. Again, I respect that.

The title was the same as this piece, 'Generosity of Worldwide Spirit?' and having it in Homebaked gave that a specific focus. Homebaked's oven was bought via a Kickstarter campaign. Donations came from all over the place. It wasn't football-specific but it's clear that its Anfield location played a part.

Football exists in that generous space though it has constant influences on it pulling it towards something very different. It's a constant battleground and it's one every football club wins and every football club loses and every set of supporters win and every set of supporters lose. You decide where your lines are and hope the club doesn't let you down a lot.

Liverpool do let us down. They've been letting us down since time began. It's existed in that space since time began. But now everything is bigger and more public. More expensive and more public. More corporate and more public. More, more, more. How do you like it?

You carve your own space out. And I think Liverpool have slightly struggled to do that themselves recently. The core of the club is so resolutely immune to corporatism that I think it cannot guide the club. We, broadly speaking, think it is all bloody stupid. The world doesn't, though. People are paying outrageous quantities of money for names on training kits. My opinion of DHL doesn't move one iota from their involvement in Manchester United, for instance. Someone's must somewhere. Surely. I do wonder. It's adding up somewhere.

Liverpool are, on the adding up, evidently getting better. More money means more good players. More good players means more good football. More good football means happier supporters and, ideally, more money. And so it goes. I still don't think they can quite crack what they are as an identity. The supporters have boxed that off and this is another conflict over space. The most meaningful charity events in Anfield during the match over the last couple of years have been for Standard Chartered's throroughly well-meaning 'Seeing Is Believing' charity.

Liverpool themselves have involvements but they don't appear to be particularly coherent. This is what I mean when I say they haven't carved their space out. Everything is political and everything is potentially dangerous.

Try to say nothing at all if unsure.

But supporters can carve space out. The generosities surrounding Liverpool's public, match-going and armchair, in Liverpool and in Leamington Spa, in England and worldwide, are absolutely staggering. They beggar belief. In terms of time, energy and money there is someone doing something that adds to the community, to the greater good, to an appeal. Hillsborough is the obvious cause but it goes above and beyond that.

Beyond the idea of simple charity, there is Spirit Of Shankly, those who serve on the Supporters' Committee, fanzines, forums. Boss Nights and Spion Kop 1906.

There is so much energy poured into making things better, different, distinctive for the Liverpool support. I've no doubt many enjoy it and it isn't all altruism by any means. But it's generous in spirit.

When I grow frustrated with the club it's often because I feel they aren't tapping into this. Maybe they are doing the right thing; letting the supporters work this out and getting out of the way. I ultimately feel there's a red horde to be tapped into. Every week at the ground. Every day around the world. I'm an optimist. I believe this horde can be tapped into for nothing but constant good. Wide-eyed and naïve, no doubt. But I've been there, seen the generosity of worldwide spirit, felt its effects. It's real.

Liverpool have to be able to interact with it better. But without simply pointing at ticket prices and the future of Anfield (the latter of which will hopefully be addressed soon), I'm all questions and no answers on this one.

Neil Atkinson

THE DIFFICULTY OF BEING LIVERPOOL

THE WAY I PICTURE IT IS THIS. Glasses are being raised in the back of a salubrious London gentlemen's club after a successful court case, an epic swindle complete. Contracts are being signed, i's are being dotted and t's are being crossed. Towards the end of the night, when it feels safe, Martin Broughton leans over the table to John W. Henry and says, 'Oh, one more thing, John. They're all mad. Completely doolally.'

I try not to criticise Liverpool Football Club and the way they operate too much. Sometimes they make this very difficult, impossible even, God bless them, but the reason I try not to is that I accept that it is very difficult being Liverpool. There is so much conflicting information we throw at them as supporters they mustn't know what to think.

The best example I can think of is one of Bill Shankly's most famous quotes: 'At a football club, there's a holy trinity – the players, the manager and the supporters. Directors don't come into it. They are only there to sign the cheques.'

We love to trot that one out. Especially when a managing director tries to push his way to the front of a photo opportunity or says something daft in the paper. But as soon as something goes wrong, for example the Suárez racism debacle, we are demanding stronger leadership. 'They have left Kenny out to dry, where are the owners in all of this?' we cry. To which a quite reasonable answer may have been, 'At home writing the cheques like we were told, lads.'

We also talk extensively as fans about a 'Scouse heart' in the team and giving young players a chance. But if a kid comes in and understandably struggles for a few games, my God, do we give him a hard time about it. There is very little understanding of the time it takes to find your feet. Just ask Jamie Carragher, who says he got years of abuse playing full back from the Kemlyn Road before he learned how to be one of the best defenders in the world.

But the main battle for Liverpool Football Club – and it has been a battle for years – is growing the club financially without compromising 'The Liverpool Way'. That phrase without definitive meaning that has tripped up so many over the years. It was 'The Liverpool Way' that meant the club shop in the city centre was closed as Liverpool paraded the European Cup through town, because we thought it would be nice to fly all the club staff out to Istanbul. It was 'The Liverpool Way' which meant Manchester United grew commercially far beyond Liverpool while we decided it wasn't really our thing.

There is, at least, now an acceptance that we need to increase revenue to compete, but we seemingly won't all agree on how this should be done. Ticket prices are the main sticking point, with most match-going fans thinking they should, on the whole, be lower rather than higher. However, there are probably some fans who go less often who would be happy to see increases if it meant better players on the pitch. This argument falters, of course, when money is wasted. Do you know we could have let over 4,000 local kids in for free each league game rather than pay Joe Cole's wages? I like that fact. It makes you want to put your head in an oven.

So if increasing ticket revenue is tricky, maybe raising commercial revenue is the way forward? But this can be problematic too when the club wants to seem both local and global at the same time. The club has to be careful to seem grounded in the traditions of the city, but also appeal to global brands and sponsors. It wants to appeal to, and sell to, fans all over the world, but has to be aware that local fans are already resentful when they can't get tickets but travelling fans can. Naming rights for the stadium is one example of something that has been raised in the past but been met with considerable opposition.

On top of this there is the uneasy relationship the match-going support has with television companies, and their increasingly creative times to play football matches, often without consideration for those who have to travel to the games. Every pound you take from them inevitably makes it more and more unlikely a fan's voice will be heard when men in suits are deciding when games of football take place.

The owners should perhaps be applauded that they have managed to increase revenues among all the contradictions and difficulties we throw at them. Especially when even commercial deals which seem to have no downsides for supporters, such as the Subway and Dunkin' Donuts deals, are moaned about by certain sections of the fan base. But we never said we'd be easy, lads. We're selfish, impatient and a little insecure. We make mistakes, we're out of control and at times hard to handle. But if you can't handle us at our worst, then you sure as hell don't deserve us at our best.

John Gibbons

THE PEN

IT STARTED, as so many of these things do, with me being a dick.

Anyone who's signed up for LFC official membership will know the club like to 'incentivise' handing over the cost of a match ticket for the chance to buy actual tickets at a later date. They do this by sending you tat. I've got a kitchen shelf stacked high with seasons' worth of unused scarves, keyrings and hastily produced, cobbled-together anthology books like, er, this one.

What I've also got are pens. Mountains of pens. If I want a Parker with a Liver bird etched on it I'll wait for my mum to come through at Christmas time. She always, always delivers on this front. But Liverpool Football Club are insistent on sending me more. I'm as keen on writing things down as the next man, but I've got pens. Everyone's got pens. I've got more pens than fingers within sight of me right now. And I'm writing this on the toilet.

So, like the dick I am, when the renewal package came through over the summer I sneered at the assortment of trinkets which fell from the gaudy box. I scoffed at the 120 People Who Made LFC book (which was actually pretty good) and the pin badge. Most of all I was really snide about the pen. Snide enough to go on Twitter and be snide in public, which generally isn't my thing.

And so I tweeted:

More tat in a box from Liverpool football club. Does anyone really want a branded parker pen?

The question was rhetorical. I don't want this item, and therefore I can't imagine why anyone else would.

The response was unexpected. It turned out lots of people actually did want a pen. Lots. Not being jaded, boring dicks, they had taken the question at face value. And so I had to devise a complicated process of selection, and send a pen to Preston. And then the previous season's to Harrogate. I may or may not have fixed the draw to save myself the cost of overseas postage.

And the moral of the story, other than don't be me, is that maybe the people who work at Liverpool Football Club do know, and care, what a lot of fans want. They definitely – definitely – don't get everything right, but whether it's doing deals with Dunkin' Donuts or creating/genetically engineering the frankly terrifying Mighty Red mascot, they quite often seem to be having a go.

The issue strikes at the core of our relationship with the club. Perhaps because the way we engage seems like such a personal bond, we allow our own preferences to intrude too much. Supporters, after all, are a disparate group. We are ostensibly connected by nothing more than our preference for Liverpool FC. There's no reason we should have the same tastes in stationery, or giant mythical bird costumes.

The club has to do its best, has to annoy most of us, has to fail to please all the people all the time. It's part of trying to satisfy a mass audience. It's nice when it feels like they're not trying actively to piss us off, lecturing us about values or putting Charlie Adam's face on things. But it's not the end of the world if they tweet a video which isn't to your taste, or send you a gift they think you might like.

It's not going to stop us winning football matches.

'A Member'

TOTTENHAM HOTSPUR 0 LIVERPOOL 5

15 December 2013.
Goals: Suárez 18', 84', Henderson 40', Flanagan 75', Sterling 89'

A GLIMPSE AT A POST-GERRARD FUTURE

'YOU GOT LUCKY WITH GERRARD, you'll be finished when he goes,' I am often told by friendly Evertonians. Actually they are less polite than that, but let's try and keep things relatively clean. Hitting them back with relative win percentages when he plays and when he doesn't seems rather pointless in these situations, and besides, I don't really believe them when I'm saying them. Throughout his career Gerrard has transformed very good Liverpool teams into great ones and average ones into winning ones, not just through his unquestionable talent, but his remarkable levels of desire and pride in his shirt.

So when he pulled up injured shooting against West Ham, it felt like it had the potential to derail Liverpool's promising season. There were plenty of other players in good form, of course, but the team looked awfully young without his leadership, and the midfield awfully small without his presence. I was nervous about Tottenham and their massive lads without him and Sturridge. It was OK, though. Our players decided to go and win 5–0 instead. Away.

Brendan Rodgers hadn't completely won everyone over by this point, for reasons both fair (lack of experience) and unfair (he wasn't Rafa Benítez or Kenny Dalglish). Overall I felt he was the best man for the job, but one of my nagging doubts was that he talked a better game than he played, or a different game at least.

One of the most refreshing things about him is that he is always willing to talk about football and genuinely seems to enjoy it, but this does open you up for criticism and critique. In particular, it seemed puzzling when he spoke so much about possession and pressing, when this Liverpool team didn't seem madly keen on either. There is no right or wrong way to play football, of course, but it did perplex me why he talked up one style of football so much, when we didn't seem to be moving any closer towards it. Things take time to integrate, but Roberto Martinez seemed to have Everton playing exactly how he wanted in less than half a season, albeit under less pressure to get results.

Tottenham Hotspur away wasn't just our best performance so far under Brendan Rodgers, but the closest we had come to performing how he spoke about wanting his teams to play. One holding midfielder, with two ahead harrying and pressing and supporting each attack. Three attacking players interchanging positions and not giving the opposition a moment's peace without the ball. Ten outfield footballers demanding the ball, all wanting to attack and probe. Against supposed rivals for a top-four place Liverpool were terrifying with the ball and relentless without. Tottenham didn't have a single shot on target all game and were lucky to restrict Liverpool to five goals.

While most fans were willing to limit their post-match analysis to 'How great was that?!' there were inevitable questions about the missing captain and how he would fit back in to a team finally playing in the style we had been waiting for, and exceeding all expectations in the process. This felt like a premature discussion to me. It was just one game, after all, and he wouldn't be back for another few weeks anyway, by which time a lot can change. However, it was hard to see him playing the role either Allen or Henderson had in that performance, while those advocating moving him further forward must have had doubts after seeing the work rate of the front three, and Raheem Sterling put in his best performance of the season by a mile.

It turns out Steven Gerrard and Brendan Rodgers had talked about where Gerrard was likely to fit in moving forward already. It's impossible to say if this game accelerated that move, but it seems unlikely it didn't go a long way to convincing both manager and player that this needed to happen sooner rather than later for the development of the team. By the time he returned to league football against Stoke City it was in a more withdrawn role, where he would excel for the rest of the season.

After this game Luis Suárez had scored more league goals than Tottenham Hotspur, by the way. This isn't really relevant to the above piece, but it's a lovely statistic. Remember this when people say Andre Villas Boas was unlucky to get sacked the next day. **John Gibbons**

HOW MUCH FUN IS THIS?

HAVE YOU EVER SEEN THAT DOCUMENTARY about the making of *Exile on Main Street*? There's one bit that has always stuck with me. The Stones are talking about the shambolic nature of the recording sessions in Keith Richard's villa in the South of France. The endless jamming sessions, everybody pissing about and not taking it seriously. But then it happens.

Nothing is said. It's just eye contact. Everyone looks at each other and they know this is the moment. Everything was leading up to this. They play and it's perfect. The perfect take.

Everything was leading up to this.

Something had been missing. We've been averaging two points a game since January, we're comfortably in the top four and the fans have started to have fun. The fans are starting to have loads of fun. But something's been missing.

It's too simplistic to say it's a big result against a big team. It's more than that. It's a game and a performance that defines this team. A blueprint. Something that everyone can look back on and say, 'Yes, that was it. That was the time when it all clicked, the time when we proved it was possible. That was the best that we could be and if we can do it once we can do it again. That was the proof.'

Up to now, Rodgers hasn't had that. For all the wins and the goals there hasn't been a game the fans would want on DVD.

That's what's been missing. Rodgers' DVD game.

Tottenham are massive lads. I don't mean they watch Soccer AM, drink WKD and read Nuts a lot. I mean they're big men. Most of them are walking at a minimum of six foot, walking with their perfect physiques, the sort of physiques that can get away with wearing white all the time. Dembele, Sandro, Paulinho, Capoue, Walker, Sandro, Chadli – massive, massive lads.

Sterling, Coutinho, Allen, Lucas, Flanagan – little, little lads.

We've got half a team of little lads.

Little lads vs massive lads at a ground we haven't won at for seven years.

But everything was leading up to this.

And it happens. The thing that was missing is no longer missing. What happens? Liverpool play the best football I have ever seen them play.

I should caveat that last statement by saying I'm 43. I've seen loads of Liverpools, all the great Liverpools from the 1970s and 80s. The 5–0 against Forest in 1988, the 4–0 against Real Madrid in 2009. I'm not daft, they were great, but what I saw today was better. This came from almost nowhere, a complete shock to the system, and it was incredible to behold.

Henderson, Sterling, Allen and Coutinho produce performances that literally transform them. On this day, they become the players they will be.

Suárez looks like what he is – the best striker in the world.

Flanagan scores the third. Jon Flanagan scores. Jon Flanagan celebrates.

Jon Flanagan scores, water dropping from the shuddering crossbar, and joy is unconfined. Jon Flanagan has a whole team running towards him. A team transformed and transcendent, a team which has become the team it will be. Brendan Rodgers' Liverpool. Brendan Rodgers' Tricky Reds.

Later in the year, at an *Anfield Wrap* event in New York, I'm asked what my favourite goal of the season is. I pick Flanagan's against Spurs. Every single one of these Liverpool players, irrespective of their position, should go to bed the night before the game dreaming of scoring goals. Jon Flanagan now goes to bed dreaming of scoring goals, and if he can go to bed dreaming of scoring goals then the whole team can go to bed dreaming of scoring goals.

Dreaming of scoring goals. Having fun dreaming about scoring goals. Just scoring goals, endless goals.

Spurs 0 Liverpool 5 was the perfect take. It was the best Liverpool I've ever seen, the BC/AD moment of Rodgers' team.

Now the fun really starts.

Everything was leading up to this.

Martin Fitzgerald

MAD SCORELINES

MAD SCORELINES BETWEEN TOP TEAMS are in vogue this decade. I remember the previous decade. Almost every game between the best sides was tight. Mascherano lost the ball on the halfway line against Chelsea at Stamford Bridge one year at 0–0. From the point he'd given it away I knew:

a)   Chelsea were in
b)   They would score
c)   We had lost the game.

That was the way these games would go. Dudek is poor against Manchester United and Manchester United win. John O'Shea scores in the dying embers of one game, Ryan Babel in another. It was rare to see anything greater than a two-goal margin between sides at the top of the table and rare to see either side score more than two. One season we lost to Chelsea 4–1 at home, and we remember beating United 4–1 away. One hurt intensely, the other was glorious. I remember Newcastle beating Manchester United 5–0 and it was tumultuous. It felt like the world was upside down.

Chelsea 3 Arsenal 5

Manchester City 6 Arsenal 3

Manchester United 8 Arsenal 2

Manchester United 1 Manchester City 6

I mean, think about that last one. Manchester United absolutely battered on their own ground. While Alex Ferguson managed them. Not that bloke they got in for a laugh this season. Alex Ferguson. Enough time has passed now that we can say it – he was good.

Tottenham then. So often spanked this decade while finishing consistently in the top six. So many batterings I won't even list them. This game, at White Hart Lane, was where we started to get in on the act of tearing rivals to shreds and setting those shreds aflame. These were meant to be our close rivals in the attritional race for fourth. They were still doing trench warfare and they suddenly found themselves in the midst of a blitzkreig.

But why are these scorelines suddenly happening with such regularity at the top of the table? It is a variety of things but I think one is that footballers are, simply, getting better going forward at a rate faster than they are improving defensively. I think the technical levels of the very best players are making it harder and harder to cope with and the coaching of those levels has improved. It takes the most intense catenaccio to stop these players from playing and from hurting your side repeatedly. I think the work rate of the best attackers has especially increased markedly – the English league now rarely sees players like Le Tissier and Merson – and the concentration levels required to stop them is immense and difficult to maintain.

It's difficult to choose standout defenders at the top sides this season. Gary Cahill has looked exceptional whenever I've seen him but has that Mourinho shell around him. Skrtel hugely impressed in the second half of the season for Liverpool. There was all sorts of talk around Mertesacker and Koscielny but that had to die down after a million drubbings. Kompany hasn't been great and Demichelis is a curate's egg. None of these names are ones which stop you in your tracks – in Vidic, Hyypia, Ferdinand, Campbell, Terry and Carvalho, this league used to have some of the world's best centre backs in their prime. Now it still has top forwards and wide players but fewer defenders you'd stake your house on.

There appear to be fewer coaches around making tactical decisions based almost entirely on stopping opponents and more making tactical decisions based on exploiting opposition weaknesses. You should always think about your opponent, but now sides enter games thinking about what we will do to them, not what they will do to us. Mourinho's sides rarely get tangled up in these games, Wenger's do. It's no accident that the Merseyside derby finished 3–3, a scoreline reflecting similar managerial approaches.

I've never had to pick myself up from a 0–5 home drubbing. I honestly wouldn't know where to start. It is something that should never happen. It will, at some point. I'm likely to watch Liverpool for another 30 years and so it surely, surely will and I'm also going to watch a Liverpool side which will be going one way, attacking far more than defending. Leaving holes. Yet it seems like a DNA thing. At our poorest under Hodgson, Dalglish and – upon his arrival – Rodgers, we have never looked like shipping a hatful at home. We've never looked like that is possible or acceptable.

I think that is the unspoken thing, beyond all the coaching and the tactics and the improvements. Manchester United got battered by City, but while they lost another derby under Ferguson, they didn't get a battering. Whereas Arsene Wenger ships eight at Old Trafford and things like it happen again and again. It's almost a viral thing. These scorelines test and change your tolerance. Some football clubs either are or become immune to them. Some allow them to happen and become weaker and weaker over time. Arsenal concede six at City, five at Liverpool, six at Chelsea and finally three at Everton this season because they've been weakened over time and that fourth place is more important than everything, including pride.

So perhaps we'll never have to see a 0–5 at Anfield. And if we do see one then I want a football manager who ensures we never see a second one. One thing does seem likely, though. Until three or four clubs at the very top of the table start employing managers who stop games rather than energise them, and who pursue the best stoppers in the world in the transfer market, we could very well be seeing mad scorelines for the next few seasons.

Neil Atkinson

LIVERPOOL 3 CARDIFF CITY 1

21 December 2013.
Goals: Suárez 25', 45', Sterling 42'; Mutch 58'

WHERE WE HAVE COME FROM

WATCHING CARDIFF CITY AT ANFIELD, hearing the chants around Mackay directed at Vincent Tan, threatening a riot, I find myself transported back to Hicks and Gillett. The football secondary to what is off the pitch. Supporters in disarray. That feeling of a football club being taken from you. I want to tell these men and women that we went through this. We went so close to the wire.

I think this is where the darkness that dogged us came from. The black hole emitting dark matter.

Supporter bases are fractious, fractured things which can be exploited for that least capitalist of qualities – loyalty. But Cardiff have seen the kit change colour. They've put up with that indignity. The 1927 Club of London and South East-based fans proudly proclaimed themselves to be the only group which opposed Tan's rebrand, and formally withdrew their support in 2012. Many others, both individually and collectively, have simply turned their backs on the club. They don't consider it theirs and want no more to do with it.

I think they've no idea how hard all this is.

This approach may be understandable, but it can't help those seeking to change the direction of the club. If you believe a football club has a soul and all the stuff about the fans being the true owners and the chairman just a custodian, why throw your own hand in and leave the man you despise with the run of the place?

I think about clambering the ivory tower and making someone like Vincent Tan listen. Vincent Tan doesn't want to listen. Vincent Tan doesn't ever need to listen. I'm so angry this is so often left to us. To supporters. There has to be checks and balances.

As for those who have remained, by allowing their anger to crystallise around the Mackay issue they switched the focus of the media narrative away from fundamental changes to the club's identity and on to a question of personnel. A much easier story for journalists to write and the public to digest, and one with a limited lifespan. He stays or he goes, the caravan moves on, you're still wearing red at home.

I think all this but I know how hard it all is. To coalesce and drive the issues around a football club. They've got it tough.

During what preceded and what became Spirit of Shankly every battle was difficult to fight. The majority of people don't go to football in order to have an argument. Those who do actually enjoy an argument – I am one of those people. Everyone has an opinion about how far you should or shouldn't go but that doesn't mean they are prepared to go that far. Marches with supporters on the sidelines cheering you on but not joining the march. Arguments over what should or shouldn't be done with people who love the football club with every fibre of their being and feel it is being taken from them. Everyone wanting the same thing, unsure of how to get there. There's no manual for it. There's no plan. Every situation is different. All you can do is care and find ways to get others to care.

It was a terrible time at Liverpool. The endless rumours about Benítez, the finances, the politics, Sky Sports News, spades in the ground. Hicks. Gillett. Purslow. Broughton. Hodgson. That second group: Ayre, Parry, Moores. Everyone tainted. Us tainted. Arguments, violent arguments on the Kop. Khmer-Rouge memos. The club was brought to its knees and was, bar the engine room around Benítez, utterly dysfunctional. And finally that engine room collapsed too, unable to sustain the ballast it had to pull forward.

I tell the stories from back then rarely. When I do it's a two-hour story with a million characters of all the people I met in Spirit of Shankly. So many good men and women, straining every sinew, taking its toll. Doing things they should never have had to do. Things no one wanted to have to do. The stories from back then aren't always happy ones. They are, though, stories about solidarity, about fellow feeling, about passion. But they aren't happy ones. They are from a time when the darkness emerged, the darkness that has dogged us.

The darkness doesn't dog us any more. I feel, on this winter's day, when Liverpool win to go top of the league at Christmas, like we've fought the darkness back. Nothing is perfect. Nothing is won. But the darkness can't get us now this season. We turn up at Anfield expectant. This is Liverpool's tenth home league game of the season. We've won nine. This young manager, these young players, led from the front by the most determined, unorthodox, glorious footballer I have ever seen, have carried a torch, fuelled with goals, refusing to be tainted by everything that has gone before. Nothing to do with him. He just wants to win at football more than anyone ever has.

Cardiff have their battles to fight. Ours are over. What's left is solidarity, the fellow feeling, the passion. We've burned the darkness off with this fresh spark. What we have left is what we all went through together. How it made us feel. And how, through what we felt, we can look at the world now on the other side. What's remained when the darkness is burned off is what powers the second half of this season in the stand:

We'll reclaim what is ours. What shysters and opportunists took from us. We'll reclaim it and you know what? More than anything, you know what? We'll enjoy the reclamation like men and women possessed. We'll have a ball. We'll have a riot.

Neil Atkinson

TOP AT CHRISTMAS

I'M IN TOP CONDITION for this early kick-off after a quiet Friday, having swerved the works' Christmas do last night. Poor form, some might say, but there was no way I was getting up and driving back to Liverpool after a night on free ale and useless canapés in Oxford. I couldn't have missed the match, and anyway it's my lad Sam's 16th-birthday weekend so I had the perfect excuse to get home pronto after a meeting down there yesterday. It's a big one for the Reds today; after the home wins over West Ham and Norwich and last week's slaying of Spurs we can go top, and stay there if Arsenal fail to beat Chelsea on Monday night. The thought of sitting down to my Chrimbo dinner with Liverpool heading the Premier League is a tantalising one, not least for the message it conveys with half the season gone.

By coincidence, but as a handy extra birthday present for Nevin junior, we're in the Red Touch Media box in the Centenary Stand today with a few of the *Anfield Wrap* lads. Despite nearly 35 years of going to Anfield, and having worked in 'business' all my adult life, I've never touched for any kind of executive ticket so this is something of a novelty – a far cry from my usual distant enclave in Block 306, stood at the back of the Kop.

In fact in all that time my acceptance of sporting 'freebies' has been restricted to sitting alongside Tommy Docherty in the South Stand at a United–Liverpool game (courtesy of Adidas) when Rob Jones made his debut, and an invitation from Saab to watch Waterloo Rugby Club take on some other crap bunch of egg chasers in 1988. On the latter occasion, my dad and I scoffed a few pork pies, had a pint and then drove straight to Anfield for Liverpool vs Middlesbrough without so much as seeing a scrum.

We're advised to get here today in decent time, so I'm in the Centenary car park waiting by 11.30 a.m. The tickets are at the posh desk for pick-up and Sam and I are both fit enough to leg it up the stairs at the expense of the shiny lift. (I've got an acute fear of getting stuck in lifts.) In the corridor upstairs there's bucks fizz waiting which is simply not strong enough to justify sipping so I knock it back in one and go looking for the oak door to our 'box'.

The best thing about being in this box is that your friends are here. Rob Guttman is here, his opening pint of bitter already downed and a bottle of Pinot on the go. He tells me of his recent weekly betting venture which is all about solace over financial gain, involving laying Liverpool in case we lose or draw, and how much it's costing him as this very real title challenge hots up. He's got Cardiff at about 12–1 today and something like 6–1 for the draw so he's quids in if we fuck it up. I tell him about my Hull bet and how we're a pair of sad bastards happy to lose money as long as our team wins.

It's only 45 minutes to kick-off now and I'm intent on getting into the wine so I get a cardboard cup (meant for coffee) and wander outside to take in the views. The spec is just above where my dad resides in the old Kemlyn Road seats. I chuckle to myself that being inside the ground at this time and not in one of The Solly, King Harry or The Albert, it's probably the first time I've seen the players do their pre-match drills since the 86/87 season, the year I departed the standing Kop. The warm-up exercises are relatively interesting to watch – for about 25 seconds. I preferred watching Roy Evans floating endless practice corners onto the boot of Kenny Dalglish.

I come back inside and view the printed team sheet (another first for me) and while I'm not looking Andy Heaton – the hostess with the mostest – fills my glass for the third time. I'm feeling tipsy and sense that this might not end well. However, I haven't committed to anything after the match, so I can always go home wrecked about seven o'clock.

Kick-off draws closer and we're joined by Gareth Roberts and his little lad, Carragh, and Neil's lovely partner Samantha. We all throw in a fiver on a Suárez hat-trick, which doesn't seem that unlikely given his prolific form of late, and take our seats as the teams line up. From this different vantage point, I'm more aware than usual of the 'ceremony' of the pre-match handshakes and Premier League anthem. What a load of shite – it's Cardiff at home, not the fucking cup final!

The Reds start with real intent and miss several early chances. It's a gorgeous day and the December sunshine illuminates some seriously impressive Liverpool inter-passing which threatens to cut Cardiff asunder. I'm ridiculously nervous and can't relax until we've made the breakthrough. To ease the tension, Heaton and I tease Gutmann, sat in front of us. He's wearing a lovely grey cashmere coat, ideal for keeping out the Christmas cold, but it has an unfortunate, decorative 'sleeve' on the back which quite obviously resembles the shape of female genitalia. It just does. It shouldn't. It obviously shouldn't but it does and this wine means it is impossible for me not to point it out. Rob takes it in good heart and reveals that he hasn't worn it for two years, though he now recalls why – he's had this grief before.

Suárez puts paid to the hilarity soon afterwards with a classic right-foot volley from Henderson's chipped pull-back – 1–0. Brilliant. Rob, Andy, Sam and I exchange high-fives. It's what happens to you when you're in a box – you celebrate like a knobhead.

We miss a couple more chances before Suárez runs through on goal in the 42nd minute. He seems certain to score past David Marshall but sees the run of Sterling, flirting with offside but just in line, and squares to his right for the tap-in. Mindful of the hat-trick bet, we applaud Sterling's goal rather than celebrate heartily and I promise myself the season's gambling from now on will be restricted to darts and National Hunt racing. However, within minutes, with the last kick of the half, Suárez brings the house down courtesy of a right-footed, swerving masterpiece – reminiscent of Dalglish at his best – to claim his second and give Liverpool a 3–0 half-time lead. He's now odds-on to complete a second-half treble. More to the point, Liverpool are going top of the league, it's nearly Christmas and it's time to indulge in animated conversation and more wine.

As it happens, the remaining 45 minutes pass by without further Liverpool goals. Suárez fluffs his best chance of another hat-trick and we lose our bet, but we're not bothered about that. We're more concerned that a facile, unchallenged Jordan Mutch header just before the hour reminds us of those early-season second-half wobbles and for a while Cardiff threaten to ruin everything. Liverpool just about weather the storm, regaining their composure towards the end and seeing out the win.

At full time, Rob (sensibly) gets off, and so too do Gareth and Samantha. Despite having had about seven glasses of wine I'm staying out, and make arrangements for our Sam to get home with my dad. With Neil and Andy for company, I'm on the loose and we head for dingy pubs between Walton Breck and Oakfield Roads, where we bump into Johnny Milburn and I get on the Peroni.

I haven't really spoken to Neil much today so between post-match alehouses I make it my business to collar him. He needs my advice. I'm telling him that his admirable *Anfield Wrap* title battle-cries are far too lily-livered for my liking; great sentiments – but they're not getting the public roused and he needs to ramp it up. These people need telling. 'We're gonna win this fucking league' – that is the general point I'm trying to make while being heroically pissed. Wake the bastards up, I say. I'm waving one of four complimentary programmes in his face while doing a pavement dance that involves me falling off the kerb every few steps. But I'm right. We need a proper atmosphere at Anfield in the second half of the season. Neil takes it all on board. The only thing more unrelenting than me is my drinking.

Later, my evening descends into carnage after we move on into town. There are various sightings of me in different places on Merseyside that night. In Leaf in Bold Street, I put forward an indecent proposal to Johnny Milburn's fiancée that involves hair extensions. I abuse Merseyside Police at Central Station. I'm seen in the Liver Hotel, Waterloo and emphatically encouraged to go home. I turn up at my parents' Christmas party destroyed and frighten the guests. I end up in bed at about 10.30 – in disgrace.

My only defence? We're top of the league at Christmas. At Christmas. It's the best defence anyone can ever have. Now, get me an Alka-Seltzer and get Match of the Day on. Season's greetings.

Mike Nevin

MANCHESTER CITY 2 LIVERPOOL 1

26 December 2013.
Goals: Kompany 31', Negredo 45'; Coutinho 24'

IS THERE ANY SUCH THING AS A GOOD DEFEAT?

LIVERPOOL'S DEFEAT AT MANCHESTER CITY told us an enormous amount about Liverpool. It also dealt a blow to the 'no one is *that* good' theory.

Manchester City are *that* good. But that's OK. Because the game told us – so are Liverpool.

This looked like a match between the best two teams in the country. That's because it was a match between the best two teams in the country. Manchester City started the game brilliantly, dominating possession and pushing Liverpool back. Then Suárez started to exploit Kompany's desire to get on the front foot and created space for everyone to play around him.

And then Liverpool cut City open, Kolarov playing Sterling onside by three yards and Sterling finishing with aplomb. Chalked off by the assistant ref. Liverpool weren't to be denied though. Coutinho's goal to open the scoring was a quite brilliant move. Liverpool were on top.

Kompany, from a corner, equalises. Then Coutinho misses the chance to score what could be Liverpool's finest goal of the season (though that is a cluttered category this season. What's the best goal Liverpool don't score? Suárez against Arsenal? Henderson against Arsenal? Suárez against West Ham. Times two? Answers on a postcard) and Liverpool concede something soft. Mignolet should do better with Negredo's goal, but everyone should do better for the duration of where it comes from. Liverpool in general should do better – just get in 1–1 at half time. But what can you do? You tell these lads they can play and play and play and then expect them to sit themselves in?

This goal is the goal Liverpool won't concede in 2013/14. This is the goal they have worked out of their system. This is the winning goal in a game between the two best teams in the league. It isn't the goal that costs Liverpool the league. There is no reason why, if we go in 1–1, City don't come out second half and find a winner. But it's a goal to learn from. There's a time to get in. There's a time to take something. You can't always be incredible and if you aren't you can't always expect a goalkeeper to bail you out.

Second half City come out and look the part. Then Liverpool reassert themselves. Liverpool are the better side in Manchester City's ground. But the goal simply isn't forthcoming. Sterling misses the game's best chance and the match finishes 2–1. These two sides absolutely went at each other for 90 minutes. As a game of football in a normal season we'd talk about this one for days. In this season?

When writing this book, re-watching some of these games, I'm knocked over by the quality of so much of what Liverpool have done. In a normal season, this is a game that stuns us, that knocks us over. And for the last three normal seasons, the last three dreadful depressing seasons, while Liverpool have got results, they haven't been involved in a game of this quality. They haven't reached this level to test themselves at this level. They haven't faced down an opponent in their own yard and said, 'We're this good. How good are you?'

But at the end of the season, by the end of this season, we've all but forgotten this game. This fabulous, proper, honest, glorious, rambunctious game of football. This riotous game of togger. Had this happened in the previous three seasons it'd be all I'd talk about. I still thrive on our 2–0 home win against Spurs in 2009/10 and that is a game which meant nothing in the grand scheme of things. This one. My lord.

Perhaps it is because we didn't win that it's slipped so easily from consciousness. But I don't think so. I think it is because there is only so much you can remember. If there can be such a thing, this is a good defeat.

However, there can be no such thing as a good defeat. There simply cannot be. I won't stand for it. Winning is what the business is. (Though Gerrard's penalty fired over against Blackburn in Hodgson's last game would love a debate about that.) There is, that said, such a thing as a good performance in defeat. There is such a thing as a defeat which means something, a defeat which sends out a signal. A defeat which shows the level players were at, a defeat which is a statement of intent. You'll have to be as good as these to beat us.

We came to your ground. We were as good as you and you can't play any better than this. Don't forget us. We are Liverpool. You are scared of us. Good. You should be.

Neil Atkinson

LIVERPOOL ARE INVOLVED; I AM NOT

DUE TO MY PARTNER working on cruise ships and being away over Christmas I spent Boxing Day on the Caribbean island of St Martin. There are worse places to be at that time of year, I can assure you of that. After spending a few hours on the beach I thought it was timed perfectly so she had to go back to work just as the football was starting. This was until I tried to find somewhere to watch the game.

I trawled the bars of the busy stretch of Philipsburg, finding a couple of places showing some German football, but that was about it. I started to feel conned by the Sky propaganda machine telling me how each big game was being viewed in 'over 200 countries by 500 million people'. St Martin didn't seem all that bothered at all. Damn you, Martin Tyler.

I finally found a back-street casino, and lo and behold they had the match on. By this time it was the second half. 2–1 down. Never mind, plenty of time to pull it back. Maybe they were just waiting for me. Unfortunately the casino in question wasn't exactly Caesars Palace and didn't seem to contain a bar you could just sit at. It was gamble or nothing. I contemplated putting a few dollars in one of the machines, but they all seemed rather complicated and besides, getting addicted to a fruit machine and not watching the football seemed to miss the point of the whole enterprise. Luckily I managed to find a quiet corner where I could see a screen and shouldn't be disturbed just as THEY TURNED THE FOOTBALL OFF FOR THE BINGO!

I looked around incredulously, waiting for someone else to agree with me that it seemed unnecessary for every screen in the building to have each of the numbers called shown on it in massive font, but it seemed I was on my own. These lads and lasses were bang into the bingo. So I gave up and found a bar on the beach front with Wi-Fi so I could follow it on Twitter on my phone.

I probably would have given up long before under normal circumstances if I'm honest. I was only on St Martin for about eight hours, and it would have been nice to see a bit more. But being top of the league on Christmas Day was a new sensation. Usually we'd given up on the league (and occasionally even Champions League places) by then but here we were fighting for the title and I didn't want to miss any of it if I could help it. So I wasted two hours in a tropical paradise marching up streets and shouting at followed accounts for not giving me quicker or better news until the game finished. Now what?

I was very happy to be away and delighted to see my partner, but I couldn't help but feel I should have been somewhere else. Had I abandoned my team and my city when they needed me? This is ridiculous thinking, of course. I am sure the fans who got tickets cheered plenty at the Etihad that night, but maybe my extra bit would have seen them through? This is how we all operate as football fans, absurdity in the face of logic. I had followed the Cardiff win on the flight over to Miami (God bless you, Lufthansa, and your free Wi-Fi) and convinced myself they would be fine without me, but now I just wanted to jump on a flight home in time for the Chelsea game and cheer the lads to glory.

I didn't, of course. That would have been ridiculous. I went for a swim on the boat and then had a nice meal with my partner instead. Overall, that period was a time where I didn't feel involved, but crucially Liverpool still were and one defeat away at the most expensive team in the league wasn't going to change that. Christmas was always going to be a tough period; it was all about getting through it with as many points as possible and kicking on again. Besides, maybe it suited us better chasing at this stage anyway. Under the radar, with everyone writing us off. That's what I told myself anyway. Eating my tea, blaming myself.

John Gibbons

CHELSEA 2 LIVERPOOL 1

29 December 2013.
Goals: Hazard 17', Eto'o 34'; Skrtel 4'

BRENDAN RODGERS' LIVERPOOL DO LOSE CONSECUTIVE GAMES

YOU'D HAVE TAKEN TWO POINTS. Three either way and it could have worked itself out. One wouldn't have been a disaster; you'd have bitten someone's arm off for four, and done unspeakable things to whoever could arrange such things for six. We got no points from Manchester City or Chelsea, which felt like a massive blow. It was nice at the top of the table, I liked it there. It suited us. You looked at the table, went to look down and then realised you didn't have to. It looked a long way up from fifth now.

Two tough away games, on paper the toughest we would play in the league, in such a short period of time was hard on the players both mentally and physically, especially after leaving Manchester feeling the opposition had been let off the hook by missed chances, a linesman's flag and a Greater Manchester referee electing to look the other way. Adrenaline can take you through a tough period when you feel the world is on your side, but can desert you when you feel it's not.

Liverpool could have got something out of this game too, but it would have been less deserved. They scored first, of course, another brilliant set piece. How many goals from that source was that already? A striker's finish from Skrtel, too. But after that Chelsea looked stronger, fitter and, crucially, wiser. The equaliser was the definition of 'coming'. What turned out to be the winner wasn't too far behind.

Liverpool had their moments. Sakho hit the woodwork but could have done better, Joe Allen was tackled brilliantly when in on goal and there were the now usual Suárez penalty shouts ignored. Good teams have good moments, we've experienced that against us at Anfield, and we were undoubtedly a good team now. We'd shown that here, at the Etihad and even at Arsenal. But we hadn't got any points from those games. Competing was progress, I kept telling myself. But then you looked at the table and found us below Everton. Actually, you didn't need to look at the table because a dozen Evertonians had already told you. They find a way. 'Ha-ha, remember when yous were going to win the league?' I needed a pep talk from Brendan, a chat with Steve Peters, a hug from Mighty Red. I had a beer.

We don't lose consecutive games. We didn't lose consecutive games. Now we have. We need a new hook. Anyway. At least Torres never scored.

John Gibbons

THE BRAD SMITH CUNUNDRUM

YOU MAY BE READING THIS BOOK IN 2017. Liverpool may be European Champions (let's face it, they probably will). Brad Smith may be the European Champions' first-choice left back. He may be being talked about as the solution to England's left-side problem (actually solved by Ashley Cole in 2004). You, being in the future and probably better-looking and richer than me, will be phoning your futuristic mates on your video phone to talk about this article's casual dismissal of football's greatest ever left back.

That's not the point, though. So wind your neck in, George Jetson.

Brad Smith, even if his name ends up in the final edited title of this piece, is not really what we're discussing here. We're discussing team selection, and what it's for.

You'd be forgiven for thinking this isn't a vexed question. In picking an eleven, you'd imagine, a manager is looking to give his club the best chance of winning. There may be other considerations, such as resting legs, but that's generally the idea. Similarly, substitutions are simple, in theory. You make a change to make something happen, or stop something happening, or keep something happening. Legs, too, can come into it here.

The players a manager picks, the changes he makes, his decisions both pre- and in-game are all sort of supposed to be about the football match, or another football match not too far away.

At Stamford Bridge, Brendan Rodgers has chosen a weak bench because he's had to. With Steven Gerrard and Daniel Sturridge injured there's little to work with among the senior players. Victor Moses is unavailable. José Enrique may not appear again this season. Jon Flanagan's promising reintroduction to the side has been cut short by injury and Daniel Agger is a fish out of water at left back.

Among the substitutes are Jordan Rossiter and Brad Smith, two youngsters we've heard a lot about but who aren't – yet – being talked up as immediate first-team prospects.

But here they are, in the squad for perhaps the biggest game of our season so far. Reflecting our small squad, our inability to get the right deals done for a second successive summer, our reliance on youth and paucity of resources just as the season's getting tough.

With an hour gone, Joe Allen is hurt. Injuries are beginning to look like our undoing. The like-for-like replacement is Luis Alberto, but it's becoming apparent Rodgers doesn't much fancy him. Iago Aspas would offer an alternative, but would leave – no, guarantee – gaps.

The other option is a more orthodox left-sided player to sit in front of Agger. In so far as Liverpool have had success in this game, it's come from stretching Chelsea. With no direct cover for Allen's energy and efficiency, this does perhaps make sense. And we have a French international left back on the bench.

But it's Brad Smith who comes on for 30 minutes at Stamford Bridge. All that reflecting our small squad, our inability to get the right deals done for a second successive summer, our reliance on youth and paucity of resources just as the season's getting tough, was all right on the bench. On the pitch it's enough to drive you mad.

During the match we're convinced this is the manager making a point, the team selection as political statement. To the fans, a shrug of impotent disaffection. To the people who run Liverpool FC, a demand for action within days of the transfer window's opening.

Later, having seen Smith demonstrate the extent to which he wasn't ready for this, having seen us slip (irretrievably?) off the pace at the top of the league, there is room for kinder thoughts. We know Rodgers backs his hunches, rewards positive contributions in training, wants genuine continuity between Melwood and Anfield.

He offers opportunities to players. It's likely he'd do this were he managing Real Madrid. It's the whole coach-before-manager thing. It's Flanagan getting in and staying in. It's Sterling, showing real promise here, seeming to come back stronger after the trauma of Hull.

As a proposition in this game, Smith offers both a sensible measure of tactical balance and an element of surprise. Chelsea's manager is José Mourinho, a hard man to outfox. But you've got to try, and throwing in a player he knows little about isn't absurd.

We also suspect recruiting a central midfielder, the player genuinely lacking from the bench today, is unlikely to be Rodgers' top priority in January. If this is a statement, it's a confused one at best. On reflection, Rodgers may this time have been too clever for his own good. But all things considered, it's likely he did it in pursuit of points, not politics.

Neil Atkinson

LIVERPOOL 2 HULL CITY 0

1 January 2014
Goals: Agger 36', Suárez 50'

TWO-NIL!

TWO-NIL! Liverpool win a game of football 2–0.

It had become a running joke, graduating from an observation. Liverpool hadn't won a league game 2–0 under Brendan Rodgers. In fact they hadn't won a league game 2–0 since 18 December 2011. Aston Villa, since you ask.

Two-nil, to me, was always the scoreline of champions. There's an ideal 2–0. It goes like this, pretty much the same home or away:

The game starts. The significantly better side win the right to play. They have control. They score. The opposition come back into it a little but the significantly better side get to half-time 1–0 up without having had to over extend themselves.

Second half, the significantly better side get themselves through a rocky first five before being better from 50 minutes until whenever they get the second. Say 63 minutes. 2–0. The poorer side accept their inevitable defeat and essentially take 2–0. The better side acknowledge this and we play out time. 2–0. Job done. Same again next week, lads?

Two-nil happens with regularity when you are good.

In 2012 Liverpool had been bad. They didn't win 2–0. But in 2013 Liverpool had been good. They still didn't win 2–0.

Liverpool ushered in the new year with an excellent 2–0 victory against Hull. It was professional, it was calm and under the circumstances it was classy. Proper teams win 2–0. So why hadn't they done it more often in 2013?

It's fascinating, really. It's indicative of this side and this manager, both the positive and the negative. It's also indicative of football in general.

This side, this manager's side, never want to stop. They want the goals to keep coming because they know the goals can keep coming. Why stop? This side, this manager's side, are built on the notion of attacking. It is what we do, what's been collectively agreed. We aren't an outfit which wins professionally; we're an outfit which scores professionally.

This impacts on the whole football match. It means teams oppose us knowing they can get something. Expecting to get chances, knowing they'll get an onslaught. They aren't ready to accept the 2–0 mentioned above. They aren't yet prepared for it. Liverpool may be good but they'll give you a chance. Liverpool may give you a chance but they might batter you whether or not you take it. Being the most exciting team in the country means the opposition buy in to the excitement. They want a bit of it.

So Liverpool ended 2013 having scored more goals than anyone else, even sides who had played more games or amassed more points. No two-nils.

This 2–0, though, showed this Liverpool side could win 2–0 if it needed to. Because today we needed to. Battered from two away defeats, at the end of a long Christmas period, we did what was required. No more, no less. And Hull City showed a side could turn up to Liverpool and accept a 2–0. They'd had a long Christmas period. They didn't have a big opening or an attempt at a grandstand recovery in them. Instead Liverpool scored in the 36th minute. Liverpool scored in the 50th minute. Hull didn't do much. Nor did Liverpool until Coutinho slalomed through four challenges towards the end of the game, firing over when he should have scored.

And so it remained the hallowed 2–0. Boring, mechanical, clean sheet, three points, 2–0.

That's that then. Let's go bananas again next week...

Neil Atkinson

THE CHRISTMAS PILE-UP

A COMMON CLICHÉ IN FOOTBALL is that a team which gets beat always wants another game straight away. I'm not sure that was the case in this instance. Liverpool's small squad had undoubtedly benefited from a lack of European football this season. Injuries aside, they had been able to generally pick the same team week after week without, up to this point, looking too tired.

Due to the hectic Christmas calendar this was Liverpool's third game in seven days and fourth in twelve. While this wasn't an impossible schedule by any means, it was one that Liverpool had largely been able to avoid up to that point of the season. With a lack of trusted options and injuries to key players such as Sturridge, Gerrard and Enrique, Liverpool picked largely the same eleven for all four of these games, with only injuries to Flanagan, Allen and Sakho forcing changes. In contrast Manchester City, who won all four festive games, were able to rotate heavily, using 18 different players with only Hart, Fernandinho and Kompany playing every fixture. It is no coincidence that a tough run of fixtures led to injuries, four in four games, during a season when Liverpool largely managed to avoid them. When fatigue kicks in, muscle injuries often follow.

So Hull City at home became very much a fixture to get through, after which we should have been able to rest players against Oldham Athletic and then have a week off before Stoke. Just find a way to win the game and move on seemed to be the mantra all round. Nothing fancy required. For once we didn't turn up to Anfield expecting a riot. Just hoping for a win.

But in the focus on your own team's frailties you can always forget about the opposition and Hull, whose fans would probably laugh at the very idea of Liverpool fans moaning about limited resources, had the decency to turn up looking shattered too. I am also a big believer that managers and players look at groups of games and aim for a certain number of points from them. After a decent draw at West Brom and a demolition of Fulham (either side of losing to Manchester United after being 2–0 up) it felt very much like the Hull side had settled for what they'd got from their four fixtures and were ready to move on to other things.

But you still have to win the game, of course, and win we did. Yet again, and not for the last time this season, Liverpool opened the scoring with a set piece, Agger heading in the corner. The second was another, a lovely free kick from Suárez. Even the disallowed goal that day was from a free kick, Suárez offside from Coutinho's delivery. This is something not often mentioned when commentators and fans talk about Liverpool's fine attacking play. It was there for all to see, of course, but so often it was a set piece that allowed Liverpool to get in front and get on top, with the flowing, eye-catching goals to follow. This is one key area the side need to maintain their excellence in over the next year.

But there are other things that won't happen in 2014/15 that will benefit Liverpool hugely. Iago Aspas won't start a league game playing off Luis Suárez, as he did against Hull. Victor Moses won't be used as the main attacking option off the bench when Sterling needs a rest. It's unlikely the manager will have to play Kolo Touré for over half an hour at right back either. While some positive things will be hard to replicate, a lot of the negatives will be easy to improve on.

After Liverpool went 2–0 up the game largely petered out, with the only notable incidents being a very welcome return from Steven Gerrard after an hour and a fabulous run from Philippe Coutinho in stoppage time which deserved a goal. We'd got through another battle, with Glen Johnson the only casualty. All other men, and all three points, intact. Of all the things that will be tougher next year, the Christmas period will not be one of them.

John Gibbons

LIVERPOOL 2 OLDHAM ATHLETIC 0

5 January 2014
Goals: Aspas 54', Tarkowski (o.g.) 82'

AN UNSEEN GAME

THIS IS A MATCH REPORT. They're increasingly rare these days, with even what some would term the 'quality' papers giving over their coverage of games of football to reporting not what was shown to the forty or fifty thousand people who paid to get in, but what was said afterwards to a handful paid to be there.

The idea of reports as something other than a recap of press conference banalities and/or 'mind games' has faded from fashion. Yet someone watching the match, mediating 90 minutes of action unseen by the reader – any reader – then writing a first draft of history and filing it on the whistle is impossibly romantic. The days when the likes of the Liverpool Echo's pre-war correspondent 'Bee', an anonymous voice of the people, dictated an entire support's mood are gone. Perhaps for the better. But gone, just the same.

Every match is screened live somewhere. Broadcast to Liverpool's pubs, from Liverpool's ground, via satellites in geostationary orbit. And then sometimes via Dubai. But Liverpool versus Oldham on a cold January afternoon was seen by pretty much no one but those of us who paid to get in. Forty-four thousand, one hundred and two of us. It simply wasn't on the television, barring an incredibly short late-night highlights package on ITV.

This, I realise now, is not a match report. It's impossible for it to be a match report. Two sentences ago, I said it was a cold afternoon, but I'm writing this some months later so I can't be sure. In fact, now I think of it, it may have been unseasonably warm in the Main Stand that day. Or was that Villa?

Without the immediacy of the on-the-whistle format, something is lost, and lost for ever. The value of the reporter as primary source falls by the minute. I wouldn't trust a word of what I'm telling you.

But you may not have seen the game, and I did. So I'm the best you've got. And this is my truth. Keep yours to yourself.

Liverpool began at a walk, an oddly uneven starting eleven looking by turns lethargic, nervy and uninspired. Luis Alberto appeared baffled by much of what went on, while Victor Moses put to rest for ever the notion that he might be a useful flat-track bully.

Oldham, more so than Notts County earlier in the season, held Liverpool at bay. Few chances were created in a first half of murmured discontent from the stands, with neither side seemingly able to fully engage with the contest.

At half-time Liverpool made changes, with Lucas and Coutinho replacing Alberto and Moses. Half the ground would have seen Iago Aspas, as forlorn as ever as the focal point of the attack, withdrawn alongside them.

But Aspas stayed on, Aspas ran gamely and Aspas scored. In front of the Kop, with a technician's poise, Aspas found the corner. It was the first real opportunity to score the game had offered, but within moments there was another. This time Aspas, enlivened, thudded a header from a Raheem Sterling cross against the crossbar. Liverpool, at last, had momentum.

That momentum was lost. Oldham regrouped and briefly threatened, probing at Liverpool with the boldness of the damned. Brendan Rodgers introduced Luis Suárez for Gerrard, saw his stand-in captain Agger depart injured to leave his side down to ten, and James Tarkowski gift the home side a barely deserved second goal. He saw these things, because he was there. I saw these things, because I was there. We saw them, and mostly forgot them. Few of us will recall this day, this cold or warm or temperate afternoon under the lights at Anfield. Except perhaps for Iago Aspas. He scored at the Kop end.

'Bee'

STOKE CITY 3 LIVERPOOL 5

12 January 2014
Goals: Crouch 39', Adam 45', Walters 85'; Shawcross (o.g.) 5', Suárez 32', 71',
Gerrard (pen) 51', Sturridge 87'

DANIEL STURRIDGE IS UNBELIEVABLE

I WONDER IF EVEN DANIEL STURRIDGE knew how good he was at football when he joined Liverpool. I'm sure he had wondered many times what he'd be capable of if he got a run of games in a top team, but whether he was sure just how explosive he would be I guess only he could tell you. There were certainly plenty of pundits and fans willing to predict how he would do at Liverpool on his behalf. To suggest opinion was divided would imply there were scores backing him, but those against were generally more confident than those for. He's the only player I can think of who we have bought to have been told he was on his 'last chance' on his first day by the manager. Not exactly signed to a fanfare, was he?

I was personally pleased when we'd bought him, and thought he was well worth taking a chance on, although I doubt very many of those who were in favour of the move fully appreciated the levels of his all-round game at that point. It always seemed unfair to me that he was labelled as having a 'bad attitude' when very few of those saying it knew anything about him. I always found the 'selfish' tag bizarre too, firstly because strikers should be selfish – in fact Ian Rush was famously told to be more greedy when he was struggling at Liverpool – and secondly because it was easy to see why he felt he needed to be up to that point of his career. He was so far down the pecking order at Chelsea he probably thought he needed to score a hat-trick to stand a chance of playing the following week, while what was he going to do at Bolton, pass to Johan Elmander?

His performances on loan are really interesting. Put this book down a second and watch his goals for Bolton again, like I have just done. His hair is longer, and he's a bit slighter, but he is basically the Daniel Sturridge we know now already. Strong, lightning fast and scoring every kind of goal, looking absolutely delighted in the process. It's remarkable that he was allowed, both by Chelsea and everyone else in the league, to go back to Stamford Bridge and sit on the bench. Was everyone so entrenched in their opinion of him already that they refused to change their mind? Or did everyone just forget to watch Bolton? Luckily there were a couple of scouts at Manchester City who still thought he was great.

We'd missed Daniel Sturridge while he was out injured, so it was good to have him back. He was only on the bench, but it was exciting to have him even there. It was exciting to have any good player on the bench, frankly, but he'd made a good impact from there before. Most notably, in the Merseyside derby earlier in the season he headed in an equaliser and, often forgotten due to Suárez biting that fella, the previous season at home to Chelsea he came on at half-time and was terrific, scoring one and setting up another.

In this game he came on with Liverpool pegged back to 3–2 when they should really have been over the hills and far away. When people talk about making defensive substitutions to see out a game, and criticise Brendan Rodgers for not doing so effectively on occasions during this season, they forget how a quality attacking sub, if you are lucky enough to be able to make it, can completely change the dynamic of a game, putting a side who were in the ascendency suddenly on the back foot. The substitution changed the feel of the game almost instantly, and within five minutes of coming on Sturridge had set up Suárez brilliantly to score.

But, Liverpool being Liverpool, they had to make sure again, which Sturridge decided to do himself. Goals can have different effects on you as a fan, depending on the stage of the game and the type of goal. Joy, relief, defiance, indifference. Every now and again they just make you laugh your head off at the sheer ridiculousness of what you have seen, and this was one of those times. It's a great save by Butland from Sturridge originally, and he could have been forgiven for allowing it to run out of play with his head in his hands, especially with the clock running down. Instead he keeps the ball up on his head a couple of times to bring it back into play before smashing it below the keeper into the net.

Daniel Sturridge went on to score in the next seven league games too, equalling a Premier League record. The selfish bastard. **John Gibbons**

YET MORE BELIEF

STOKE – THE PLACE DREAMS COME TO DIE. In their first season in the Premier League we managed two points and zero goals against the Pulis threshing machine and lost the league by four points, thus the Liverpool Hate-Affair with Stoke Away was born.

In the subsequent four games at the Britannia between then and this match we managed a run of DLLL, so it was hardly the fixture we needed to see in our quest to get back to the recently vacated top spot. Pulis was gone, but in my eyes little had changed; one whispering Welshman I can't bear had been swapped for another, and the should-be hod-carriers' spine of Shawcross, Chadam and Jonathan Bleedin' Walters was still there and still making my skin crawl. City, Chelsea and Everton had all failed to win here prior to our trip, so it was with a sense of trepidation that we set off on our journey to the land that *totaalvoetbal* forgot.

Stoke being Stoke, it was cold, wet and windy – not even Lionel Messi himself could have done it tonight and were surely in for another war of attrition against Mark Hughes' men. But who needs Lionel Messi when you have Aly Cissokho? A trademark Cissokho thunderbolt followed by the Luis Suárez nuisance factor and within no time we are 2–0 up and cruising towards half-time.

Christ, we're good up front, like *really* good.

A non-jumping Kolo and a slipping Gerrard later and we're going into the break at 2–2.

Christ, we're dodgy at the back, like *really* dodgy.

Two quick breaks later and we've scored four away at Stoke. FOUR. Away. AT STOKE.

Christ, we're good up front, like really good.

Madness up front.

Hang about, how has that gone in? It was straight at him.

Christ, we're dodgy at the back, like really, really dodgy.

Madness at the back.

IS DANIEL STURRIDGE JUGGLING THE FUCKING BALL ON THE GOAL LINE?

Christ, we're good up front, like really, really good.

Madness up front.

In a way this game can be seen as a microcosm of our season – wobbly and leaky at the back, conceding soft goals from individual errors, vs the breathtaking forward play of our front three, scoring goals at will. Up until this point, the players and manager hadn't really given us much indication of just how crazy this season was going to be – sure, we had experienced/endured one of the maddest Merseyside derbies in history, and we'd forced Daniel Levy to exile AVB to Zenit, but those games aside it was shaping up to be a fairly normal, if promising, season. That is until today.

No one scores five at Stoke, least of all us, and this performance, along with the recent game at Spurs, was perhaps the first indication that the players had failed to read the script for a typical Liverpool season. They certainly believed, and this was perhaps the first time the majority of fans dared let themselves have a little dream too. The City and Chelsea games were still far too recent and felt like a reality check at the time, but sticking five past Stoke in a game like this let us put reality back on the shelf fairly sharpish.

Ben McCausland

LIVERPOOL 2 ASTON VILLA 2

18 January 2014
Goals: Sturridge 45', Gerrard (pen) 53'; Weimann 25', Benteke 36'

LOSING MY SHIT ON TWENTY

WE SHOULD ALWAYS REMEMBER football managers know far more about football than we do. All of them, even the rubbish ones, know loads about football, how footballers work, tactics and how best to go about winning games. They are also both fortunate and unfortunate enough to have their decisions judged by a crowd of self-proclaimed experts every week – but the rest of us are most definitely fortunate in that we can say what they should have done, safe in the knowledge our theories will never be tested.

I think I've seen enough footballers over the years to know a bit about it at least, but if a bizarre set of circumstances led me to be the manager of Liverpool, the players would probably revolt after less than a week. Actually Lucas wouldn't, because he's a lovely fella, but the rest of them would be banging on the chairman's door before I could get to the end of telling them about all the trophies I'd won and formations I'd mastered on Championship Manager.

That's not to say we shouldn't still debate the manager's decision, of course. For many of us, overanalysing substitutions, formations and transfers you would or wouldn't have made is all part of the fun of being a football fan. But it should also be done with the caveat that it's much harder for the fella who is actually being paid to make these decisions for real, and he probably has much more information and is much better qualified to do it than any of us.

Saying all that, it's the most frustrating thing in the world for a manager to make what you think is a wrong decision and have it play out in front of your eyes exactly how you thought it would. You start to doubt all the sensible talk I went through above and instead start screaming: 'JUST DO ALL THE THINGS I'M TELLING YOU TO DO, WILL YOU!'

It's a bizarre situation when a manager wins a game 5–3 away, then feels he needs to make the team more attacking. To be fair, Sturridge probably had to come back in, and it was always going to be at the expense of a midfielder, but I hoped to hell it wasn't going to be at the complete expense of balance.

When the teams were confirmed, we looked exceptionally open, especially after what happened against the same opposition the previous season, with Aston Villa dominating us in midfield and breaking through the centre of the pitch with little or no resistance. It looked like a team that was finishing a game desperately searching for a goal rather than starting one with 90 minutes to break down a mid-table side at home.

There was some talk after the game that Brendan Rodgers felt under pressure to put on a show in front of our rarely spotted owners, who were in the stands that day, but there is no real evidence that was the case, especially given how frequently Linda Pizzuti tweets her love of a 'clean sheet'. It just seemed very unnecessary to me, a sledgehammer to crack a nut. Did we really need that many attacking players to break down Aston Villa?

Some will say we picked similar personnel at other times during the season with considerable success, but that ignores the roles the players were being asked to play. If picked in central midfield, Philippe Coutinho will be disciplined in his position and as tenacious as he can be in the tackle. When picked wide left, he sees his role as a third forward, with little consideration for what is going on behind him.

It would also be fair to say we won games playing similar formations that season, but this doesn't factor in that Jordan Henderson was often one of the wide players, and would naturally cut inside to offer an extra presence when necessary. While Raheem Sterling is a wide player willing to work hard without the ball and help out his full back when he can, it's not his natural game to come into central midfield like Henderson.

Therefore, it could have been said Liverpool were playing more of a 4–2–4, but this doesn't tell the whole story either. Henderson has a natural inclination to get about the pitch and fill in space, of which there was a lot to fill, but by trying to play everywhere he was effectively playing nowhere. This left Steven Gerrard very isolated and he must have wondered how a 33-year-old had ended up playing midfield on his own.

It took all of 45 seconds for Aston Villa to 'break down' Liverpool, Agbonlahor finding an extraordinary amount of space so early in the game, but firing wide. Throughout the first period Villa looked the more likely to score. It was no real disgrace for Skrtel and Touré to struggle to contain talent like Agbonlahor and Benteke, but infuriating that Villa's midfielders seemed to consistently have so much time to pick them out. All the time Brendan Rodgers just stood there, seemingly forgetting it was up to him to sort this mess out.

After hitting the post, Villa finally scored through Andreas Weimann breaking into the box, with very little interest from any of our lads in tracking him. At which point the manager decided we probably weren't doing very well, and he should probably try and change the formation. I very rarely get angry at football games, especially those connected with my club. In fact, the thing that annoys me most about going to the game is those who come out with constant negativity and bile when they should be there to get behind the team. But on this occasion, I may have stood up and casually informed Brendan Rodgers the time to change the formation was 24 minutes ago, when it was already obvious his questionable tactics were unlikely to come off.

It was something like that anyway. It may have contained 14 more swear words, some of which I invented myself on the spot. My dad, who was sat next to me, still does an impression, complete with flailing arms and higher and higher-pitched voice. Although at the time he just asked me if I was all right, with a rather concerned look on his face.

The formation change didn't really work, largely because the players didn't seem completely sure what it was, and Aston Villa scored again. Luckily Liverpool managed a goal back out of nothing just before half-time, at which point the manager decided it might be a good idea to bring Lucas Leiva on. This did little to calm me down, however. Why wait that long if you can see it's needed? Rodgers had shown he had the confidence to make a first-half substitution if necessary the previous season against Wigan, so why not now, when it was never more clear?

Fairly quickly after half-time Liverpool were level, through a Gerrard penalty. But they'd put so much energy into having to come back into the game, they didn't have anything left to finish it, and it somewhat petered out.

So what happened then? Did Rodgers underestimate Aston Villa? Perhaps –

they certainly approached the game with a more attacking mindset than he might have expected – but I think it's more likely he overestimated Liverpool. There have been a couple of times in his reign, and Aston Villa at home the previous season is one example, where he seemed to think the players he had available were a little bit better than they actually were, and that the opposition would submit rather than go out thinking they were well capable of winning the game themselves.

If that's the case, you would much prefer that to a manager like Roy Hodgson, for example, who seemed to approach every Liverpool game constantly fearing the worst. However, that wasn't what I was screaming at Rodgers after 20 minutes.

John Gibbons

WE ARE ALL ABOUT TO BE VERY WRONG ABOUT STEVEN GERRARD

I WENT MAD AS WELL.

I took it personally. For months I'd walked around this city both literally and metaphorically, telling anyone who'd listen that Liverpool were going to win the league. I'd talked this team up, it had gone and won at Stoke. Scoring five. I'd taken it personally. I know this isn't healthy in any way. But this felt personal.

I went mad. Absolutely mad.

I was watching the best footballer I'd ever seen in bits. In absolute bits. Steven Gerrard is the best footballer I have ever seen. And it was an unmitigated disaster against Aston Villa. It hurt. It broke my heart.

I'd taken it personally. It was my birthday night out. These bastards are doing this to me on my birthday night out, when I'd walked around this city talking them up. These bastards. Liverpool exposed again and again. Opened up. Turned around. Hurt. Flayed. Punished. This isn't mentally healthy. The bastards.

It didn't stop. Villa found the most space I've seen in this ground since Marseilles in 2007. The midfield, like that day, was an enormous green space with the occasional opposition lad popping up in there. After that game against Marseilles there was talk that Momo Sissoko just sat in the dressing room in tears. The footballers feel the football and they know, more than we do, whether they were any good. They know far better than we do. I'd taken it personally but when sanity began to descend all I could do was think about the captain. It had broken my heart. God knows what it did to him.

I rewatched the terrific *Queer As Folk* recently. In it a character goes into a 'straight pub' and says: 'There are people talking in sentences that have no punchline.' That makes me think straight away of Liverpool. You go out in Liverpool – and you should, it's the greatest pint in the world for a variety of reasons – and everyone has a punchline. This isn't about Liverpool people being any funnier than any other – far from it – more that everyone's always got a line, everyone's always got an angle. Everyone's about to tell you something. That night, on my birthday night, it was Steven Gerrard. I saw a million people and all everyone wanted to talk about was Steven Gerrard.

There were huge concerns over whether or not he'd be able to do this. Huge concerns over Lucas going off injured. Huge concerns over the side that destroyed Tottenham not having Gerrard in it. Huge concerns over whether or not the manager would have the balls to drop him if that was what it took. There were huge concerns over whether or not we kick on from here. Orders suddenly looked tall to all and sundry.

All and sundry were about to be proven dead wrong.

Because while they must feel it more than we do, they can do something about it. Managers can do something about it. And Steven Gerrard is about to go on and make a strong case for himself being player of the year. In the season Suárez scores 30 goals, you could make a strong case for Gerrard being player of the year. It is all in what he and the manager do next. Ten days later Henderson shifts all around him. Coutinho buttresses him and Liverpool beat Everton 4–0. Barkley doesn't expose Gerrard, as so many Evertonians say he will in their corners to one another on this dreadful night. On my birthday night. Barkley will expose him.

Nope. Doesn't happen. Quite the opposite. Gerrard exposes Barkley.
That day, that night, he must have been heartbroken. He must have despaired. For himself and the city he carries. And then he redefines the position in this league. He does what Pirlo has been doing in Italy. Can you imagine? He has ten days. They – he, the manager and his teammates – have ten days. And then he does what Pirlo has been doing in Italy to mass acclaim. And keeps doing it for the rest of the season. The Merseyside derby arrives and he and they, but mostly he, throws all the punchlines back down all the throats. Because he is Steven Gerrard.

He's done it before. It's my birthday. I'm 33.

He'll do it again. It's my birthday. The captain is older than me. He'll still do it again though. You watch.

A colossus.

Neil Atkinson

BOURNEMOUTH 0 LIVERPOOL 2

25 January 2014
Goals: Moses 26', Sturridge 60'

LUIS SUÁREZ IS THE BEST FOOTBALLER EVER TO PLAY FOOTBALL IN YOUR GROUND

THE BOURNEMOUTH SUPPORTERS BOOED SUÁREZ. All game.

This sort of thing had pretty much stopped by this stage of the season. Suárez had won his abusers round by simply being brilliant at football. There were still moments, but on the whole things like: 'Luis Suárez – he looks like a rat', to the endlessly abused tune of 'Sloop John B', had stopped getting trotted out. People had even stopped singing to him, intriguingly coyly, that they knew what he was.

That's because they now actually knew what he was – one of the best footballers you will ever see play in your ground. Maybe not the best, but one of them.

However, I'm pretty certain he's the best footballer Dean Court – for sponsorship purposes now the Goldsands Ground – has ever seen. Literally – the oft-abused 'literally' – the best footballer that has ever played on this pitch. The supporters who turned up that day booed him all game.

I probably find this more troubling and annoying than Luis Suárez does. I find it troubling because they think it's part of the game. They think it destabilises him. Or at least it should. If you are right, boo them all. Give them all down the banks.

However, Suárez got it especially badly. Mainly because he's good. Or because that's what the Bournemouth supporters think supporters do.

My friend Adam has often remarked that Manchester United are the club of the North West. So often you go to grounds like Wigan, grounds like Blackburn, and you hear Manchester United cover versions of their favourite Liverpool-hating ditties casually slung out there. Again, it's what football supporters do, isn't it? It's rivalry, this. That's what this is. Rivalry and that. What they have at the football. That's what we'll do. Because of television, the tiring cover versions have escaped the North West and gone nationwide now. You can hear about your Liverpool slums up and down the country. Everywhere you go.

And yes, it is what football supporters do. Insofar as you can be, I'm genuinely all right with verbal abuse from Manchester United supporters. It's underpinned by a ship canal and a million years of inter-city rivalry. I'm not precious about it. They can fill their boots. But Manchester City don't get dogs' abuse everywhere they go. Chelsea, Arsenal, Spurs don't have a set of songs lined up slaughtering them. We do. Because it's what football supporters do, isn't it?

There are a thousand reasons why we get it and no one else does.

Bournemouth therefore get their big day doing what football supporters do. They give the best player their ground has ever seen a torrid time while Liverpool win without playing well, Sturridge killing the game on the hour mark. I wonder afterwards if they enjoyed it. What they got from it. Best player I ever saw was Thierry Henry. I talked about nothing else for days, his acceleration, his touch. I hope they did the same. I hope they didn't talk about how he looked like a rat.

I'm worried though. Worried they asked everyone if it came through on telly. The day they got to do what the big clubs do. Like Stoke. Like Fulham. They got to do what the big clubs do. Abuse the best player ever to play in their ground.

Neil Atkinson

LIVERPOOL 4 EVERTON 0

28 January 2014
Goals: Gerrard 21', Sturridge 33', 35', Suárez 50'

A STATE OF SHOCK

HEADS HAD GONE in the days leading up to 28 January 2014. Well and truly gone. It could be blamed on the fact that days earlier, we'd drawn 2–2 with Villa. At home, at Anfield. And two months earlier, we'd fought out an away draw in the first Merseyside derby. A draw born of the brilliance of Daniel Sturridge, a draw we nearly didn't have. And now we were facing the Ev again. At home, at Anfield.

'I've got a bad feeling about this, you know,' said everyone, ever. 'They gave us a game at Goodison, you know. Just got a bad feeling.'

They did give us a game at Goodison. It was a proper derby. I enjoyed it, personally. I think I was totally smashed on mojitos at the time, which helped. But such a fiery contest hadn't done the confidence of a lot of people much good. 'It could go either way, this,' appeared to be the general consensus, among the more positive. A higher-than-average percentage, I noted, were expecting Roberto's newly confident gang of lads to give us a pasting. The Blues fancied it as well. Not many of them said it, obviously, but you could tell.

Neil, our friend Adam Melia and I had seats together in the Main. Very near the away fans. Our position afforded Adam an excellent opportunity to perfect his critically acclaimed derby day mimes in front of an appreciative audience, which helped to settle the nerves somewhat. And 21 minutes later, Steven Gerrard settled them a bit more, with help from Luis Suárez, who couldn't have been less arsed about being pelted with coins during a corner.

Less than 15 minutes and two Daniel Sturridge goals later, 'I've got a bad feeling about this' was a distant memory. Replaced with: 'I can't fucking believe this. Can you fucking believe this?'

Anfield was giddy. Full of joyfully shocked faces. Blues getting off for half-time ten minutes early. In the second half, a Suárez goal on 50 and a missed Sturridge penalty five minutes later meant the most overheard comment while filing out of the ground was: 'Ah, it was a shame not to get five, wasn't it?'

Four-nil. One goal short of what could be described as a 'crushing defeat', we decided. Four-nil and we were a bit annoyed. (Obviously we weren't actually annoyed. But it would have been nice for Dan to have got his hat-trick, wouldn't it?) Looking back, you could argue the derby was the point at which our expectations and hopes had begun to properly change. It suggested our 5–0 battering of Spurs the previous month (see, I could confidently type battering there – five goals and that) certainly wasn't a flash in the pan.

As an aside, I did feel bad for Roberto Martinez. But that's just because I love him. I don't know anyone who doesn't, to be honest. The difference he and Brendan Rodgers have made to Merseyside in just a few short months is phenomenal and both Reds and Blues have been exceptionally lucky to each land a hugely talented and classy (a dreadful word, but an accurate one) football manager at the same time.

Anyway, I think, after all that's happened since, many of us have forgotten how mad and brilliant that day was. The fact that the even madder 5–1 victory over Arsenal came just two weeks later has eclipsed it somewhat. Not that I'm complaining. More eclipsing of 4–0 derby wins next season, please, Brendan. We'll be fine with it, honestly. But it was the point at which we really started to have fun. It was the point at which we began to realise what Liverpool had become in just a few short months. And, even more remarkably, it was before the full magic of Raheem Sterling had been unleashed.

It was also the point at which I realised I needed new glasses, because I could see fuck all. And I've got new glasses, so I've got Brendan to thank for that as well. It's easy to say with hindsight that there was a feeling we were only going to get better from that point. But there was. Match reports talked of excitement about our potential return to the Champions League and at that point, it felt like it was assured.

But in dark corners in pubs, after 10 p.m. and several shorts, if you listened really, really, REALLY hard, you could hear the first few tentative whispers that weren't from Steve Graves or Neil Atkinson. You couldn't be sure where they were coming from, or if you were making it up. Maybe it was time to go home to bed. But no, hang on, there it was again.

'This could be on, you know. I don't want to speak too soon, but I think this could be on.'

Who said that?

Kate Forrester

DANIEL STURRIDGE LOVES A LOB

'OH, BEHAVE YOURSELF, LAD.'

My words in October as Daniel Sturridge held off a West Brom defender and looked to chip the keeper. Behave yourself. Because there was no way on earth it …

… it dropped in.

I was right behind it. Right behind it. The arc of it was utterly remarkable. In a season with a billion brilliant goals it could well be the most brilliant. Suárez had scored a hat-trick. Scored a header from a million miles out. Sturridge lobbed a keeper who was about three yards off his line while holding off a defender. It was utterly outrageous and it was all we talked about after.

Daniel Sturridge can make everything you know about football wrong.

He's done that since he arrived at Anfield. Loads of lads saying his attitude wasn't right.

His attitude is perfect. His attitude is everything I want in my number nine. His attitude is the answer to my life. He demonstrates that against Everton.

Let's talk about his attitude. He bosses the life out of Everton before he scores. His every touch is the essence of centre forward play. He holds it up, oozing class. Pulling and pushing it about the place with his feet. It's never been as easy as this. I've seen all sorts of centre forwards watching Liverpool but none made centre forward play look like the most natural process in the world.

Let's talk about his attitude. He scores his first and Liverpool's second. Eases through and pings it past the onrushing Howard into the far corner at the Anfield Road end. It's never been as easy as this. He arcs his celebratory run past the badly kagooled Evertonians, not once taking his eye off them. Finally he turns away, congratulated by Henderson. I've seen all sorts of finishers watching Liverpool but none made finishing look like the most natural process in the world.

Let's talk about his attitude. Touré clears long, Sturridge appears on the end of it. Has a look here. Has a look there. Has a look elsewhere. Clip. It's never been as easy as this. The ball goes a million miles up in the air. Sturridge stops. Watches. It drops. It drops. It drops. It bounces and hits the roof of the net. Sturridge remains still. Stares at the Evertonian hordes as they rush towards the front of the stand. They fume. He stares at the fume. The best fume in world football. Liverpool 3 Everton 0. Sturridge stares at the fume. Stares them out. The Liverpool players hanging off his outstretched arms. I've seen all sorts of needle watching Liverpool but none made needle look like the most natural process in the world.

This is what being good is about.

They'd fancied this, the Evertonians. They'd fancied this game all week and then the class turned up. This is what being the best number nine in the country looks like. His attitude is the answer to my life.

He went on to miss his pen for a hat-trick. Who cares? Him. Us? Nah.

But the next day he comes to town in a flash white car. Parks it by Castle Street. Has a mooch about the place. Struts about the place. He scored two for Liverpool in a Merseyside derby. In a 4–0 Liverpool win. He gets to strut about the place. He gets to be Daniel Sturridge. These are the perks. This is how you deal with the fume. How you have off lads in kagools. Own the place.

Let's talk about his attitude. Loving lobs. Loving life. This charming man.

Neil Atkinson

WHY I WAS REALLY, REALLY, REEEEALLY WRONG ABOUT RAHEEM STERLING

NEIL CAME UP WITH MOST OF THE IDEAS FOR THESE CHAPTERS, and I laughed when he gave me this one. Cheers, mate. But, as reading this book will tell you, he also often says that being right about football is overrated, so bearing that in mind I will happily go into just how wrong I was on this one.

Raheem Sterling made his first-team debut aged 17 years and 107 days and was seemingly lauded for his performance by everyone except me. I couldn't really understand what all the fuss was about. Yes, it was impressive that he didn't look particularly fazed, and it was certainly welcome that he had done so much running around, but he hadn't actually done anything with the ball. And besides, I wasn't interested in looking for positives when we'd just been beaten at home by bloody Wigan.

By the start of next season he was a regular under Rodgers. During a challenging period for the club he was seen as a shining light, but again I wasn't sure.

Don't get me wrong, I was impressed with certain aspects of his game, particularly his strength for his size and his tactical intelligence for such a young player, but I still thought it could go either way for him. I was well aware of the concept of young players improving, but there had been plenty of young attacking players in this country over the years who had seemed full of promise but had ultimately failed to deliver. I wasn't yet prepared to go to town on a wide forward who scored just two goals all season.

For the first half of this season he notably struggled, seemingly being mentioned more for court time than playing time. By the middle of December it wasn't looking great for him, which is when I sent this email:

> *Question is, in January, who is coming in and saying 'I'll have Sterling for £12m'. I don't see what team is doing that.*

I'd like to point out I wasn't actually advocating selling Raheem Sterling for £12m, although I probably would have sent him on loan. This was for a hypothetical game for *The Anfield Wrap*, in which contributors were asked what they would do in the upcoming transfer window. When the valuations were being worked out I said 12 was too high for Sterling and suggested seven was more realistic. £7 million. For Raheem Sterling. Now I didn't have to tell you any of that – I'm not in a situation yet where my private emails are likely to be leaked by a disgruntled temp – so please bear this in mind if you are tempted to bring it up whenever I next try to pretend I have the first clue when it comes to football.

You would have to add a zero to the end of my miserly suggestion now for Liverpool to be even tempted to sell. But in my defence, did anyone expect that second half of the season from Raheem? A time when he went from behind Victor Moses in the pecking order to one of the best players in the country.

A development of a footballer is rarely in a straight line, it's usually in spurts. Raheem Sterling is the only footballer I have ever seen improve 15 to 20 per cent from the previous week. He did this a few times this season, and Everton at home was one of them. By this stage he was barely recognisable from the player who had struggled so badly at Hull less than two months before.

He'd had a good January, but against Everton he was imperious. Firstly, he did a great job of keeping Leighton Baines back, such a threat for Everton when he is allowed to push forward. Leighton Baines had other things to worry about that game. Namely, 'How on earth am I meant to stop this young lad who is playing like this?'

For the second goal he wins the ball brilliantly, showing a much undervalued part of his game, before having the coolness under pressure to slip it to Coutinho in space. He also won the penalty Sturridge missed, timing his run on goal brilliantly and drawing the foul from a keeper, who'd had enough. But to reduce a player's contribution to involvement in key moments shows a misunderstanding of football (and yes, despite the above, I'm still going to lecture people on misunderstanding football). All game Sterling posed Everton problems with his pace, his intelligence, his touch and his work rate. Premier League defenders thought they had a hard enough time worrying about Luis Suárez and then we added Sturridge. They were pulling their hair out with them too, and then we added THIS Raheem Sterling. The more you can pre-occupy a defender's mind, the more space it leaves for others. No wonder Suárez loves Raheem Sterling.

Raheem Sterling has made me look daft, and I don't care who knows it. Being right about football is overrated. Who wants to know all the good things that await us? Surprises like this are the best thing in the world.

John Gibbons

TRANSFER DEADLINE DAY #2

31 January 2014

NOBODY REALLY KNOWS WHAT THEY ARE DOING

FOOTBALL IS BIG BUSINESS NOW.

That's what they say. They especially say that when they want a forelock to be tugged. You know how it is. Big business.

So why do Dr Dre's headphones go for more money than Manchester United are valued as being worth as the season ends?

Football is significant business but it isn't big business. Let's allow, though, the idea it is, just for a second. Loads of people in big business get things wrong all the time. Loads of people are on the blag. You know them through your work and by the fact big businesses fail. So don't rush to tug the forelock.

Football though. Significant business. In the summer window just gone supposedly Manchester United left the idea they need a central midfielder till the last minute. They could have signed Fellaini for significantly less than they did. They reputedly had teams of lawyers running round Bilbao trying to sign Herrera. Arsenal go for Higuaín. Then they go for Suárez. They settle on Özil. Three very different players. Chelsea buy back a player for far more than they sold him this winter –

surely someone somewhere feels a bit embarrassed and concerned for his job over this. Liverpool are trying to pull it together for Konoplyanka on the final day after Salah fell through, struggling to decipher release clauses in Ukrainian.

Transfer deadline day is your six-monthly reminder not to take those engaged in the business of football too seriously. Every transfer deadline day there are teams scrounging round looking for players. Football is big business, so they say. Yet you don't see any big businesses doing their recruitment like this.

This matters. I'm OK with football actually being bigger money than headphones, and if it gets better at the old capitalism then one day it might just be able to be bigger than headphones. That dream isn't dead. I'm OK with that. Because this six-monthly disaster is an aspect of football's exceptionalism, and football's exceptionalism matters. We have reminders of football's exceptionalism all the time but they are usually against us. We don't get to turn our nose up at our club's product and go and find a better one. We don't have the opportunity to say that the prices are too much at Liverpool but Everton is more affordable for a similar product. We have to strain every sinew to say no to our football clubs and they know it and they exploit it. We're captive and it is an exception.

Because we love it. Because football is wonderful, is beautiful, is an exception from so much of our ordinary lives. Its exceptionalism is everywhere and so it should be. No one is creating fanzines, podcasts, websites devoted to the Home Direct group. There isn't a book coming out called *Make Us Dream: Home Direct 2013/14* and if there was, you wouldn't be buying it. Football is a spectacular, maddening thing, even when nobody knows what they are doing and is seemingly on a mission to display their ignorance.

So please don't wheel out Christian Purslow to tell us how this works. Don't take it ever so seriously, don't take yourselves so seriously. Many of the people involved in football were businessmen. They might be businessmen again one day. But when the clock ticks down, they are all vaudeville. Jim White is actually right. He's the yellow-tied ringleader and while these men – almost all are men – might like to tell themselves they are players, they are the real deal, as far as the men – almost all are men – running Tesco and Home Direct and Beats are concerned, well, ringmaster White, bring on the clowns.

Neil Atkinson

HOW MUCH FOR SALAH!? THIS MUCH FOR KONOPLYANKA?

THIS WAS THE SECOND TIME me and Neil, and a rolling cast of several thousand others, have done a radio show lasting hours and hours on transfer deadline day. For this one nothing at all happened, including at Anfield, despite me telling everyone all night I thought we would get someone in. This was largely fine for the radio show itself; me and Neil can blab on about nothing for hours, no problem, but it would have been nice if Liverpool had signed another good player.

In the end we had to go with what we had. It would be foolish to try and predict what kind of impact this had on our season. For all the games where more strength on the bench would have benefited us, including the very next game away at West Brom, there were others that might have played out differently had our new man started. There are no guarantees he would have hit the ground running, and he'd have certainly wanted playing, probably at the expense of Sterling. The fact is, though, Brendan Rodgers wanted at least one more player to help our charge for the title and the powers that be were unable to get him one.

The thing that confuses me the most is the process and valuations, with particular reference to Salah and Konoplyanka (who I thought when we didn't get him, 'Well at least I won't have to learn how to type it,' and I now don't even get that saving grace). Salah was the one we went after first, so one would assume he was our first choice. This was supported by the words of his agent, who said we had spent months telling him we thought he was really great and that we were deffo going to buy him. We then put the name 'Mohamed Salah' into our magical valuations machine and it seemingly came up with a figure of £8m upfront, which we decided would be our final offer. Chelsea then came in with £12m upfront, Basel said thanks very much, and he went there.

OK, these things happen, sometimes you get outbid. I would argue that if we are saying someone is not worth £12m, then he shouldn't be a main target for Liverpool at all, but that's a separate argument for another day. There's still time left, so on to the next one. The next one seemingly being Yevhen Konoplyanka, who from now on I'm going to call The Yev. Now The Yev is presumably our second choice, bearing in mind we went after him second. This is usually how these things work. So we put The Yev's name into the magic valuations machine and it seemingly comes up with a figure of £15m. Wait, what?

For what it's worth, I felt sorry for the powers that be on this transfer. It sounds like they had done everything in order only for Dnipro to pull every trick under the sun to prevent it going through before the deadline, from 'Who's Yevhen Konoplyanka?' to 'Sorry, all the pens have gone' to 'LOOK OVER THERE (legs it)'. But the overall question remains, if we valued The Yev at almost twice what we valued Salah, then why wasn't he our first choice anyway? Surely the best thing to do is go for the best player if you have the money and aren't seemingly trying to get anyone else? Unless the magical valuations machine doesn't factor in talent at all, but other things. Such as how easy his surname is to type.

Chances are by the time you read this you will know if we have fared any better in the summer of 2014. I just hope the magical valuations machine has sorted out any glitches it might have so our list of targets makes a greater degree of sense. Try turning it off and on again, lads, that often works for me. Failing that, just reinstall the java. Or maybe throw it in the bin and just pay a bit more for someone the manager wants.

John Gibbons

WEST BROM 1 LIVERPOOL 1

2 February 2014
Goals: Anichebe 66'; Sturridge 24'

THE TURNING OF THE SCREW

Liverpool have scored about a billion goals up to this point this season, winning by three, four, five.

They've dug in, winning 1–0 at home when under the cosh. They've freaked out, winning 5–0 away from home with panache. They've been pegged back by half-time and won with style. They've been 2–0 up, conceded and kicked back on.

They've won every kind of football match except one.

Here is the list of Liverpool games this season against sides that aren't in the top seven they've failed to win, up to and including West Bromwich Albion away this season:

Swansea away, 2–2
Southampton home, 0–1
Newcastle away, 2–2
Aston Villa home, 2–2
West Brom away, 1–1

In each of these games Liverpool have been level or behind with 20 to go and haven't forced the game in their favour. Newcastle also were down to ten men.

There is no list of games against sides that aren't in the top seven where Liverpool have scored a goal to equalise or go ahead in the last 15 minutes.

The first thing to point out – and it is important to point it out – is that it is a short list and only contains one defeat. In the four seasons that precede this one, this list, by February, would be far longer and that's because of what's been discussed above – scoring first and standing firm or scoring first and setting fire to the game. One reason there is no list of games where Liverpool have scored to equalise or go ahead in the last 15 minutes against the poorer sides is that there have been few occasions they have needed to.

The second thing to point out though – and it is important to point this out too – at no point in the last 15 minutes of any of those games listed above have you felt Liverpool have had their opponents under relentless, error-inducing pressure. That they would crack their opponents' will. That they will grind them into the dirt, until they are limp, exhausted, giving up chances, begging to be put out of their misery, submitting to the sweet relief of the grave. In none of those games can I recall a goalkeeper pulling off miracles in the dying embers, defenders straining sinews to keep out another red wave, the football match cracking like a walnut in a vice, shell pinging off and about to have an opposing manager's eye out.

They haven't turned the screw.

There are two reasons for this, each equally valid. The first is being able to make changes from the bench, replacing quality with quality, introducing fresh legs as capable as the players being replaced at their freshest. Talk of transfer committees, priorities and that slippery bastard value is valid here but has been well and truly rehearsed on pages preceding this one, and John will talk about the bench in a second. It's good to delegate.

The second is that this side isn't one built to do gradual, unstoppable accumulation of pressure. It's either all over you, pulling you apart, or it isn't. It's a blade, not a steamroller, but a blade which can blunt itself over 90 minutes. The players instinctively look to stab, stab, stab. They don't try and shepherd the game through its final stages, create an ever-smaller pen for the sheep opposite, put the fear into them. Instead it's the jugular with every lunge, letting the sheep scatter and having to start the process again if unsuccessful.

One of the things we love about this Liverpool side is that they aren't a metronome ticking ever faster, they are a hands in the air banger. Tops off.

Tops off is brilliant. Tops off is why there are only five games on that list, why any lead Liverpool have over those behind them can have the goal difference point added to it, why Liverpool are magic and David Moyes is tragic.

But the problem Liverpool have in the second half of their season is that the skill that is evidently absent is likely to be required that bit more often. Liverpool now aren't a surprise. Both Pepe Mel and Paul Lambert have set up and then tweaked sides stocked with poorer players into a team that can frustrate Liverpool across 90 minutes in the last month. Liverpool's away games are against sides fighting for their lives and the oft spoken of tough home games are surely going to be tight on occasion. Liverpool are more likely to have games of football that are on a knife-edge with 20 minutes to go – it is inevitable that Liverpool will be all square or a goal behind with 15 to go at least three times between now and the season's close. There needs to be an answer when this question is asked.

A solution could be found. It could be on the pitch, in the form of slipping Sterling to full back to allow another attacker. It perhaps could be on the bench, in the form of Alberto, a man whose glorious lack of pace necessitates the game slowing and whose decision-making Liverpool could possibly make greater use of. It could be on the training pitch – and it probably will be, looking at the wonders this manager has worked on Liverpool's attacking – instilling patience into a young team when it feels as though every second is heart-stoppingly vital. Finding that extra pass that leads to a clear opportunity soon rather than a half-chance now, popping the ball off and getting everyone ten yards further forward rather than turning into trouble. There is such a thing as trying too hard and Brendan Rodgers' Liverpool is far more likely to be guilty of that than the opposite.

It could even be buttressing the bench, occasionally starting one of Sturridge or Suárez or one of Henderson, Coutinho or Gerrard from it, recharging their legs for challenges to come while being able to introduce them as time ticks on should the eleven on the pitch be struggling to finish the job. A big call, yes, and more likely to ensure tops remain on, but Liverpool now need the points, not the dancing.

Liverpool have shown almost everything this season. Everything to be considered a very good side that can for the first time in years look at the mountain of greatness, take a pencil from behind the ear and at least start jotting some ideas down about scaling it.

They've been irresistible. Now it is time to be inevitable.

Neil Atkinson

THE BENCH

LIVERPOOL WON A LOT OF GAMES in the first half this season. They won a fair amount in the first half of the first half, truth be told. But this can't always be the case, no matter how good you are. Sometimes it won't quite go for you; sometimes the opposition will be tougher than you think. Sometimes you need something big at the end.

You can achieve this through different means. Superior fitness will sometimes tell, a mentally tougher team who refuses to drop points can often prevail over one who is less confident, or a home crowd can roar a team to victory. But the really good teams usually do it by bringing about £60m worth of talent off the bench.

Ah, the bench. Nothing tells a smaller team that the dice are loaded against them quite as much as the players the bigger team can bring on. You think you have done great, you're tired but holding out for a draw? Here's last season's top scorer who we can't be bothered playing anymore, along with the captain of Argentina. If that fails we've got a winger warming up who we didn't really need, but cost more than half your team combined. Imagine how much that deflates the opposition. I've given up just typing it. However, for a club of decent resources, our bench was never too scary. Certainly not that day. When you were looking for a game changer against West Brom there wasn't one among them.

Iago Aspas started Liverpool's first three league games, all wins of course, but lost his place even before Suárez returned from his suspension and barely featured again, either from the start or the bench. Bizarrely he seemed to get thrown on when we needed a goal against top teams, featuring home and away against Chelsea, but not when we needed them against poorer teams when you would presume he would find it a bit easier to contribute. I never really figured that out. In this game our number nine was left sitting on the bench while we toiled for the winner.

The two who were brought on were a defender in Martin Kelly and Joe Allen, a good player but not exactly the man you want to throw on when chasing a game. Unless you planned on winning it by being more neat and tidy, something I doubt is ever Luis Suárez's intention. Aside from those, the other options not used were Victor Moses, who started his Liverpool career brightly enough but soon decided it wasn't for him, Luis Alberto, who had shown signs of promise but had only really been trusted in certain situations, and Jordon Ibe, who was about to go on loan to Birmingham City. No wonder the opposition never looked too flustered.

You couldn't help but get the feeling that half the time this season there were some on the bench who were there solely to make the numbers up, who would only get on if we were 10–0 up or Steven Gerrard's head fell off. Many of these players were not even particularly trusted to give key players a rest when dominating. Liverpool used only two substitutes, for example, in five-goal demolitions of Tottenham Hotspur and Norwich in December, and one of those in both games was in stoppage time. This despite it being a relatively busy period of fixtures.

There were pros and cons to having a tighter group of players during the campaign. How younger players like Flanagan and Sterling got chances and were able to play week after week. How together they all looked, with team spirit never better. How they all seemed to grow in understanding through minutes on the pitch. But West Brom away was definitely one for the 'cons' column. You can sneer at rich clubs stockpiling players all you like, but with 20 minutes to go you'd have killed for Edin Dzeko.

John Gibbons

LIVERPOOL 5 ARSENAL 1

8 February 2014
Goals: Skrtel 1', 10', Sterling 16', 52', Sturridge 20'; Arteta (pen) 69'

A HALF-DAY IN THE LIFE: MATCH REVIEW

At this stage in the season, I was asked to write match reports in the immediate aftermath of football matches. I had never done it before and had long complained about the format. You, the reader, have watched the game. Either in the ground or on television. And if you've missed it, there's ample opportunity to see the key moments. Too many newspaper match reports were becoming dominated by key moments along with managerial quotes. There was no longer any sense of a day or an occasion.

So I decided that was what I wanted to do for a readership of Liverpool supporters. Give them more colour, try to find new ways to describe what they'd seen.

Some were more successful than others and the successful ones are in this book, tweaked and tidied as they were often finished in pubs. And they are titled and then hyphenated as 'Match Review'. It'd be outrageous to call them reports. As you will read …

WOKE UP. GOT OUT OF BED. Realised it was 5.15 a.m. Fucking hell, I am a bag of nerves.

Checked my phone. Text from Gibbo received late last night. He was in a bar.

It was badly Wool. Name redacted to protect the innocent.

Drank some water. Pondered this. Champions elect or fourth dogfight. Fucking Arsenal. The rock where too much has appeared to have foundered. Bag of nerves.

Back to bed. Liverpool still going on outside my window. Shouted conversations. This city never sleeps. It has murder instead.

Don't really sleep for half an hour. Contemplate again how amazing professional footballers are. These lads are getting their head down. They have a job to do. I'd never sleep if I was a player. When very young I ran cross-country to a decent standard. Used to keep me up nights, the anxiety of it all.

9 a.m. – Wake. Decide to make a full breakfast for me and Brockle. Go the Tesco in my pyjamas. Loads of red on the streets. Gangs of lads, gangs of girls, gangs of families. A coach. We don't talk enough about the energy match day brings to this city. It vibrates.

I'm only buying sausages.

Get 200 quid out. Need to pay for my derby tickets as well. Don't begrudge that but it's a shocker. I'll hand £150 over today. I can afford it, just. I'm lucky, I know that. I just wish it was a little less.

10 a.m. – Brilliant breakfast being prepared. Served up with a ton of plate discipline. Plate discipline is important. If I want to mix it up, fine, but you should never have your breakfast decisions made for you.

Dave Sutton wants to meet. He's with Phil Blundell. I want to meet them but want to spend time with Brockle. Doing film and TAW stuff I let the side down sometimes. A 12.45 kick-off further pressures the weekend. She'll meet us post-game for a ludicrous pub crawl she's devised with Steve Graves but it's good to sit and be.

I'm thinking of the knife edge. Games on the knife edge have been far too rare since 2009 but this is one. The knife edge is where you find out about your football team. Your club. What we can do.

10.45 a.m. – Realise am dead late now. No shower. Sorry, world. Teeth brushed though. Instead I prioritise getting some port into a hipflask. My hipflask debut. Today this feels like an extra holding midfielder. Another line of defence. The port is great but being an amateur I spill a fair amount. I might be shaky.

This is it, in my head. Do or die. I have spent a season telling everyone who will listen you might as well come first as come fourth. Liverpool are the champions elect. Liverpool are good enough. If they don't show that today then the darkness is back in abundance.

11.15 a.m. – Head out to meet Marjo who is getting the ticket money. Dave and Phil gone. Head to Dr Duncans where we will meet Steve Graves and Kate. Then Mike Girling. Sanguine about selection. Me and Steve have two speedy pints. Girling arrives. Get a taxi.

12.45 p.m. KO to 2.30 p.m. Final Whistle

You've seen the game. Some observations quick:

'Four-nil and you still don't sing'

No. But at 1–0, at 2–0, at 3–0 and at 4–0 we roared. Roared and roared.

Singing is overrated. It really is. An enormous god-rattling scream of fuck off you, just fuck off, fuck off with your battle for fourth, we'll do this instead. We'll not conform to our nightmares. We'll claw upwards. It's the noise that gets them, not the clever verses. The bone-jarring noise.

And that argument with pre-informed destiny, with the narrative of what this season should be, of that's enough now, Liverpool. You don't sing that, you scream it. You rage it. The atmosphere at 4–0 went from the sublime to the ridiculous. You have fucked off. We have imposed our will. What do you do now?

Sit there. Mildly shocked.

Skrtel's second – Hyypia-esque

A wonderful curving header. Where did that come from?

Aly Cissokho is clearly a great lad

He's a Houllier left back. Wins his battles. And now gets in opponent's faces.

Jack Wilshere plays football like a bad Evertonian

Gerrard's pen

The foul of a man who has been tackling everything, sees that and thinks, 'Yep. I'll have this as well.' Tra-la-la-la.

Henderson goosed on 80, making one more shuttle

One more. Then another. Then another. But it isn't just the running. The quality and intelligence was magnificent.

Second half in front of us it looked like Flanagan was calling the line

Coutinho sending everyone the wrong way; Arteta, who bestrode the Emirates, being put on the deck by Suárez; Sterling desperate for a hat-trick

This Liverpool team, the maddest I've seen, the maddest in the country

Germanic, explosive, overwhelming. It is lightning football. The opposition get a free kick, I wonder about how we will break. Concede first against Liverpool at your peril.

At the time of writing Arsenal are top of the league having shipped 11 at Man City and Liverpool

Look me in the eye and say this Liverpool team can't win the league. Look me in the eye and say they can't. The league is bananas. We should win it as the most bananas. It is only right.

3.30 p.m. – The Post Office on London Road. Finishing this up in our first pub of the crawl. Told you it was a mad one.

Mad team. Mad day. Mad pub crawl.

It.

Was.

A.

Joy.

To.

Be.

Alive.

That.

Day.

My.

Friends.

Football can get a lot wrong. But it can also do this.

Neil Atkinson

THE BEST 20 MINUTES I HAVE EVER SEEN

TWENTY MINUTES INTO THIS GAME against the Premier League leaders and Daniel Sturridge is stood, chest out, arrogantly eyeballing the Anfield Road end as bedlam erupts all around him.

Twenty minutes into this game against the Premier League's tightest defence and we have scored four times.

Twenty minutes into this game against the Premier League's tightest defence and we could have scored eight.

So this is what '88 must have been like. This is the best 20 minutes of football I have ever seen, in fact, this is the best 20 minutes of anything I have ever seen.

This is better than the Little Larry Sellers scene in *The Big Lebowski*.

This is better than the 'Talent Trek' episode of *Phoenix Nights*.

This is better than the third Bruce encore at Wembley Stadium.

I have honestly never known a 20 minutes like it. We would have annihilated anybody in those first 20. ANYBODY. In fact, we would have got the better of a Spain '08 – Milan '89 – United '99 – Holland '74 Dream Team that day, such was the exhilarating and inventive football we were being treated to.

The pace and ferocity of our pressing, the determination in our tackling, the clinical nature of our finishing – Arsenal could have thrown all seven subs on and we would have still put four past them.

Remember that Suárez volley that hit the post? Ten defenders and two keepers wouldn't have been able to do a thing about that. Jesus, that Suárez volley. (And bloody hell, the subsequent Kolo miss …)

Even before we saw the wriggly arm dance on 20 minutes, Sturridge had missed a relative sitter as wave after wave of Liverpool attacks crushed Arsenal.

Henderson vs Özil and Coutinho vs Wilshere and his Joe Cole tongue were no contests. Özil took a clattering from Hendo in the build-up to the third and shrank further away from the action after that – he simply didn't fancy it. Hendo's harrying and aggression cowed him, making him look like a £42m luxury and Hendo a £16m bargain. I hope Hendo knows how much we love him.

Coutinho and Wilshere was a different story. Wilshere at least showed some fight (in his narky, niggly way), but was simply outclassed by the Brazilian. The shining light of English football, the great hope which the national team is going to be built around, could not get close to a fella who will be watching the World Cup on the telly. On the few occasions when Coutinho has been utilised in the deeper central role he has blended his outrageous skill with surprising, serious steel, and today was no different. When Coutinho is on song he makes it look so easy, as if he is just messing about against an under-8's team, and Wilshere and his tired dog's tongue didn't like it one bit.

Interception, run, through ball, goal, 4–0. Coutinho made it all look so easy.

The fourth inspired a strange phenomenon on row 60 of the Kop, something I'm not sure I've experienced before, that is – celebratory laughing. Instead of the usual screaming and shouting, everybody was just laughing their heads off. Full-on belly laughs, the kind of laughs that are closely followed by tears. Grown men jumping around like loons, laughing maniacally. Taken out of context, the men in white coats would be taking the lot of us away to a padded cell, but it was the natural emotion at this point. Like I said, I had never seen anything like this first 20 minutes.

All in, we got five and we could have got ten. Suárez didn't score, which is some going for a one-man team. The one they got felt like a blow – conceding goals from a silly mistake is always more galling but unfortunately this was becoming a common theme for our team this season. We escaped one in the first half when Mignolet inexplicably punched the ball against Flanno, but we weren't so lucky when Gerrard inexplicably dived in against Oxlade-Chamberlain.

Had we lost this game we would have been 11 points behind Arsenal, but we didn't lose this game – we won this game so convincingly and so exhilaratingly that we should have been given ten points. As it was, we only got the three (and tipped the goal difference between us and Arsenal on its head too) and we were now five points off the top, with the bit between our teeth and a pretty favourable run-in – we couldn't, could we?

Bogart and Bergman might always have Paris, but no matter what happens this season, we'll always have those 20 minutes.

Ben McCausland

NO ONE GOES FROM SEVENTH TO FIRST

YOU SHOULDN'T GET WOUND UP by what other people say, for a whole host of reasons. One is that a lot of other people are idiots, and idiots are generally best ignored. Another is that people are wrong all the time, so if someone is saying something you don't agree with, there is a fair chance they are wrong about it. So the best thing to do is to wait and see and laugh about it later.

I rarely follow this advice myself. I got wound up by people writing us off all season, even if they were nice people making a reasonable point about squad size and depth and all that. The one that really annoyed me was that 'no one goes from seventh to first'. Why, why don't they? Well, the main reason is that teams who come seventh aren't normally very good. But we had proved ourselves this season to be very good indeed. We'd beaten Everton 4–0, we'd scored five at bloody Stoke, we'd competed well with everyone who we had faced. How we got on at the start of the season before when we barely had any players was no longer relevant.

Every piece of sporting achievement you have loved has been unlikely. Every single piece. Unlikely things happen in sport all the time. Atletico are doing a number on La Liga while Liverpool are doing a number on Arsenal. We love sport because it is unlikely. Voices, however gentle, wrapping themselves in the blanket of 'can't be done' should be smothered in it. This is the adventure we have been looking for.

Besides, why can't an outsider come from behind and shock everyone? A 100–1 shot can win the Grand National, after all. Sceptics will say this is because horses are more unpredictable than humans. I'd say they just don't have journalists in their ear telling them what they can and can't do. They just go out and do it.

For this is the key thing for me. We talk ourselves out of things all the time. We get told what we should be doing, and act accordingly. We essentially allow others to talk us out of what we can and can't achieve. If Istanbul had been over two legs instead of two halves it wouldn't have happened. Doubt would have crept in, everyone would have had their say. 'Liverpool have got no chance, they were completely outclassed, the opposition are just too good.' Instead we didn't have time for this nonsense to get in our minds and we just went and won instead.

I'm not having anyone talk us out of anything anymore. We are Liverpool, the kings of improbable victory, the enemy of logic. You can't go from seventh to first. Who fucking says?

John Gibbons

FULHAM 2 LIVERPOOL 3

12 February 2014
Goals: Touré (o.g.) 8', Richardson 63'; Sturridge 41', Coutinho 72', Gerrard (pen) 90'

THE DEMONS:
MATCH REVIEW

DEMONS. ALL DAY. DEMONS. THEY WON'T SHUT UP.

Fulham away. I hate Fulham away as a fixture. Hate it. The formbook goes out the window. For every Yossi late winner there is Lee Mason sending a billion of ours off.

All day the demons. Rory Smith saying Liverpool won't win. I like Rory. He's wrong. But it's sense he's speaking. We've lacked gumption after big wins.

All day the demons. The noises. The 'don't get carried away' sense shouts. They love them. I've seen them. Roy Henderson, Iain Macintosh and Paul Tomkins. Good men possessed into saying it can't be.

The tantrum-havers. Don't say it. Don't dream of saying it. We'll only let ourselves down if we say it. It's unseemly.

The demons, they speak through them.

Blocking them out has grown harder and harder as we get closer to kick-off.

Don't let the demons in.

First bad call of the day – watch the match on a stream. The demons love a stream. Stuttering. Imperfect. Solitary. Your relationship becomes just them and you. No us. A me. A me. A me. And what do I think?

I think everything. I hear everything. I hear the demons. I hear can't do.

Don't let the demons in.

Kick-off. Don't like it. They look urgent.

Kolo. Oh Kolo. Oh Kolo. You poor bastard. All the security you were meant to bring reduced to an argument with God.

The shape isn't great and they are countering us. Not meant to be this way.

The equaliser. Oh my lord. The pass is genius. The pass is beauty. The pass is matched by the finish. Gerrard. Sturridge. Demons beaten back.

Pressure though. The Reds had done pressure. Actual pressure when not playing well. Isn't this what you have been waiting for? I think, though I could be wrong, I'm a spineless fool. I'd rather they'd just played well.

Half-time I walked about six miles around a one-bedroom flat.

Second half more pressure. Waves of pressure. Twenty-four hours in A&E going on behind me.

Christ almighty.

Stream jamming. Swarms of red. Waves of red. Post hit. Endless pulsating red hordes, smashing into – oh for the love of Mike. 2–1 Fulham. Disastrous defending.

The demons are at the door. Clawing. Biting. Hammering. Jamming. Stream jamming. Gnawing their way into my skull.

Brockle urges. Loads of time, she says. Stare them down, she says. Go out, man, she says.

Coat on. Shoes on. Open the door. Stare them down. Duke Street's finest bar. Name redacted to protect the guilty. Silent Sleep's Chris McIntosh doing the bingo in front of the match. This truly is strange torment. The match on. 2–2.

Two fucking two.

With humans not demons.

More pressure. The Reds doing ugly. Doing it well enough?

Liverpool look more likely. Begin rationalisation process. We haven't lost ground this weekend. Everyone else has dropped points. So 2–2 is OK. It is. It is. It is, right!

Terrible decision on Coutinho from the referee. Aspas going spare behind the manager. Go 'ed, Iago. Start him Sunday, Brendan. Start him.

Penalty. PENALTY.

Gerrard will score. No demons. No rationalisation. Not now. No doubt as he steps up. None. Look at him. Walk. Around. Him.

And Liverpool see it out. Come from behind away from home. Grind it. Pressure. Win when not playing well.

But rewind. Walk around him. Look at him. Wheeling away. Shirt in his hand, screaming, a football team descending on him, a city collapsing in on him, his shoulders broad a thousand times over, broad again, holding an entire city up. Steven Gerrard.

Walk around him.

Look at him.

I dare you to look at him. Demons. Naysayers. The *reasonable*. Look at him. Battle for fourth, is it? His jersey a circular blur. Just about getting back into the CL, is it?

Let's be clear. Fourth place this campaign would be a significant achievement for the football club. One which should be applauded and welcomed. Everyone walks away head held high. We know that.

But he's walked among the stars. You dream of it, he's done it, except one thing. Everything you can in club football. He's done fourth, he's done third and he's done second. He has never done first. Nor has he wheeled away, his jersey in his hand, his heart pumping, our hearts exploding, in a February league game.

Look at him and tell me this isn't about first. Look at him go. I'm weak as a kitten. He is strong enough for us all. He is our Atlas. Look at him go.

Look me in the eye and tell me you don't think of first. Look me in the eye.

Support.

Believe.

A joy.

Neil Atkinson

KOLO: A TRUE BELIEVER DETERMINED TO SCUPPER

I WATCH LFC TV A LOT AT HOME. By this I mean I watch LFC TV a lot when I am in bed hung over when an hour of Robbie Fowler scoring goals is about all I can cope with. Which I guess also counts as 'a lot'. The problem with doing this is the adverts they show in between, which seem to be charities telling me that all the bad things happening in the world are my fault. This isn't what they actually say, of course, but it's what it feels like to a man with post-alcohol depression trying to work out how far the amount he spent the previous night on Jägermeister could go to help an African village which has no water.

Anyway, one of the things I half remember watching at the start of the season, in between trips to the toilet and crying into my pillow, was Kolo Touré speaking to an Ivory Coast teammate at Melwood. I've no idea what he was doing there, maybe you just get to invite your mates to Melwood when you play for Liverpool, but in a not-at-all-staged conversation, the other player asked Kolo Touré what he thought Liverpool could do this season, to which Kolo Touré replied, 'Win the league'. At this point the other player, like everyone else sensible in the world, tried to talk Kolo out of it, suggesting that top four was a more realistic target. Kolo Touré, to his credit, was having none of it.

This kind of talk from Kolo happened a lot throughout the season. If you google 'Kolo Touré Liverpool can win the league' you get bullish quotes from 4 November after defeat 2–0 at Arsenal, and 19 January after drawing at home to Aston Villa, and many more besides. You even get quotes from 13 May 2014 saying we are going to win it in 2014/15, God bless him.

It is fair to say that Kolo Touré was a firm believer in the Liverpool title surge when many weren't. I also think it's fair to say that this belief, coupled with his early-season performances, had a profound impact on both the rest of the squad and the fan base. Kolo had been around championship-winning squads, and if he said this was one, then who were we to argue?

It didn't go wrong for Liverpool, but it certainly went wrong for Kolo. So what happened to him? It was quite possible his legs had gone when we got him, and adrenaline could only take him through so many early games before we learned his true level. I also think he was at the point of his career where, fitness-wise, he needed to be playing every week, and bringing him in and out of the side wasn't doing him any favours.

That said, by Fulham away Touré had started seven games in a row, so he certainly shouldn't have been rusty, but mistakes were starting to occur at an alarming rate. The pass to Anichebe arguably happens to all footballers at some point, especially those who play in teams who want to pass it from the back. Even Steve Gerrard has been through his fair share of passing to an opposition forward, usually Thierry Henry, to see them score. The own goal against Fulham, however, looked depressingly like an over-the-hill player who simply could no longer get his body to do what his mind wanted it to. In the spirit of fairness it should be pointed out that the ball took a bad bobble, which Touré wouldn't have been expecting; however, he seemed to have enough time to adjust his body to the position of the ball, but was quite simply unable to do so.

Kolo couldn't seem to get his head together for the rest of the game, to the point of clumsily barging the referee over in the middle of the park, and arguably didn't recover for the rest of the season. He was out of the team, pretty much for good, by the next game against Arsenal and became fourth choice from then on in. It was a shame really, for a man who seemed to embody so much of the early-season optimism, to become seen as a liability, the biggest embodiment of Liverpool's defensive fragility. But I hope he is remembered as he should be, as the man who came in, kept three clean sheets on the bounce, and told us we were all going to win the league. Someone had to, and I'm glad it was him.			**John Gibbons**

COUTINHO'S STRANGE CAMPAIGN

IN A SEASON OF UTTER MADNESS, Fulham summed it up pretty well. The days preceding the game saw serious doubt as to whether it would actually go ahead, with Fulham claiming that the planned Tube strike would see all of their casual staff unable to get to the ground – it was more than likely an excuse so they could have a rest, having being involved in a really funny 2–2 draw at Old Trafford that saw them lead for most of the game, go 2–1 down and then equalise at the death. Probably fair enough to have a bash really, more so given the leggy and somewhat stupid foul by Sascha Riether in injury time that led to the match-winning penalty.

The game was mad from the get-go. We found ourselves 2–1 down with about 20 to go. Stupid goals, one a comical Kolo own goal, the other goal that confusing and surreal I couldn't figure out which of three people was most at fault for it. Our goal came as a result of a Steven Gerrard pass that good, that beautiful, that perfect, that I saw someone tweet PornHub and ask them to stick the six-second Vine on their site.

The game-changer was Phillipe Coutinho with something that summed up his season. A pot-shot from the edge of the box that was neither here nor there, and needed a large chunk of luck and some particularly average goalkeeping to end up in the back of the net. He did loads of ambitious pot-shots all season. Loads. To the point that it became very annoying.

I love flair players. I loved Luis Garcia. I love players who'll do things a bit different, a bit left field, daring. I like a maverick. He'll stick two fingers up to the miserable old bastards who infest Anfield by doing something marvellous after they've moaned for the previous hour. The reason you've sat in that seat for 50 years and seen loads of glory is cos you weren't a footballer yourself, mate, so stop trying to tell one what to do.

Who can forget that twist of the hips from Coutinho against Arsenal that should have seen Mikel Arteta have to pay £50 to get back on the pitch? He's a beautiful player when he's on his game. When he isn't, you almost feel like he's trying to make a point about how much of a maverick he can be. Just keep it simple, mate. Christ, he's done my head in this season. The back end of last season Coutinho was a thing of beauty – everyone just walking out of grounds up and down the country laughing that we'd managed to nab this lad from Internazionale's bench for £8.5m. His performances at Wigan and Newcastle in particular were majestic.

This season, however, this season he's been crackers. Moments of genius have still been there, but far less evident and regular. The aforementioned twist and shake on Arteta and subsequent through ball to Henderson was without doubt the high point. While he's drifted through some games doing loads of nothing, you can't even say he's been poor, because he hasn't. It's been the season of your typical maverick.

I'm considering getting a really big megaphone for next season so I can shout, 'Oi, knobhead, you're shit at shooting from outside the box, do a through ball, you're dead good at through balls,' extremely loud every time he shifts the ball out of his feet, drops the shoulder and nine times out of ten drags the ball disappointingly wide. Coutinho shots and the subsequent goal kicks cost us about 20 minutes I reckon. I've not checked this; this isn't a verified stat. It's just a rough guess that happens to be correct.

To be fair to him, there's probably a good reason why he's been up and down (although the word down is a little harsh) – he started the season against Stoke in front of Gerrard, Henderson and Lucas and was the creative fulcrum. After it became clear that Raheem Sterling was the future of this club, and most importantly a 'number ten', he started being shunted around a little, the role we all thought was his taken away by the young pretender. To his credit, his head didn't drop, he worked hard and he realised what he needed to do.

Even with all of the frustration he brings, he's been really important in what we've done. Clever, industrious, and he really enjoys a tackle which for someone of his build and nationality isn't something you'd expect. He's second only to Henderson for me in the ability to press and harass, and while I've complained a little, I wouldn't have him any other way.

In this, the first game where you suddenly saw Liverpool stick their backs to the wall and tell the world the Reds were genuinely in the mix, Coutinho provided the impetus. I'd known for months, loads of us had known for months, that we were in the shake-up. That we were as good as anyone else and we weren't going anywhere. But the marker, four days after snotting Arsenal 5–1, had been thrown down in good fashion. The Reds were in this title race. Game two of the glorious eleven. As I walked out of Craven Cottage that night the real belief filled the air. It was beautiful.

Liverpool 2013/14. We're all mavericks now.   **Phil Blundell**

ARSENAL 2 LIVERPOOL 1

16 February 2014
Goals: Oxlade-Chamberlain 16', Podolski 47'; Gerrard (pen) 59'

THE EMIRATES

THIS WAS GOING TO BE A DODDLE.

Arsenal – poor, fragile, five goals worse-off Arsenal coming up against rampant, confident, five goals and a last-minute peno to the good Liverpool. We had Suárez and Sturridge up front, they had a postman. This was going to be brutal. Then the texts started coming through:

> *'THE SHITE AT HOME'*
> *'Lad, we've got The Ev at home next round, am not messin'*
> *'We've got your fucking shower. At fucking Anfield. Fuck off'*

This was going to be a procession into the semi-finals – swat Arsenal aside today with minimum fuss and then don't let Everton off so easily this time and give them a real hammering – six, maybe seven, yeah, that sounds good.

It didn't take long for this bravauro to disappear – just the length of time it took Sturridge to miss two relatively easy chances in the first five minutes.

'But he usually buries them!'

'That's their reserve keeper an' all, lad.'

Ah balls, it was going to be one of those days. I knew it, our whole end knew it. The players didn't know it – they manfully strove to get themselves back into it, not realising that Howard Webb had also decided it wasn't going to be our day.

Arsenal time their goals well, the first putting an end to our early, frenzied pressure, the second one minute into the second half, before 90 per cent of the stadium are back in their spacious, luxurious, ergonomic, reclining, massaging Emirates chairs.

Seriously, how good are those seats? Parking my arse in those seats at half-time is usually the only worthwhile part of the day out at the Arsenal.

Scandalously overpriced train ticket? Check!

Similarly priced match ticket? Check!

Nowhere around the ground for a pint? Check!

Strangely small-time home fans? Check!

I would like to just add at this point, that I have no axe whatsoever to grind with Arsenal – my grandad was a proud Arsenal man and my good mate Gareth is a season-ticket holder down there, but there is something very odd about modern Arsenal. Or perhaps it's just the Emirates Experience which is odd. Highbury was all right – a 'proper' (i.e old and a bit shit) ground – like a less bile-filled Goodison.

It was never the most intimidating place to go, but thinking back to games such as that one when Poll went mad and sent everyone off, they could muster a decent atmosphere in there.

The atmosphere at the Emirates is pitiful. I blame that dreadful middle tier which seems to be all corporate and no doubt rakes the Arsenal in plenty of match-day revenue, but ironically kills any kind of traditional football match-day experience for the people at the match. I am a firm believer that a football stadium should be 90 per cent peanut gallery seats and the 10 per cent corporate should be tucked away somewhere where they can see us but not negatively impact on us shouting, jumping, swearing and creating that atmosphere they have paid through the nose for. Wembley has exactly the same thing, and Wembley is just as bad.

Also, that wavy design all around the top. What on earth is that about? It looks like the architect had been on the ale the night before, or was maybe something he drew in his first year at uni and thought he would submit it to Arsenal's board for a laugh. Sit in any seat in the Emirates and you could be in any other seat in the ground, such is the lack of identity in this Pride Park-on-steroids of a ground.

The majority of the fans are a strange bunch too – very banter-y and *Soccer AM-y* – very haircut-y too. There seems to be a lack of passion around Arsenal these days, like the game is a big laugh and it doesn't really matter. I don't want to make out like football is the be-all and end-all, but it does matter. It matters more than the Arsenal fans let on.

Whether these fans are a by-product of the move to the new ground or just an exaggerated version of the modern football fan (or maybe even just Cockneys, though Cockney Reds aren't like that) I don't know, but there is something very disingenuous about a good number of them.

Reading this back, it certainly does seem like I have an axe to grind with Arsenal, but I genuinely don't – I hate them far less than I hate most other clubs. And they've got fucking lovely seats.

Anyway, having accepted our fate long before the final whistle, we had been reduced to thinking up postman puns in relation to Arsenal's raw young striker Yaya Sanogo's previous career ('Do you think when he goes to see Wenger he always knocks twice?' and 'Another first-class delivery from Sanogo' being two personal favourites).

We kept on plugging away, and chance after chance came and went but our end never had the smell of blood in our nostrils, we were never baying and scream- ing and bellowing – something just didn't feel right today. As that prick Webb blew for full time we filed out of the away end, with one phrase tumbling from everyone's lips.

'Ah well, concentrate on the league.'

Ben McCausland

I DON'T LIKE TALKING ABOUT REFEREES

TWICE A WEEK I have to get behind a microphone and talk about football. It's easier than you'd think. I get together with three or four other people and we talk about Liverpool. We have very, very few rules. But one is this:

Only in the most extreme circumstances do we talk about a referee.

There are three reasons for this. The first reason, the smaller reason, is that they are, on the whole, trying to do their best in a difficult environment.

The second reason, the medium-sized reason, is that it is dull. Duller than ditchwater. So what, a referee got something badly wrong. What about the rest of the game? It suits a televisual agenda that loves to boil football matches down to moments and those moments down to controversy. We can have a big chat about a defined five seconds of football, no need for anything bigger. Managers are questioned on it in the immediate aftermath, emotional, engaged. This falls over into back-page headlines. I'm broadly OK with all these people doing this. They have their rules of engagement and we have ours. We get to define ours and say, 'This isn't for us.' We get to do that when we own and control what happens behind a microphone.

Howard Webb's performances against Chelsea on 29 December and Arsenal on 16 February during this glorious adventure of a football season broke my rule. The seeming desire not to give big decisions underpins both performances. Two penalties were too big at Arsenal and …

WHAT ON EARTH WAS HE POINTING AT AGAINST CHELSEA!?

I can't stop thinking about this. At the time of writing almost five months have passed since Eto'o cut clumsily across Suárez and Howard Webb stuck his arm out and pointed at who knows what against Chelsea. He cannot have seriously been saying that Eto'o got the ball. I can't stop thinking about it.

This Liverpool side have gone both beneath and beyond the big moment. When you sweep teams away you rarely get into big moments. How can five seconds define a game when Liverpool can win them in five minutes?

HONESTLY, WHAT WAS HE POINTING AT?

Yet when you get into big games, they are more likely to have big moments. You can't get beyond them all and you can't pick yourself up after them all if you feel like they have gone the wrong way. In the FA Cup Liverpool were better than Arsenal. Not a bit better, but a lot better. They camped inside the Arsenal half and refused to let them escape. They pushed and probed and created but one bad refereeing decision meant Arsenal got off the hook.

It was astonishing to see. Less than six months ago Arsenal were imperious against Liverpool in this ground. And now they could hardly get a kick. This is something worth talking about despite the defeat. This is a footballing marvel. Arsenal and their crowd were reduced to emptying the ball up the pitch and cheering it being emptied with gusto. They were hanging on for dear life. But …

WHAT IS HE PLAYING AT!?

It disrupts your perception of the football game. Words like 'injustice' are tricky in footballing parlance. It's a game, a diversion, a distraction. It may be the best game, diversion, distraction, but it remains just that. It might have the hopes and dreams of millions around the world on its shoulders. It might feel like everything. But it isn't everything. However, you take your 'injustice' and it clouds the rest of the football match. Suárez was fouled. It was a second penalty. And then that's all everyone talks about. Everywhere you go, it's all everyone talks about.

We shouldn't talk about it. We really shouldn't. This is the third and biggest reason why I hate talking about referees:

Liverpool were better than Arsenal. Arsenal scored more goals. Howard Webb didn't give Suárez a second penalty, nor did he send off Steven Gerrard. The neutral arbiter of events got things badly wrong, as he did at Stamford Bridge. The issue the neutral arbiter of events had on both occasions was seemingly the absence of decision making about events; trying not to be seen as someone who ruins the game. After less than a minute back in December Eto'o committed a red-card foul on Henderson at Stamford Bridge. But give it and you get accused of ruining the game; even if you get it right. Imagine what happens if you get it wrong. Suárez wins two penalties. But if either isn't a penalty you get headlines all week telling you that you ruined the game.

What talking incessantly about referees does – the rule I try so hard not to break – is redefine the concerns of refereeing. The neutral arbiter of events instead becomes a participant who can be rated. He can have marks out of ten. How he manages the game – not neutrally arbitrates events, but manages the game as a spectacle – gets rated. Gets talked about. So if you talk about him, you compromise him. Atkinson's Observer Principle: 'What impact does constant slagging off of the observed have upon the observed?' These lads don't run round, blow whistles and then disappear back into cryogenic storage. They know they'll be pulled apart. And it wouldn't be human not to think about that at the moment when Luis Suárez, known gamesman extraordinaire, goes down for a second time. If he's conned you twice, well, let me guarantee you, my friend, you are getting it in the neck all week. So exactly how sure are you?

If we talk and talk and talk and we add to the talk and talk and talk then we are part of the problem. And that's why I hate talking about referees.

Still though. What *was* he pointing at?

Neil Atkinson

LIVERPOOL 4 SWANSEA CITY 3

23 February 2014
Goals: Sturridge 3', 36', Henderson 20', 74';
Shelvey 23', Skrtel (o.g.) 27', Bony (pen) 47'

MORE OF A TRY THAN A GOAL: THE WINNER

IT WAS GOOD FUN watching Manchester United this season. Even with plenty of quality in attack they had a wonderful habit of huffing and puffing and crossing the ball and getting beat. It reminded me of the worst days of Liverpool, wondering how it seemed to be the hardest thing in the world for us to score a goal, while the opposition seemed to find it so easy.

Of course, it wasn't always like this, which is why you have to enjoy these things while you can. For a while watching Manchester United play was the most frustrating thing in the world. They undoubtedly had a great ability to carve teams open and score at will when they were on song, but I would pull my hair out at how many goals they scored when they weren't. How many penalties did they get? How many soft ones did the opposition seem to let in against them? And how many bloody own goals?

What I probably knew deep down at the time, but wasn't prepared to admit, was how they were kings, even when not at their most fluid best, at building pressure and forcing opposition errors. All the criticisms above have probably been levelled at Liverpool this season, but we know now that they are nonsense. Do the right things with the ball for long enough, and eventually they will pay off, one way or another.

This was a strange old game. Liverpool went 2–0 up without playing particularly well, and then forgot to kick on from there. At 3–3 Swansea sensed they could get an unexpected point and sat back, while Liverpool finally realised this game would take some winning, but found it difficult to move through the gears having played so lethargically so far. This is when a team needs to be patient, trusting that quality pressure will pay off, and that is exactly what happened.

Liverpool scored exactly the type of winning goal that, had it been Manchester United, would have led to me throwing the remote control at the television, calling them 'spawny bastards', but it was the result of doing all the sensible things you should do when looking for a winner. Getting the ball to your best players in quality areas. Getting other men in the box around them. Following up on chances in the hope that something breaks.

Something did break. Suárez's shot bounced off Henderson towards the keeper and he was following it up to kick into the goal with the keeper on the floor. It reminded me of a rugby league team putting a grubber kick into the in-goal area hoping it would bounce around long enough for an attacking player to fall on it. In this case the attacking player was Jordan Henderson, a blur of energy, reacting before anyone else and bundling over the line. More of a try than a goal. Spawny? Simply good.

If Jordan Henderson had been born in Sale instead of Sunderland he would have made a good rugby player, I think, willing to run the ball downfield all day, and tackle anything that moved. I'm glad he's a footballer, though, and I'm very glad he plays for Liverpool. They probably wouldn't like his hair anyway.

John Gibbons

'THIS DEFENDING IS DECADENT'

THE TITLE QUOTE comes from highly respected television journalist Peter Marshall. I watched the Swansea game next to him. Sitting next to Peter is brilliant, I heartily recommend it. He's utterly absorbed in the contest. He lets out involuntary noises and shouts so loudly. He's in the contest. Not thinking about his tea or his work or where he's going out afterwards. He's in the football match. And in this football match he turned to me and said, in his fantastic presentational burr, 'This defending is decadent.'

This defending is decadent.

Liverpool struggled to cope with Wilfred Bony. That is the essence of Wilfred Bony. It's what he wants to be, a defender's nightmare, a player you can't contain. But leaving the centre backs aside, Liverpool had Henderson outrageously high up the pitch, clearly on instruction, leaving Gerrard, as against Aston Villa, sitting utterly alone. Bony is uncontainable but now he has unmarked runners joining and Liverpool are pegged back from 2–0 to 2–2 with alarming ease.

This defending is decadent.

What matters here is the team. The wide players aren't coming back in, Henderson is staying high and Liverpool, as a whole, look far too relaxed about Swansea having the ball. Liverpool get in at half-time 3–2 ahead and will surely shut up shop before pulling away.

Swansea make it 3–3. Decadent.

It's disturbing, this. Even at this stage of the season Liverpool's approach is disturbing. As a game of football to watch when you are convinced this side can achieve something astonishing, it hurts too much. Palpitations aren't even the start of it.

Decadence.

Peter's right, of course he is. But he's also wrong. This Liverpool side could have reinforced pillars at the back if that decision had been made. There's a theoretical problem with the way we set up but it is based upon not needing reinforced pillars. Football teams have to be about something and the way Brendan Rodgers sets his team up isn't about decadence, it's about having good players and trusting them to be good.

Last season I was saying to people, what worries me about Rodgers' football is that you need to have eight really good players in your first eleven to play it. At least eight. Benítez needed sevenish. Houllier six. Hodgson four.

But now we've seen eight really good players. How we've seen it. In the five league games that precede this one, Liverpool have scored 20 goals. Make that 24 from six after this Swansea win. It's been mind-blowing football.

But what happens when all the good players don't play really well? They can't every week. What happens if one or two misfire or if the manager has perhaps picked the wrong one or two for the occasion? What happens if you have the really good players and it just isn't quite right? Well today, Liverpool won 4–3. They got away with it. Against Fulham, they got away with it 3–2.

What would happen under Benítez, Houllier or Hodgson in that circumstance? Under Benítez you'd probably eke three points out somehow. It wouldn't be pretty. Under Houllier, eke something out though a strong chance of a draw. Under Hodgson a draw or quite possibly a defeat. All these results by a single goal and with fewer than three goals in a game.

Good players having off days happens everywhere. Up and down the country, it happens. It's what happens next that matters. And while it may appear decadent to play in this way, its basis is anything but. It's being certain that these players are the good players and letting them be. Occasionally they are going to let you down to some degree, but look at what empowering them and their ability has done. Set up in a manner which has safety nets all around them and you aren't empowering them to succeed, you are planning for them to fail.

Having the players to do this doesn't worry me. Having the players to rotate in order to do this next season doesn't worry me. Keeping the intensity to ensure the single-goal victory, whether that goal is the first, the third or the seventh, is what worries me. The collective defending might be decadent but the collective ethic is anything but. While that remains the case, seven-goal thrillers might just have to be borne.

What a shame that is.

Neil Atkinson

SOUTHAMPTON 0 LIVERPOOL 3

1 March 2014
Goals: Suárez 16', Sterling 58', Gerrard (pen) 90'

SUBJECT. VERB. OBJECT.
A MATCH REVIEW

Brockle said to me: 'Your match reports are horrible.'
We're calling them reviews, not reports.
'Horrible. Don't know how people are putting up with them.'
People seem to like them. Came as a surprise to me, actually.
'Sentences without subjects. Subject. Verb. Object. That's how the English language works.'
It's malleable. And it's fascinating to make it malleable around football where it mostly doesn't get to do much.
'Who do you think you are? Gogol?'
I like the idea of solving the problem of what happens writing-wise after a match everyone has seen and invested their soul in.
'Horrrrrible to read. I hated that last one. Couldn't finish it.'
The last one was a bit disjointed I grant you. I may have been in the throes of a breakdown though.
'Don't care. Couldn't finish it.'

WE PUT NARRATIVES AROUND FOOTBALL MATCHES. We reject disjointed.

Before. During. After.

We impose the rules.

Subject. Verb. Object.

We find narratives and we apply them because it is how we humans tend to see the world. But by imposing that narrative we impose a structure that doesn't entirely exist or apply. Football matches are full of random things happening which are often completely unrelated to random things that have gone before. That humans want to shape this into something is natural but false.

That tackle in the 27th minute? Had to have meaning from either before or after. Couldn't just be a tackle. The shot in the 34th told us this. The save in the 68th told us that. We struggle to accept the randomness of football in the same way we struggle to accept the randomness of the universe. Football is as much about the way you adapt to the random, the way you anticipate the unanticipate-able, about the way you embrace the madness as it is the way you plan for it.

Luis Suárez is the best at this in the world.

Luis Suárez has reached a pact with the random. He will do its bidding and it will do his.

Luis Suárez plays every moment of the game as though it is its own moment; crystalline, pure. For Luis Suárez the game is afoot. The game is always afoot. It is here and it is now and therefore we play and we play and we play and we play and we play. And we win. And we win and we win and we win and we win. Or we die trying.

Luis Suárez is the best footballer at dealing with random I've ever seen. Luis Suárez doesn't just expect the unexpected, Luis Suárez is the unexpected. He's footballing Chaos, terrifying opponents, taking the expected football universe off its axis and realigning the reality of defenders into a far darker place where all the old certainties dissolve into a primordial swamp and instead the hindbrain twitches with fear. What is he going to do to me next? How does he hurt us now?

Christ, he's now even making Liverpool's throw-ins look good.

Southampton were much the better side at the football first half. But Liverpool were better at the random. Liverpool got lucky with the post, the goalkeeper responded brilliantly. They did random better than a Southampton side who showed their class once again.

It was an agonising first half. The pain is what you are in this for. The pain means this is real. And you know this is real. Really real now. Because you feel this pain.

Sterling's finish back against the momentum of the play was lovely. The sort of thing that pleases the life out of my dad. He'll talk to me about it tomorrow. We still talk about Fowler at Leeds, treble season.

Agger responded to being substituted and criticised by the manager. Yet again, the manager knows what he is about. And fair play to the player.

Gerrard vacating his zone may drive me mad. But, by Jove, he can pick a pass.

Liverpool's shape after scoring the second was excellent. We've spoken loads about this.

Liverpool showed they could shut the life down out of a game. A clean sheet.

Around the 80th minute Suárez tried to trip someone up with his head. Think about that for a second. Think about how many other people earning over five million pounds a year are doing that. Throw my head in at that lad's knee. That'll help the cause.

The rest of today lies on the floor in bits. Destroyed by the happiness of the football match. These bits will need picking up.

All stories pound towards their conclusion, their conclusion is written in the events of the game, in the context of the season. All plots lead to death. The plot so many of those who shape football's plots want to give this Liverpool season is that it runs out of puff. It runs out of steam. It finishes. It dies. It cannot be. It doesn't make any sense. I predicted this. I did not predict that. It cannot …

Before. During. After.

Subject. Verb. Object.

All plots lead to death. Unless they lead to Luis Suárez. Sense is in short supply in these parts these days. Sense rode out of town. Instead we have unpredictability. We have madness. Even calm madness.

And in this most chaotic of seasons wouldn't it be right if …

I mean, wouldn't it be appropriate if the man who embraces randomness, when everything is so very random manages to …

… And there we have it. There you go again. There I go again. I'm as much to blame as anyone. Imposing the narrative. Any narrative.

Before. During. After.

Subject. Verb. Object.

What do we know, definitely know, from today? That the joy of those goals was all-encompassing, overwhelming. That it blasts you. That it was three more points.

What can we speculate about? That you'll spend the next 10, 20, 30, 40, 50 years of your life imposing narratives on this thing which was this much fun; banging on to friends/children/grandchildren, that you saw these Tricky Reds. The trickiest Reds you could ever have conceived of. The trickiest Reds there have ever been. Brendan Rodgers' Tricky Reds.

Ten to go. Ten. Liverpool are second and the game is afoot. The game is always afoot. It is here and it is now and therefore we play and we play and we play and we play and we play. And we win. And we win and we win and we win and we win. Or we die trying. You either embrace that with every fibre of your being or you are dead already.

Don't fear the fact that all plots should lead to death. Instead look at them unfold. Look at this, this glorious surprise, this red lava streaming down the mountain, enveloping everything in its path from a volcano so many thought had fallen dormant. A volcano too easily written off as dormant for too long. Many of those who had written it off are now running screaming from their homes as the lava inexorably streams towards them.

Don't you dare look away. Don't you dare get scared and flinch, however tempting it is on a day like today when the agony hits. Don't you dare run from the joy or rationalise it into what can't be. What's the worst that can happen now? We die trying? The plot will have been worth it. Every twist. Every turn.

I'm out. And will be all night. With Steve and John and Brockle and Kate and Laura and Nick and Liz and Dan and two Robs and Ben and and and and. (Come to town. Always come to town.) Steve will end up on John's shoulders. Why? Because we are going to win the league. (Come to town. Come and play with us.)

So now, after the agony, we have the joy and the pieces all over the floor. I'll pick them up tomorrow. I'll impose the structure tomorrow. I'll reduce in the week. Make sensible. Presentable. Subject. Verb. Object. Tonight though we drink and dance and talk talk talk in a city that throbs throbs throbs.

Right now you are going to believe us (about the random). In 20 years we'll be boring you (about the inevitability).

Subject. Verb. Object.

Liverpool. Win. League.

And if they don't? Well there was a period, a long period, in which I wondered if I'd ever have this much fun from football again.

Neil Atkinson

OUR FIFTH FORMATION OF THE YEAR

ANOTHER GAME, ANOTHER TACTICAL SWITCH. On paper it looked like Liverpool were going to set up in a fairly familiar 4–3–3, but it became clear during the opening passage that Philippe Coutinho was actually playing at the tip of a diamond in midfield. The fifth formation of the year.

Many armchair Liverpudlian tacticians had long advocated a diamond formation as a possible way forward, wondering why it hadn't been at least tried already. The fact was that, while it had been very effective in Europe, it had never really caught on in the Premier League. This could be to do with the traditional way the game is played in England, with wingers looking to hit target men. However, with Liverpool arguably playing a more European style, favouring short precise passing over crosses into the box, there was no reason it couldn't work. It also seemed a good tactic to contain an opposition who played a similar way, with numbers in the centre able to rush a team looking to play through the middle from the back.

I would imagine the main reason Rodgers wanted to try this formation was to get Sturridge and Suárez working as a genuine partnership up front. This was important in the long term, not just to get our two most deadly players in more dangerous positions, but also in keeping them both happy. Suárez and Sturridge had generally taken it in turns to play wide when playing 4–3–3 or 4–2–3–1, and seemed happy enough to do what was best for the team against the big clubs, but it always seemed likely it would be a tough sell to get either of them doing it for any considerable length of time. Both players naturally pull wide to find space, but – crucially – on their terms, rather than as part of a pre-defined role. Those who argue players who are paid by the club should do as they are told ignore the importance of managing personalities and keeping key players happy in times of transition. It's much easier to get Luis Suárez to play left side when you have just won the European Cup, for example, than it is when he has spent the previous summer trying to move to a more successful club.

From an offensive point of view the formation largely worked well. Liverpool found width through full backs, looked dangerous whenever they could get it to the front two, and of course scored three goals. My issue with a diamond formation is that your team is built around your number ten, with everything naturally going through him. The AC Milan team of around 2005–07 that played it so well had Kaka pulling the strings, for example, at the time one of the best players in the world. Philippe Coutinho isn't at that level yet and struggled with the responsibility of the role, seemingly preferring it when he starts from deeper or wider and can choose his moments to influence the game.

There were also issues with the formation defensively. This might seem a strange thing to say after keeping a clean sheet away at a good side, but Southampton had several good chances in the game and probably should have scored more than once. Henderson and Allen seemed to struggle with their off-the-ball roles slightly, looking to push on to Schneiderlin, Cork and Davis but getting caught out behind them, with Lallana and Lambert frequently outnumbering and finding space round Steven Gerrard. With greater quality ahead of them, it could have been a different match.

So despite a fantastic win at a difficult ground the jury was still out on the formation at this stage. I remember thinking that I wasn't sure if we would see it again after this game, it felt like something specific to target Southampton's numbers in midfield that wouldn't necessarily be used against other teams who were stronger down the flanks. I had no issue with it as such; I just felt the lack of a genuinely reliable top-class number ten was the main thing holding it back. Turns out we had one. He just hadn't told anyone yet.

John Gibbons

IF THEY WERE THAT GOOD, THEY WOULDN'T BE EIGHTH

I DISLIKED SOUTHAMPTON GROWING UP. We didn't seem to win there ever and everything seemed utterly joyless. Until 2001 they played in one of those terrible stadiums that everyone said was a leveller, and then they moved to an identikit thing in the middle of an industrial estate. Then in 2004 they disappeared. All was good.

Sadly, eight years later they came back. When they did come back we had more misery, we turned up there last season and lost 3–1 – it was embarrassing. Not only that, but I spent about two hours walking round looking for a pub and couldn't find one. We submitted and had a pint in the ground. It absolutely lashed down as well. There weren't any positives to take from that afternoon.

This season it was a nice day, we had a good little stop-off in Winchester on the way, we had loads of fun on the train back to London and one of our party disappeared for five hours and reappeared at my flat grasping chicken and chips at 3 a.m.

It was a good day. As match-going experiences go, the two trips to Southampton have been polar opposites. Any ill feeling or dislike for them has gone. That's how good this afternoon was.

This Southampton team are a mad one. The world and his wife raves about them to such an extent you'd be forgiven for looking at the league table and really wondering how they have ended up the season six points ahead of Stoke and seven points ahead of crisis club Newcastle United. Well, how did that happen? Oh yes, I know, they finished exactly where they should have done.

There were plenty who came into this game with feelings of great trepidation. Feelings of 'This is the game we'll slip up and lose ground' circulated widely. But why? We're Liverpool. We've scored 12 in our last three league games and they got beat at West Ham the week before. Pessimism and a refusal to believe we were the real deal permeated.

We were playing a mid-table team. Admittedly they've got some very good players, but they're very overhyped. Plenty of their players will go on to do better things, Lallana, Shaw and Schneiderlin are three players who could grace any side in the top six of this league, while Shaw might even grace the side who finished seventh. Last summer they signed a £13m centre forward, an £8m centre back and a £12m centre forward. Southampton aren't a collective gaggle of journeymen who are cobbled together, they're a group of international footballers who managed to come eighth. Well done, lads. You're worse than Manchester United and better than Stoke. Why has what they've done this season been seen as some massive shock?

To be fair to Southampton, in the first half they gave us a game. Mignolet pulled off a quite brilliant reaction save to get us in at 1–0 at half-time. After half-time though, it was all about us. We got an early second and controlled the game in the manner that you think Brendan Rodgers wants us to, we took time out of the game, kept the ball really well and didn't allow them a way back in.

The contrast between the two sides was quite clear. We were possible champions, they were trying to hang on to the coat tails of teams chasing the top four. Listen to the common narrative, however, and they're the side every team should be basing themselves on, when the reality is they got promoted with a good set of players, splashed a decent chunk of money two summers running, and made themselves better than loads of dreadful sides.

Because that's what you've got down at the bottom of this season's Premier League – loads of absolutely terrible teams. The Premier League is at its weakest since its inception and Southampton have carved a nice little area for themselves in the upper mid-table – that area where you don't actually do anything much, you just swim in a sea of nothingness once it becomes apparent you're too good for relegation and not good enough to be a European contender.

And then the season ends and you either spend loads of money to become a European contender or you lose all your players, fall back into the pack and then within two or three years you get relegated. A little bit like Blackburn after they decided to dispense with Sam Allardyce.

This summer could see Pochettino, Lallana, Shaw, Schneiderlin and Lovren all depart, while Jay Rodriguez picked up an injury that could see him never really recover to be what he was, and then there's the owner who isn't really bothered. Their future isn't bright. Whereas Liverpool ... Liverpool.

Phil Blundell

MANCHESTER UNITED 0 LIVERPOOL 3

16 March 2014
Goals: Gerrard (pen) 34', (pen) 46', Suárez 64'

OUR BALL – OUR GAME

IT'S PROBABLY FAIR TO SAY that my relationship with Mancs isn't typical for a Merseyside-born Liverpool fan. I've worked in Manchester more than anywhere else, and even spent big chunks of my late teens in the city due to an ex-girlfriend studying there.

So I know it pretty well. I've got mates there. I've had a fair few nights out there and – unlike some – I'm not bitter about every single thing associated with the city and its people (I was once warned by a fellow Liverpudlian against spending 'the Scouse pound' while within the boundaries of Greater Manchester).

Manchester's been pretty kind to me and – whisper it – we're actually pretty similar as a bunch of people; like a laugh, like music, like footie, like clobber. But I still want us to batter them at footie. Not just win. Dominate. Humiliate. Score loads. Climb the perch. Flick the Vs.

I want that because I want Liverpool FC to be successful. To fly the flag for the city. I want to feel proud. And I want good reason to walk into my Old Trafford office on a Monday morning with arms stretched as wide as my smile. Because God knows, I've had enough stick coming the other way down the years.

Yes, sadly, for the majority of the time detailed above, Manchester United have been a more successful football club than Liverpool. Since the Reds lifted the title in 1990 – and won at Old Trafford with two goals from John Barnes along the way – Liverpool had won just four more times in 27 attempts in all competitions in front of the Stretford End before this game.

We'd had our moments, of course, notably the 4–1 of March 2009. But despite going to Old Trafford several times, in the cup and the league, I'd managed to miss those rare bright spots. In fact, the only Liverpool victory I'd witnessed there was against Chelsea in the FA Cup.

Against Manchester United it was always the same story in my experience. The occasion seemed to get to us. Players played within themselves. We missed sitters. We played in patches. Decisions went against us. And they were seemingly never beaten. They always found a way to nick a draw or grab a win.

Or, maybe I was just a jinx. Either way, they'd had it their own way for far too long.

With that in mind, emotions were torn as I walked to the ground. If ever we were going to pull down United's kecks in public then today was surely the day. The Southampton game had felt like a monkey off the back of the team. They were off the leash, playing confident, care-free, flowing football and they could do it anywhere now. Home. Away. Bogey grounds. You name it. And it was easy to see why. Trying to plot Liverpool's downfall must be a nightmare. You stop Suárez, you face Sturridge. You stop them, you've left Sterling.

Compare and contrast to United under David Moyes. M16's answer to Roy Hodgson. A man who sucked everything Manchester United out of Manchester United with his defeatist attitude, negative tactics and safety-first approach. He even said Liverpool were favourites for this game. A Manchester United home game. Brilliant. And how we laughed. But they'd be up for this. The history, the rivalry, that indeterminable edge to these games. Even Moyes couldn't take that away. They'd be up for this. It was Man United–Liverpool at Old Trafford. Of course they would be up for it.

Before the game, I had a natter with Steve Armstrong, a contributor and seller of long-standing fanzine *United We Stand*. He seemed quietly confident. Even if he wasn't, there's no way he'd suggest otherwise. Some of those buying the fanzine seemed less certain. There was lots of 'hopes', 'mights', 'maybes' and 'erms'.

A lad in a replica United top with an accent that couldn't be more removed from Mancunia butted into our pre-match conversation.

'Where's the Stretford End, mate?'

Perfect timing.

'This is going to end up in something you write, isn't it?'

Yes, Steve, 'fraid so.

So to the game. The away end was cocky and confident, the piss-taking in full flow. A similar swagger was soon on show on the pitch. There was belief. Arrogance. Control. This was a Liverpool side that knew what it was doing. Knew it was better than them. And the ground? The history? The fact it was *them*? So what? We're boss and we know it. They're worried and it shows. The ball's ours. Come and get it, lads.

Sturridge wastes a chance almost straight from the off. Missed opportunities in this corner of the North West had in the past been accompanied by the feeling of inevitability that we would be made to pay for it. This is different. This time the squandered effort is accompanied by a feeling of inevitability that they will be made to pay for it.

It's coming, Davey. It's coming.

A 'David Moyes Is A Football Genius' banner was unfurled as Liverpool continued to stroke the ball around like it was a barefoot kickabout in the garden of the family home with only a toddler to tackle and a dog keeping goal. Frowns to the left of me, jokes to the right. The behaviour of the rival sets of fans said it all.

A Suárez shout for a penalty turned down, another Sturridge chance missed. And yet still the Liverpool corner of the Theatre of Broken Dreams smirked, shouted and sang. It's coming.

Rafael – one of the few United players to show any kind of fight in a game that should always be a battle – was beginning to lose his head and after seeing yellow for clattering Gerrard, he handballed in the area. Clattenburg gave the penalty, Steven scored at the Stretford End and Liverpool led. The skipper barely celebrated. It wasn't done yet. But no one told the away end. I bear-hugged an old bloke next to me and fist-bumped a young lad with a Uruguay flag in front of me. I'd never met either of them. It was that kind of day.

When a second penalty came our way early in the second half following the pretty vacant Phil Jones' decision to take down Joe Allen, Gerrard tucked it away with ease. It was simply a matter of how many now. Liverpool were superior all over the pitch. More intelligent, passing the ball better, and quicker, and playing with the belief that had so often drained away in the past on this patch of grass.

Gerrard missed his chance to emulate big Jan Molby and bag a hat-trick of penalties for Liverpool when he hit the post with another spot kick but our end just laughed. Being awarded three penalties at Old Trafford was mad enough. Not being arsed about missing one was insane.

This was embarrassing for the Mancs. It was Drago pummelling Creed on the ropes. When Suárez made it 3–0, Steve Round could have shouted: 'Throw the damn towel.' Like in *Rocky IV*, though, it was far too late. Moyes was down and out.

Meanwhile, these hugs with this old fella, well, I was starting to wonder if we should exchange numbers.

So the first time I'd seen us win at Old Trafford and what a win. Jon Flanagan dribbling around players like he was playing three-and-in on the Vernon Sangster car park, Henderson and Allen not giving United an inch. Sterling bossing the number ten role in one of the world's biggest games aged 19. Our defence barely troubled.

And all in the back yard of our rivals.

United ended the match with ten men after Vidic was sent off. They were lucky they didn't end the match conceding ten goals.

Work on Monday was great. Eye contact avoided, audible groans, new-found concentration on computer screens. I didn't bother with the outstretched arms in the end. I didn't need to.

They knew.

Gareth Roberts

COMMENTARY IN NEW YORK CITY

A GROUP OF US were over in New York for this game with *The Anfield Wrap*, essentially putting on parties and shows for Liverpool fans. Wherever we go to do these events, we always get a great turnout, showing how the club deeply touches people in all corners of the globe. New York was no different, with all three nights selling well, and the passion of the support in the city there for all to see.

Our home for the weekend was Legends Bar, right under the Empire State Building. At some point it was suggested that we should do the match commentary from the bar during the game. I can't remember who came up with it, but everyone seemed to think it was a good idea. I would imagine I thought it was a good idea too if, as I half remember, it was suggested late night after we'd all been drinking heavily.

It seemed like less of a good idea when we arrived at the bar early on the Sunday and it got busier and busier with fans of both clubs. A series of conversations ensued which were essentially:

'Are you sure you want us to do this? I don't think most of these people know who we are or care what we think.'

'Yeah, yeah, definitely.'

'Are you sure though?'

'Yeah, yeah, it will be great.'

'But, really though?'

While this was going on other people were sorting out microphones and plugging us in. My girlfriend, mystified by the whole thing, went shopping instead. The match started and we took a deep breath and began speaking out loud. No one threw anything at us, so it was already one up on if we had tried to do similar in a bar in Liverpool. And that would just have been my mates.

We didn't supply commentary as such; everyone could see which players had the ball and who was passing to whom. We just made comments on how we thought the game was progressing and things that had caught our eye. We described how it was going to Old Trafford as a Liverpool supporter. Neil banged on about how good he thinks Michael Carrick is. And we both made jokes about David Moyes. It seemed to be going down well, particularly the David Moyes jokes. I was just getting comfortable with the whole thing and planning a possible career change in my head when an irate Irishman approached.

'You're everywhere, you conscious bastards. Turn that down.' (He said 'conscious'. 'Conscious' is not a typo.)

'It's a microphone, mate. I can't do that.'

'Just turn it down, will you, I don't want to hear it.'

'I appreciate your concerns, but I don't think you understand how a microphone works.'

The gentleman then disappeared, presumably to find whoever was in charge of the PA. Or to boil his head.

Everyone else was nice, however. We even had a couple of Manchester United fans join us on the microphones at half-time to talk about how their team needed to improve. The second half was nice and relaxed, of course, so we could just talk about Liverpool's dominance and how great Luis Suárez was. And laugh at David Moyes. Until Neil said he likes to celebrate a big win with a double whisky and the bar brought us a round of them. Everything got a little hazy. Never mind, it was only six hours until we were onstage that night.

Overall I enjoyed our first foray into commentating. Would I do it again? Probably, I'm a terrible show-off. I'd want a fair guarantee that we were going to win though. I don't think anyone needs to hear my escalations from nervousness, to despair, to fury that accompany a defeat any louder than they already are. I'd had that fair guarantee that day. Liverpool were always going to win. I knew, before a ball was kicked, there was no way they could beat us. I was always more worried about the commentary. **John Gibbons**

SHIP CANAL: A MATCH REVIEW

THAT'LL TEACH THOSE BASTARDS for building the ship canal.

Samuel Greg and Daniel Adamson, your boys took one hell of a beating.

I'm writing this in Legends Bar in New York after doing 90 minutes' commentary. Thanks to them and NY Kopites for the maddest hour and a half of mine and Gibbo's life.

It's half-eleven here. What do you do now? Who do you get in touch with? We've just beaten Manchester United 3–0 in their own ground, it's half-eleven in the morning and I'm having to touch the wall of a urinal for support. Simultaneous high and low ebb this.

Mike Nevin has just said to me that he's never seen a Liverpool performance like that at Old Trafford. He's ranking it high in the context of all-time Liverpool performances. Chelsea drop points and Liverpool go to Old Trafford and do, well, THAT.

That said, it's David Moyes' Manchester United. And that's something almost sad to see. Not quite but almost. My friend Adam Melia, who was distraught after 2008/09, who is refinding his sea legs at a wonderful rate, says this: 'The two sets of supporters who talk best about football in this country are Liverpool and United.'

He's right. In my top 20 pints worldwide are Steve Armstrong, Andi Thomas and Chris Clarke. Remarkable men to talk about football with for different reasons. All United fans.

Steve came on the show on Friday. He thought we might lack the depth to go all the way. Sensible, but look at that. Andi's been writing we're the most fun in the world but it might drop off. Sensible, but look at that. I haven't seen Chris for a bit but he'd be telling me, 'City will fuck it up, you know. It is ingrained.' Sensible. Tattoo it on your eyelids. Listen to Chris.

Look at that. Look at it. Keep looking. Keep talking. Say this: 'And now YOU are going to believe us.' Those United lads, who know more about winning the league than any in the last 20 years, those United lads, whether they like it or not, they believe us. They can't look away.

What strikes me is the sheer quality of the performance. Liverpool were the better side in all departments. Almost as though it was a choice. We won't be tricky today. We'll just be boss. That wasn't Brendan Rodgers' Tricky Reds, that was the Champions Elect.

Henderson shuttling around, Sterling, Allen and Coutinho all able to beat a man in centre mid, the great innovation of this side. Sterling was magnificent.

Gerrard. Gerrard. Gerrard. He scores his opener and doesn't celebrate. Work to be done. He scores his second and goes bananas. Me and these lads? We've nailed it. We know it. He could lead them, lead me, lead you, lead thousands, those brilliant thousands at Old Trafford, through the jaws of Hell.

That is what the business looks like. What Captaincy looks like. Captaincy capitalised deliberately. Because it deserves it. He was phenomenal. Stopping him from running the next nine games? All the best.

They are so fit, so strong, they have their own identity. This gang of brilliant lads, trusting each other. Every win breaks new ground. Every win is a new trick. A new idea.

There is a sudden certainty to this side. They know what they are about. Solid saves from a goalkeeper, a much-maligned (not least by me) centre back partnership clicking – Skrtel especially was excellent – problems such as Flanagan exposed getting solved in real time.

The front two scare the life out of everybody. Distorting every game.

Still, this was a Moyes outfit they scared to death. We could see the Moyesness dripping off them. Liverpool today didn't vanquish Manchester United – you ask Steve, you ask Andi, you ask Chris. They'll be back. They may well have vanquished the man who demonstrated you don't have to win anything to be a winner.

Tonight though, Steve, Andi, Chris, your boys took one hell of a beating.

What do you do now? Who do you get in touch with? I've got to talk aloud in no time and I am definitely too happy and probably too drunk to pull it together. It is daylight outside. We have an age to kill and cannot drink any more. How on earth do overseas supporters cope? I'd be living in a bin within three weeks, and coincidently that's what Brockle's just told me I look like I do as soon as she turns up.

Rodgers doesn't look like he lives in a bin. He looks a winner. He looks a man setting winners up, getting them to do the right things everywhere. He talks like a winner. 'Our Ball. Our Game.' Victorious. Glorious. The Champions Elect.

Walk around them.

That will teach the bastards for building that ship canal.

Walk around them.

Neil Atkinson

CARDIFF CITY 3 LIVERPOOL 6

22 March 2014
Goals: Mutch 9', 88', Campbell 25';
Suárez 16', 60', 90', Skrtel 41', 54', Sturridge 75'

LET'S GO CRAZY: A MATCH REVIEW

THIS ISN'T JUST ABOUT ONE GAME. It's about two – let's go crazy. Maybe even three – let's go nuts. Because:

And then there were three. After Chelsea's demolition of Arsenal, this league will be won by one of Manchester City, Liverpool and Chelsea. I'm telling you that now.

Arsenal are now three points and insurmountable goal difference behind Liverpool.

To finish ahead of Liverpool – not Chelsea, not City – Liverpool, Arsenal now need to better the result in two of Liverpool's last eight games. That's 25 per cent of the remaining games.

It isn't happening for them now where the title is concerned. And I'm glad. Not because I think Mourinho is a nicer man than Wenger. Or because I think a side built as Arsenal's has been isn't as noteworthy as the squad Manchester City has amassed aggressively and at expense.

But because if you ship six at Manchester City, six at Chelsea, five at Liverpool, you could never be worthy champions. You could never deserve the

Football League.

Liverpool would be worthy champions.

Liverpool deserve the Football League.

Chelsea would be worthy champions too, I suppose. Today they were a Liverpool cover act, cutting Arsenal to shreds. They learned from what we did all those weeks ago when a defeat could have destroyed us. They got their education from the Kop.

Liverpool verged on unworthy for the first half today. Cardiff were compact, aggressive and attacked the space Liverpool struggle to cover in the diamond – where Flanagan, Agger, Gerrard and Allen were all at the ragged edge.

These Liverpool players have enough credit in the bank to have an honest discussion about this. Gerrard isn't a pure holder, Agger lacks aggression on occasion, Allen doesn't have Henderson's engine and Flanagan remains a youngster for all his outstanding composure shown so far. The change for Cissokho was right and proper.

On the other flank Henderson's pass for Johnson for the first equaliser was sublime while some of his others went astray. And Johnson was at his Rolls-Royce best. A man of the match performance in a game where Suárez got three and Skrtel got himself a brace with some fabulous work in the opposition box.

Liverpool were, all in, not at their best.

What a team.

They scored six goals.

You've seen us play far better this campaign.

Six goals. And it could have been more.

What a team. They astound me. Delight me. Confound me.

They are by far the trickiest team I ever did see. I really love their peaches, want to shake their tree.

They played brilliantly from the 46th minute until they made it 2–4. They decided the game needed running and they ran it. They ran rings around Cardiff. For that period it was their ball, their game. They seized it. Before then Cardiff had been better set up to hurt Liverpool than Manchester United had managed. Fair play to them.

This is why this Liverpool side can do this. This is why they actually are as worthy as anyone else. Why not us? Let's go crazy.

City scored five. Liverpool and Chelsea scored six.

And then there were three.

But two of them have to come and look at the Tricky Reds. Walk around the

Tricky Reds. Be spun around by the Tricky Reds. Right round round round round.

And so further analysis proper tomorrow. This is my evening. Spinning. Drinking. Dancing. Singing. Out since noon with Steve and Kate. Brockle and Girling. Rob, Ben, Rick, Becci, Claire and Nick. Out since noon in a city which believes if Red and is terrified if Blue.

And then there were three.

Let's roll. Brendan Rodgers' Tricky Reds. Never bowed, never beaten. Eighty-two goals and it isn't April.

Lad. Lad. This league isn't going to win itself, lad.

Let's win it. Sunderland next. Let's go crazy. Let's go nuts. Are we going to let the defending bring us down? Oh no, let's go.

And then there were three. Let's go crazy.

Neil Atkinson

DON'T LOOK BACK

I ALWAYS FLINCH A BIT when I hear the term Against Modern Football.

Are there problems with modern football? Of course, it's generally too expensive and its governance at a local and global level is highly questionable.

Is it right that these issues should be highlighted? Yes, organisations such as Stand AMF, the FSF and journalists like David Conn do a great job in bringing some of these issues to the fore.

So what's the problem? Why the flinch?

Despite the obvious good work they do, I can't help feeling that some of the arguments against modern football stem from a position of false nostalgia. And in my view, all nostalgia is false, it's a con. I'd much rather enjoy today, today is always more fun than yesterday.

Whatever your thoughts about modern football, it is a fact that it is less racist, homophobic and sexist than it ever was. You're less likely to be a victim of violence or prejudice. You're less likely to be treated like a subhuman underclass by the very agencies that are there to protect you. You're more likely to watch the game, if you can afford it, on a pitch covered in grass rather than mud. You're more likely to watch it in a stadium that has a safety certificate. You're more likely to see better players, who have trained better, eaten better diets and, as a result, play better football.

There are loads of good things about modern football.

There were loads of things wrong with football when I was growing up in the 1970s and 1980s. There has never been a time when football has been perfect.

Maybe this nostalgia for a golden age that never really existed is related to the changing demographic of football supporters. The average age of an adult football supporter in the UK is 41, the highest in Europe. Football supporters are still overwhelmingly male. So what we have here is loads of lads in their forties. Lads in their forties can be terrible lads. I should know, I am one. They'll do anything to waive their responsibilities and feel 18 again.

I have a mate who has a season ticket at Wolves. He hates modern football. He also hates modern music. He's not that keen on modern telly and, if I'm being honest, he's never quite gotten over Marathon turning into Snickers. Remember that fashion when young lads would wear their jeans around their arse to show off their box-fresh underwear? He really hated that too. He's one of them. A grumpy middle-aged man. Nothing would make him happier than standing at the match, going to see The Wonder Stuff and then going home to watch Auf Wiedersehen, Pet while he eats a Marathon, or a tube of Spangles, or a huge bowl of Angel Delight.

But it's a con. It wouldn't make him happy. It wouldn't make him happy because he's never happy.

He'd be happy if he got on board with things like today, with all its imperfections, and threw himself into it like he probably did when he was 18, when nothing was perfect either.

Is there a bit of this in the Against Modern Football movement? Possibly. Next time you're at an AMF event let me know how many people under 20 are there.

Anyway, Cardiff away.

Yeah, mad that, wasn't it? Nine goals. NINE GOALS! We came from behind twice and moved into second place. My overriding memory of the day was of our fans, though; an away end that definitely had an average age under 41. Huge gangs of young lads, and noticeably a few young girls, singing songs about winning the league in spring sunshine. Having the time of their lives singing songs about winning the league in spring sunshine.

Anyone can sing about winning the league in autumn and winter but you know you're in with a chance if you're singing it in spring. For these young fans, this is the first time they've been able to sing these songs, to feel this way, and the pure unadulterated joy is etched across each fresh face. These fans, this team, they're not looking back. They can only see a future. No backward steps. Today, they were very much into modern football.

I only hope they stay that way when they get older.

Martin Fitzgerald

LIVERPOOL 2 SUNDERLAND 1

26 March 2014
Goals: Gerrard 39', Sturridge 48'; Sung-Yueng 76'

SHUTTING LIVERPOOL DOWN

AFTER THE CHELSEA HOME GAME an Evertonian, whose opinion on football I respect greatly, tweeted: 'It's nice to see another team at least ask a different question of Liverpool.'

I disagreed with him on this, as I felt many teams had come to Anfield asking the same question. The question presumably being: 'Just how many defenders can we fit in our own penalty area?' They just weren't as disciplined, talented or bloody massive enough to get the right answers.

Sunderland came to Anfield with three centre halves and wing backs who forgot to attack. In front of them Bridcutt and Cattermole got deeper and deeper, with Cattermole almost playing as a fourth centre half at times. Because of that, chances were understandably hard to come by, with most of Liverpool's shots coming from range.

Had Rodgers known just how defensive Sunderland were going to be, he probably would have started Sterling and pushed Coutinho further back. But you never know how the opposition will approach a game at Anfield, so having criticised him for being too attacking earlier in the season against Aston Villa it seems unfair to complain about a slightly cautious selection. Especially when it was expected that Sunderland, who had a good record against top sides and needed the points, would have more of a go.

Much was made of Liverpool shooting so much from outside the box, but I would argue if the defence are deep and not pressuring the ball a shot from the edge of the area is a decent chance for a top player. In fact, I felt Liverpool's players could have got their shots away more than they did when in good positions. Working the space for a shot at goal from a central area isn't the same as desperately hitting the ball under pressure from a defender because there are no other options available to you.

It was also written after the game that Liverpool had 'needed a set piece' to break the opposition down, which seemed silly to me considering many of our opening goals had come from set pieces that season and it had been expertly won by Luis Suárez. When the defence is so deep, plentiful and well organised, it takes guile and nous to break it down, and match intelligence can also come in the form of winning free kicks in dangerous areas. Not that Suárez had much say in this one, being crudely brought down after getting ahead of the defender.

Liverpool scored again through Sturridge after half-time and then took their foot off the gas somewhat. Much was made of Sunderland's spirited response to going 2–0 down, but once they had opened up and tried to attack they should have been picked off with ease. Suárez got in the way of another Sturridge effort that looked to be going in, then shot wildly after a gorgeous first-time touch past his marker, and Coutinho made a mess of a lob through on goal, when he should have just fired it in. Sturridge was also unlucky to hit the bar. All this happened before Sunderland managed to score and get back into the game. Other opportunities were missed through poor touches or picking the wrong option.

Much was made of Sunderland making life tough for Liverpool, but the point was they had been broken down, and if Liverpool had played properly at 2–0 the papers would have been praising a resounding victory the next day. And that's before we get into the fact that Vergini should have been sent off in the first half. But the scoreline meant the story had been written. Counter-attacking Liverpool struggle against a deep-sitting defence.

Still, at least the bigger teams still to come to Anfield would look to play a more expansive game …

John Gibbons

ROUNDHEADED: A MATCH REVIEW

AND ON WE GO. And on we fucking go.

That wasn't nice. That wasn't fun. That wasn't Brendan Rodgers' Tricky Reds. That wasn't the People's Champions. That was the champions elect.

They didn't play well.

It wasn't pretty. It can't always be pretty. That's conventional sense. It can't always be pretty. In a sense, in this league-winning season, it is as conventional as it gets. Liverpool score two against a side digging in, they get on the front foot but are just about repelled.

Tonight I was with two young lads at their first game, Aden and Eli. They would have hoped for more.

We aren't used to this.

The problem with being endlessly unconventional is that the return of convention is terrifying. We've become used to the wild and unexpected. Banal only hurts.

And on we go.

The diamond today seemed that bit too functional. The full backs struggled to impact. For 45 minutes Sturridge was human. And then he was superhuman.

Aden and Eli, they come, they are brought to see Cavaliers. They got Roundheads. That they can get both or either is worthy of more than a nod.

And this is the thing. The front two can be off-song but they are worth a goal and an assist. At least. The positives include Suárez's single-minded hold-up play when the game was on a knife edge. Blamming it into a Sunderland player with two to go felt as good as a goal.

I have to be honest, the alehouse bell-end in me loves that sentence. He blammed it into the defender. It felt like a goal. I've needed that even if we haven't. This makes more sense to my basic mindset.

My mindset has become basic. Just win. Just fucking win. Well, that is that. They won. They just fucking won.

Few impressed. Liverpool never felt in control of the game. Johnson added ballast. Gerrard was solid but needed company. Suárez showed a thousand times. Coutinho prompted and probed and looked to find. Brave all game.

Three points. All the points. All three of them. No dancing. No singing. No spinning. Just teeth-gritted points.

It is seven to go. We'll take 2–1s in all seven but God knows that will hurt.

It will feel against nature. In vanquishing the darkness and taking us to the light Liverpool have made 2–1 victories seem unnatural.

Sunderland deserve credit in among this. Yes, the referee was poor, yes, they were rough, but they fought for their lives. They were tactically sophisticated first half and fought for their very being. This is something we overlook, when we look at our rivals' remaining fixtures, when we look at ours. What we are all up against will fight for their lives.

We have shown we will fight. We won't step backwards, we won't panic, we won't flinch. We are prepared to blam the ball into defenders.

We are one point off the pace. There are seven games to go. And this is the supposed dark side of what the business looks like? Are you kidding? I remember winning 2–1 at home in March when nothing meant anything. This means everything. Win again Sunday. Throw the gauntlet down.

Aden and Eli don't know it but all the three points in a run-in are equal. These are no different. Lad, lad, this league won't win itself, lad.

Grit your teeth. Hold your breath. Call the lads in on the Anfield Road and God bless you for it. This is what the business looks like, there's no dark side in this. It might well hurt but it is right it hurts.

Embrace the agony. We have more to come.

And on we fucking go. It can hurt. Let it. It should.

Neil Atkinson

LIVERPOOL 4 TOTTENHAM HOTSPUR

30 March 2014
Goals: Kaboul (o.g.) 2', Suárez 25', Coutinho 55', Henderson 75'

PROCESS

OFF THE PITCH, IT'S BEEN A BATTLE ALL SEASON.

Convincing yourself that you can win the league after 24 years is a process.

Convincing others, that's part of the process too.

The process:

Pre-season

We're definitely not winning the league. 100 per cent. Mark my words.

I know it's mathematically possible, I know I'm an optimist but it isn't happening.

This is the start of the process.

Throughout the Souness, Evans and early Houllier years, I would always start the season thinking we would win the league. We were Liverpool. Liverpool won leagues. Leagues after leagues. This temporary 'not winning the league' thing is exactly that – temporary.

Just a matter of time before we do it again. This season, yes THIS season, this season is our season.

The further I've come from 1990, though, the less hopeful I've become. This 'not winning the league' thing had become permanent. Even 2008/09. I looked at the table, I did the maths but I never imagined the trophy. I never saw it in my mind's eye being tossed around the Anfield pitch by players just crowned as champions.

Before a ball is kicked, I get asked to predict where we'll finish this season.

I predicted fifth.

I remember thinking, 'Fifth wouldn't be bad, we'd be going in the right direction.'

That's how far I'd come. Hopelessness, the start of the process.

Day 1 – Liverpool beat Stoke 1–0; Mignolet saves a last-minute penalty

Euphoria. The process needs euphoria. That's all it takes.

I see my mate Dave after the game.

'We're going win the league, Dave. Last-minute penalty saves are what winning the league is all about.'

Dave raises an eyebrow and orders a Stella.

I'm being an idiot, of course, trying to get maximum enjoyment out of a temporary moment. Dave knows this and gives it the short shrift it deserves, the miserable sod. Dave's got a longer journey than me ahead of him.

October – Arsenal Away

We're not out of it. It's October and we're definitely not out of it.

Before the game I have a chat with Neil Atkinson at an *Anfield Wrap* event in London. Like co-conspirators in on a secret mission we convince ourselves the phrase 'Liverpool will win the league' doesn't sound daft. We replace 'Liverpool' with other clubs and realise phrases like 'Chelsea will win the league' don't sound less daft. It's a secret though, hushed conversations in darkened corners.

Convincing others, it's a process.

Neil and John Gibbons then take to the stage in front of 600 people and tell everyone we're going to win the league. They don't want this to be a secret. They want the hearts and minds.

No one laughs, that's a good start. The secret's out. People are on board.

We get outplayed at Arsenal. People fall overboard.

Part of the process.

Christmas – Top of the League

Top of the league pigs in blankets.

Top of the league bucks fizz on Christmas morning.

Top of the league haircuts and Christmas presents. Top of the league crackers. Top of the league decorations and chocolates. Top of the league cold cuts with pickle.

We'll lose to Man City and Chelsea before the New Year.

Hopes are dashed, the process again, but we'll always have Christmas. No one else had Christmas, it was ours.

7 February – Mike Nevin on *The Anfield Wrap*

We've slipped to fourth.

Eight points behind leaders Arsenal.

The league looks out of reach; things will go back to normal soon.

And then Mike Nevin goes on the radio the day before the home game against Arsenal.

Mike Nevin goes on *The Anfield Wrap* and says: 'If this was the 80s, people would be saying we were handily placed.'

MIKE NEVIN GOES ON *THE ANFIELD WRAP* AND SAYS: 'IF THIS WAS THE 80S, PEOPLE WOULD BE SAYING WE WERE HANDILY PLACED.'

Mike Nevin knows. Get Mike Nevin in that dressing room. Get Mike Nevin round Brendan's house. Brendan, put a portrait of Mike Nevin up in your house.

Mike Nevin knows. Mike Nevin is calm.

Mike Nevin has convinced himself and he's now convincing others. The process.

Handily placed? You've got to love him for that.

When all hope had gone, when we were all nearly done with the process, along came Mike Nevin.

We'd win the next game against Arsenal. God, did we win that game.

We'd win the next ten too.

Game after game, possibility replaced with actuality. Game after game, the whisper of 'it's on' getting louder and louder.

It's on. It's on. It's on. It's on. It's on. It's on. It's on. It's on!

During this period I often look back at the Nevin moment and I tell myself this was when it started for me. This was the pivotal moment when I started to believe.

I'd speak to John Gibbons months later and it had a similar effect on him too. Mike Nevin, convincing others.

And now here we are.

Spurs at Home

And then it happens, the process is complete.

Now you're gonna believe us.

Everyone has convinced themselves. Everyone has convinced everyone else.

Liverpool are going to win the Football League. Today you can feel it; today you can almost touch it.

I'm imagining the trophy.

Spares? Anyone got any spares?

No one has any spares.

EVERYONE is now on board. Dave is now on board.

No one is left out.

Let's all meet the coach early as it comes down Anfield Road. Let's show THEM how on board we are.

Let's get in the ground early and watch their pre-match routine. We need to show THEM that we believe. THEY, the team, THEY have convinced US. WE now need to convince THEM.

Let's sing Rodgers' name. Let HIM know what HE has done.

Let's remember what we became when we beat Spurs 5–0 away from home. Everything before had led up to that, everything since has led up to this.

Let's beat these Spurs, this day, 4–0.

Let's go to the top of the league.

Let's go to the top of the league with six to go.

Hearts and minds. Handily placed.

Martin Fitzgerald

BEING MADE TO WATCH TOO MUCH FOOTBALL

BEFORE THE GAME I bump into Mike Nevin, which is nearly always a pleasure and only occasionally a chore, upstairs in the Twelfth Man pub near the ground. He looks shattered, like a man who's just had a baby and had to go back to work. But instead of late-night feeds it's afternoon football that is doing for him.

'I can't cope with all this, Gibbo,' he said to me. 'I've never watched this much football in my life.'

They don't warn you about this bit. When you think of a title challenge you imagine becoming obsessed with your next game, but not those of your fellow challengers. By this point of the season I could rattle off our rivals' fixture lists without pause, and had become an expert in the current injuries of all their opposing teams. Before we even got to think about playing Tottenham on the Sunday, we had two Saturday fixtures to get through. Firstly Chelsea playing away at Crystal Palace. I watch this game on a stream on my phone through an app I probably shouldn't tell you the name of. The fact I can't really tell who is who does nothing for my nerves, so I abandon it and turn instead to Soccer Saturday, shouting: 'NO ONE CARES, LAD' every time someone has the nerve to try and update me on Swansea vs Norwich and having a heart attack every time someone in the background makes a noise that might mean a Chelsea goal. It doesn't. Crystal Palace win the game.

At that point I should have just gone bowling or something. Taken my mind off it all and checked the result later. Instead, of course, I stay glued to my seat and watch Arsenal vs Manchester City. My tension isn't helped by idiots on my Twitter feed debating if a Manchester City win isn't better for us in relation to getting fourth. Do one, you cowards, and take your fourth place with you.

Manchester City start wonderfully well and go 1–0 up. People say it's 'ominous' when a team plays badly and wins, but I much prefer it when our rivals are rubbish than when they look brilliant. Rubbish makes me think their luck will run out sooner rather than later, brilliant makes me think they'll never lose a game again. After a win at Old Trafford earlier in the week, although who doesn't nowadays, it felt to me like a win at Arsenal would have given Manchester City unstoppable momentum going into the run-in. Instead Arsenal get an equaliser and then look the more likely to go on and win it, before Manchester City elected to close the game off. This confused many at the time, a team taking a result that brought the title race into our hands as well as theirs. Maybe they just thought it was a good point with what had gone on before and was likely to go on after. Maybe we just couldn't remember what it was like to watch a team who were really good but didn't want with every fibre of their being to score at least seven more goals before the final whistle.

Mike said he didn't cope very well in the second half of the game at all, with the current Mrs Mike Nevin forcing him to have a drink in the end because he was 'doing her head in'. A similar thing happened to me a few weeks later watching Chelsea vs Sunderland, pacing around my flat while my girlfriend packed away the shopping on her own because I had to 'concentrate'. In the end she brought me a glass and said, 'Have this.'

I asked what it was and she said, 'That hazelnut vodka we got in Poland. It's all we've got in. But it looks like you need something.'

I held it until the final whistle and then drank it in one go. My girlfriend said I had celebrated the winner like a Liverpool goal. I said they were all Liverpool goals now.

And now here we were, me and Mike Nevin, looking at each other in a pub, having to go and watch ANOTHER game of football. Having to put ourselves through it all over again, after an agonising Saturday where we hadn't even played. Pressure seemingly increased rather than decreased by the events of the previous day. They don't warn you about this bit. They should.

John Gibbons

UNBUTTONED. UNDRESSED. MATCH REVIEW

WHEN THE FINAL WHISTLE went in The Excelsior last night after City/Arsenal all I heard was people saying to each other: 'It's in our hands. It's in our hands.'

Today we grabbed it. Seized it. Knuckles white, grip tight.

In our hands.

We are Top of the Pops. Six to go.

Der der der der der, der der der, der der der.

Top of the pile.

A proper number one. Entered at six. People fell in love with them. Kept buying it. More people, the housewife's choice.

Number one in April. With a bullet.

Return of the Mack. It is. Return of the Mack. Come on. Return of the Mack. Oh my God. You'll know the Mack is back. Here I am.

Here we are.

The first half was an explosion, the atmosphere sublime before the own goal.

And whatever goes beyond sublime after it. Nerves gone, everyone roaring the champions elect towards the promised land.

Johnson's odd season continued in the own goal; the only thing more unpredictable than him is Spurs. Coutinho's goal divine, his changes of pace effortless in a team which could simply rush past him. Flanagan looking for more battles to win, his own won early, covering across with panache. The centre halves not taking any nonsense.

The front three interchanging with such understanding. Each occupying every position along the line, knowing exactly what they are about in and out of possession.

Sterling was devilment personified, holding the world off just as Gerrard holds it up. He twisted and spun, found angles and mischief everywhere. This is how to be man of the match.

The word 'undressed' has fallen into misuse in football. Just as Larkin thought the sexiest word in the English lexicon was 'unbuttoning', the sexiest in football's is 'undressed'.

Tottenham Hotspur were undressed.

Time and again they were undressed.

Sturridge's back-heeled attempt, Suárez's missed header, Henderson firing over when it just needed to stay low. These weren't the modern statistics' definition of 'clear-cut chances', they were undressings. Emphatic exposure of the shortcomings of opponents. These opponents, by the way, finish top seven.

This on a day Suárez wasn't great. Lovely, lovely goal, but not at his best given his fury over that brilliantly saved header. That doesn't matter as much as it once did. He's been the catalyst in making this the best football team in the land.

It's National weekend and we've hit the front. Six out. We've hit the front. Six to jump.

Trickyred hits the front of the Grand National six out. Rodgers sits motionless in the saddle, the 25–1 shot smooth while all around him horses are clipping fences.

Check your slips.

Skyblue, the classy 9–4 favourite, from the Sheikh Mansour yard looks suddenly uncomfortable. Grinding Machine is being shown reminders by Mourinho while Fourthenough is tailing off.

(Moyesnoise has the screens around him. 'Nobody wants to see this,' opines Scudamore.)

Six to jump. And he hasn't had to reach for the whip.

Trickyred is travelling beautifully. His form has belied his price since around last year's National. Rodgers the calmest man in the racecourse, punters on Trickyred excitable, those on his rivals terrified.

Setting the pace. Liverpool.

We've looked at those around us and seen flaws. Do we have them? Yes. But we've been hopelessly flawed not so long ago. Now? We're the best team in the country and perhaps, those outside, perhaps there should be someone better. There isn't, though. There is nothing out there for us to fear. Not this year. Not next.

Belief itself is no longer anything to be scared of. Ridicule of belief is nothing to be scared of. Hope is nothing to be scared of. What can be done to us now, that hasn't been done to us in the last ten years? We are invulnerable now, regardless of what happens from here.

The notion that it is 'the hope that kills you' has gained popularity in recent years. This is bullshit. Render it as such. It is Evertonian thinking that Evertonians have grown out of. It is badly, badly English. I remember being hopeless and I was almost dead. Hopelessness nearly killed me, let's not recall it quite so fondly.

This is being alive. It's thrilling and exhausting and overwhelming. It is unbridled. It is unbuttoning. It is undressing. Hope is wonderful. It, like Liverpool, is the business. The Business.

This is Liverpool. Tra-la-la-la-la.

Neil Atkinson

WEST HAM UNITED 1 LIVERPOOL 2

6 April 2014
Goals: Demel 45'; Gerrard (pen) 44' & (pen) 71'

GAUNTLETS: A MATCH REVIEW

THE GAUNTLET. I love the word 'gauntlet'.

West Ham United felt like a gauntlet. Won six from the last nine. Big Caz. Big Kev. Big Mohamed. Big. Bigness. All the bigness. You want to run the gauntlet of bigness? You'll need balls to do it. Have you got them?

Liverpool have. But they have more than that.

My third favourite thing in football is watching lads solve problems on the pitch. From about 25 Liverpool began to solve the problem of West Ham. It was a big problem and it was solved and it eventually resulted in the Liverpool penalty. They were coming closer and closer.

It was a crazed decision to overrule the linesman. Absolutely crazed. This, though, is the West Ham lottery. It is what they do. They want the game to take place in the zone where infringements are constant. Some are given for them. Some are given against them. Some aren't given at all. This is a tactic and it is a valid one whether we like it or not. Morality doesn't come into it.

For 45 minutes West Ham played as well as they could at their tactics and Liverpool struggled at times and then began to solve what they were up against.

My second favourite thing in football is managers solving the problem. The Lucas change proved inspired. It wasn't a diamond. It was a parallelogram. It promoted patience and brought about strength. It was sense on toast but sense twisted. Bell-ends like me would have sat Leiva in next to Ste Gerrard. Bell-ends like me are wrong.

All the pre-match talk of second balls. Liverpool have fifth balls. Sixth balls. Balls coming out of their ears. Balls and brains.

That is as hard as any game will be for these Reds from here on in. It will not get tougher than this. West Ham were brilliant at being West Ham.

The second. What a pass from Lucas Leiva. What bravery from Jon Flanagan. What balls and technique and assurance from the captain. He's gorgeous. Grown into himself in every way. I've never admired him as much. Wherever he is I am.

In this run Skrtel has been magnificent. He showed as much today. This is what winning your battles looks like, especially when up against the unplayable Caz.

Both Liverpool's front two worked hard. Neither played well despite Suárez's two glorious efforts.

Balls run gauntlets. Brains then beat gauntlets.

What is a football season if it isn't a gauntlet? You start with zero. You have to work past 38 barriers. Some will batter you and bruise you. You overcome. Some will beat you. You overcome. Some will throw the ball into the air and you overcome.

I've become boring. Have we? Have you? I say the same things. To you. To people I meet. To myself. To you:

—   This team has been hewn in Luis Suárez's image. It hunts.
—   This team is brilliantly coached by Brendan Rodgers. They improve every few games. They get better at football.
—   This team is led by Steven Gerrard. Shepherded by Steven Gerrard. Fostered by Steven Gerrard.

Boring.

I say to myself upon opening a door: 'This league won't win itself, lad.'

To myself upon cutting meat: 'Looks championship material, that.'

To myself in the mirror when having a shave: 'Just got this league to win. We'll have a look after that.'

Boring. Boring, boring, boring.

But we were never being boring. We had too much time to fill for ourselves.

We aren't being boring. The Reds, every week, they make amends.

My first favourite thing in football is Liverpool winning.

And the gauntlet. You want to throw the gauntlet down to someone?

Anfield. Sunday. Forty thousand people screaming at God. That's a gauntlet.

Five to go.

The Mighty Boys in Red.

Neil Atkinson

LET ME TELL YOU A STORY ABOUT THE GIANT ANDY CARROLL

THIRTY-FIVE MILLION POUNDS. Was a lot of money that, wasn't it? I don't think it'll ever make sense. Not a single person will ever get their head around that one. Whether you wrote the cheque, banked the cheque, or stand on the Kop or the Gallowgate, or even if your name is Andrew Carroll you will never be able to figure out how Liverpool managed to say: 'Yeah, we've got this money here and I reckon that Carroll lad is worth £35 million.'

He wasn't, he isn't, and he never will be. It was all probably a millstone that was too big for him to ever overcome.

There were high points, of course – that left-footed bullet against Manchester City, the FA Cup final goal that should have been a brace, and the goal that saw us in that FA Cup final in the first place. A late winner against Everton. I'll be honest; a late winner against Everton normally seals you forever as a hero in my eyes. But it wasn't enough. I can't figure out a single way how Andy Carroll would ever have really been a success at Liverpool, never mind justifying that monstrous price tag. Well, I know of ways, but his talent just wasn't going to allow him to achieve them.

He initially left Liverpool on loan in August 2012 and joined 'Big Sam @ West Ham'. At the time it basically meant that our forwards were Fabio Borini and Luis Suárez, plus whoever we were able to sign in the next 48 or so hours before the transfer window closed. Some said it was a gamble, some saw method, some saw idiocy. The proof of the pudding would be in the eating.

Personally, I saw sense in letting him go. Carroll wasn't a Rodgers player. He wasn't going to fit in his side that needed movement and fluidity. It was very logical. It was the complete opposite of the approach I think Rafa Benítez would have taken. The long-ball game was the short-term pragmatic approach. Long term we wouldn't be using Carroll while short term the obvious argument is that he'd have done a job. Rodgers wasn't interested in the pragmatic approach of trying to win a game in any way – to me he wanted to win his way and his style and approach were being implemented from day one. I suspect Benítez would have said: 'Forget the style, he will help me win.' He would have done – this after all is a player that Benítez nearly signed for Liverpool. We'd have finished better than seventh in 2012/13, of that I have absolutely no doubt, but the long-term game would have been set back further for me.

A six-foot-four outlet that would hold the ball up and allow direct football just wasn't for Rodgers. It was a policy that many disapproved of at the time, but one that has borne fruit, and beautiful fruit at that. Liverpool as a footballing entity is further advanced now than if we'd have shoehorned Andy Carroll in and tried to win football games in November 2012. Maybe it would have got us into the Europa League last season? This magical ride we've been on might not even exist? I could be bringing things together that just shouldn't be, and people will be reading this disagreeing, but I think pragmatism was an issue that held Rafa Benítez back – the first two seasons were wonderful, a European Cup and an 82-point season which was made possible by Momo Sissoko and Peter Crouch doing brilliant jobs, and then in 2006 he decided that the pragmatism was going and a brand of football was coming. It was the third season of it, 2008/2009, when it all clicked. That's not to complain, as I thought those five years were brilliant, it's just an example of pragmatism and long-term ideology not going together that wonderfully.

This game was the first time we'd come up against him since he left and he gave exactly what we knew he had. West Ham were quite obviously very happy to throw balls up to him, and he was happy to have balls thrown up to him. It was a battle. And Liverpool battled. A glorious battle, a fight, a rumble. It was tremendous.

Their goal? All Andy Carroll. Illegal admittedly, but he was a complete nuisance, he beat a defender, caused the goalkeeper problems, and Guy Demel poked it home from close range. When you throw your body around you're going to break laws, and a barge and a hand to the goalkeeper's face definitely breaks laws, but as we saw on a regular basis when he was here, he also gets wrongly penalised. Somewhere along the line a valid goal will have been written off due to anti-Carroll refereeing. 'Decisions all work themselves out over the course of the season,' or something.

West Ham's goal was all Andy Carroll, and while our goals were from the penalty spot, they were very much not Andy Carroll in style. The first penalty saw a Gerrard ball fizzed out wide to Suárez, and Suárez tied James Tomkins in that much of a knot he was able to kick the ball at his hand and get a penalty. The second was a through ball to a full back. A ball that if Andy Carroll was on the pitch might have instead gone to his head or chest to generate a second ball. I'm speculating here and feel a little harsh on Carroll, but the approach is different, and the ideas are different. If you're struggling to break a team down, it's easy, lazy, that you go to the big man and win the header. We didn't do that. We passed through what resembled a brick wall. We got the win by patiently passing.

Carroll getting short shrift accelerated a quick passing game. We removed the easy, lazy option. It was bold. It was brave. And while we'll only know what might have happened had he stayed if we were in a parallel universe, it's hard to envisage how keeping Andy Carroll would have seen Liverpool better now than they are today. And that is all that matters.

Phil Blundell

LIVERPOOL 3 MANCHESTER CITY 2

13 April 2014
Goals: Sterling 6', Skrtel 26', Coutinho 78'; Silva 57', Johnson (o.g.) 62'

GRASPING: MATCH REVIEW

WALKING OUT THE GROUND THERE IS LOADS OF SINGING. Loads of harassed faces. I bump into Ben Jono. Collapse on to his shoulder. This is overwhelming. Everyone is exhausted and exuberant.

This is the essence of tired and emotional.

I was terrified for Arsenal. A wreck. That was it. Are these what I thought they were? Are they a brilliant football team?

I was horrified for Fulham. Clawing at my face. Are these what I thought they were? Are they a serious football team?

Today I woke up. Did the dishes. Decanted the port. Had a shower. Then the panic set in. What do I wear? Long day ahead. Breakfast at 11. Expect to be out all night. Looks chilly. What do I wear? What coat? Knitwear or just shirt?

Duncan there overwhelmed. Shaking his head. See Steve Graves. In excelsis deo. Some lad grabs me. Put that in your Anfield Wrap. Oh, we will. You are telling me we will.

This morning the football didn't come into it. Manchester City are a brilliant football team. The football was the least of my worries. Manchester City are a serious football team. Liverpool will win.

Team news. The manager has a decision to make. Decision for him seems as straightforward as my morning. All in. He's urged the crowd to be all in. He's gone all in. He's said to his team they are to seize the day.

Now you're gonna believe us.

Agüero starts from the bench.

Seize the day.

Walking to the ground with Mike Girling. 'This,' he says, 'is what you are in it for. If this isn't for you then find something else to do.'

It's been a year of days. I've seized them. I'm not letting them go. Do not let them go.

Now you're going to believe us.

I'm sitting alone today. I mooch up to my seat. The emotion of it is suddenly overwhelming. I am nearly in tears. Not because I'm worried about the game, but for what the game is, what it means. For a long time I wondered if we'd ever be in this position. Sages suggested we'd be looking at a long journey to this point. And I honestly, honestly, honestly wondered, as awful as it is to admit, if I had a long journey in me. Everyone sensible counselling caution, almost revelling in the length of the journey. Talking to you about process and cycles. Extrapolating this, analysing that. Rome not built in a year. It was at odds with what I think of this city and its football. At odds with how I think full stop. Just do it and work out if you had permission to do it afterwards.

This isn't a title decider. Nothing silver is won today. Arsenal wasn't a title decider. Fulham wasn't. However, today's game tells the rest of the world, those who don't follow us, the story Arsenal and Fulham told us. We are a serious football team. A brilliant football team. Tug your forelock in front of it. Genuflect if you feel the need. These lads are The Business.

So The Business:

• The noise when they came to the corner flag Kop end at twenty-two past one was intense.

• The silences and tributes were impeccable.

• The opening explosion was something to behold. The crowd, often maligned, was wonderfully intense. As intense as what was in front of it. And the utterly relentless Raheem Sterling eased his way through City, taking an age to slot home. Such precocious ability so aggressively harnessed.

• I see stories of the season everywhere I look. But this second half of the season surely belongs to Raheem. Dzeko urging his teammates to sharpen. Coutinho hunting for his life.

- They targeted Liverpool's right with numbers, wanted to break quickly on Liverpool's left. They looked to pressure Henderson in possession. They made a virtue of the necessity of Yaya Touré's substitution.

- They are good at football. The crowd's constant barracking was terrific and necessary.

- First half Manchester City were good at football but not Liverpool at football. Liverpool kept coming, Sturridge should have scored, Gerrard elicited a fantastic save from Hart. Skrtel was never to be denied on an occasion like this.

- Liverpool kept coming, got themselves into a nervy funk before half-time when lesser sides might have just shut everything down. However they should, again, have got a third. They kept coming. Champions elect.

- What a team we have here.

Then Manchester City destroyed all my certainties. Destroyed all our certainties. They started the second half brilliantly. Milner made a huge difference but David Silva was remarkable. For the first time in a very long time Liverpool simply couldn't cope. We were the ones undressed. The lazily maligned Demichelis had Suárez as much in his pocket as anyone has managed this season.

Now you're going to believe us.

We have played Manchester City twice and they have been two proper football matches. They are a proper team. Splendid. Three points each feels a fair outcome.

Coutinho's superb third turned the game into something akin to the rearguard actions that started the season. Liverpool clung on, Henderson jumped in, Lucas arrived. The crowd was magnificent throughout. Not taking no for an answer. We will not be denied. We will not be moved.

We're going to win the league.

On the final whistle I finally burst into tears I threatened when I got to the ground. I find out when I get out of the ground the captain did the same. It was, from me, undignified weeping, no battle cry, no call to arms here. I was shaking, snot everywhere, quivering and sweating. My shirt unimportant. My hipflask empty. My head emptier. My heart bursting with pride.

I had wondered through the summer gone if we'd get back here, I had wondered through that summer if I had a long journey in me, if we had a long journey in us. Then it had hit me. We self-select. We have the best player in the league and we have the best finisher in the league. We had it all in our grasp and Liverpool have grasped. They've grasped and grasped and grasped. They've taken every opportunity open to them and no one could ask for any more from these players. This is why I cried. It's practically impossible not to be emotionally engaged by effort and quality which feels superhuman after seven months of believing, of knowing they could be superhuman. They vindicate belief. They take it onto a higher plane. I believed in them, they believed in themselves more. I had such faith in them. It paled into insignificance next to the faith they had in one another. I thought them to be genuinely good. They knew they were actually excellent.

They've shown themselves to be brilliant, be serious and be hewn from iron. What a performance in both halves. Resilience in spades.

We've done this much. We are the only side that controls its own destiny in mid-April. No one gave us permission to do it. We just did it.

Four to go.

Neil Atkinson

THE SANITY OF MANCHESTER CITY

SOME FOUR MONTHS PRIOR TO THIS GAME as we walked out of White Hart Lane I turned and said to Mick: 'I tell you what, mate, I think that fourth spot is ours now.'

Fast-forward 18 games and 55 goals scored and I have got Mick in a headlock in the middle of Pogues, slurring into this ear: 'I tell you what, mate, that league is ours now, mate … IT'S OURS.'

Testament to the incredible journey our team had taken us on since the turn of the year. Belief was sky high, and why shouldn't it be? We had just beaten a very, very good Manchester City side and for the first time, the title was ours to lose.

Having missed welcoming the player's coach into Anfield against Sunderland for boring work reasons, I was curious as to what all the fuss was about as we assembled on the Anfield Road on this sunny Sunday. That was until the bus pulled into sight – and as bangers, flares and smoke-bombs simultaneously burst into life and the crowd roared, 'WE'RE GOING TO WIN THE LEAGUE', I lost my shit. For the minute or so it took the bus to work its way through the crowd I screamed at the top of my lungs, straining every sinew in my body as I punched the air and attempted in vain to make contact with whoever was behind that blacked-out window. For all I know, it wasn't even the players' bus.

We took our seats inside the ground a full 30 minutes before kick-off, the earliest I have been inside a ground since the 2005 Chelsea semi-final, and the atmosphere was tremendous. While not reaching the fervent, almost feral heights of that night, it was still probably the best I have known for a league match. The Kop was full of flags and banners and song after song was booming out. The impeccably observed minute's silence to remember those who died at Hillsborough only served to ratchet up the noise and intensity at kick-off.

City surely knew what to expect in the first few minutes, but stopping it was another matter entirely. Sterling, all muscle and twinkling toes – a juice-head ballerina – went that way, and Kompany and Hart went that way and Anfield exploded. These starts cannot be stopped, it has been like a full season of the first 20 minutes versus Real Madrid at Anfield. We are swarming City, Anfield is shaking to its foundations.

Yaya Touré tries one of those mad banana shots he quite often pops in the top bin, but it goes wide and he's hurt himself in the process. He trudges off to a very sporting round of applause from the whole of Anfield. It is easy to be sporting at times like this, isn't it?

Gerrard should score from a corner, but no mind, Skrtel does immediately after. Two-nil up before the half-hour in the 'Nothing is Getting Decided Today Title Decider', is this real? My glasses, which have been on their lazzies since Kevin punched them off my nose celebrating our fourth at Cardiff, are three rows away, the fella from two rows behind me is now four rows in front of me and upside down and the Kop is still celebrating wildly as City kick off.

Half-time on the concourse and the scenes of jubilation are such that I fear a conga line might break out at any point. We return to our seats for the second half and await the inevitable glut of goals from the boys in red.

Pellegrini does that thing managers do when they want to make a show of a player and hooks Navas on 50. Milner on and immediately linking up nicely with the wizard that is David Silva. We are getting picked apart here. City are dead, dead good. Their goal on 57 minutes is no surprise, and is probably the best team goal I have seen at Anfield since Marc Overmars finished off a wonderful spell of Barca keep-ball in 2001.

Their second five minutes later is a hammer blow. We are all over the place and David Silva is a toenail away from putting City in the lead. I get that depressing feeling of 'We're not going to win this, in fact, we're going to lose this quite badly'. I have had that feeling a few times before – I got it the minute AC Milan qualified for the final in 2007, I got it halfway through the Chelsea semi-final in 2008 and I had it at Old Trafford every season for a decade. Just that horrible, negative dawning that no matter what, this isn't our game today, well played City, blow the whistle and give them the three points, ref. Maybe it is my problem, maybe I need some sessions with Dr Steve, let that blasted Inner Chimp out.

However, something very peculiar happened at 2–2. Manchester City took their foot off the pedal and our windpipe, and began to let us back into the game, and we managed to pick ourselves up off the canvas and start landing some shots back of our own. Granted, they brought Agüero on, which is hardly letting someone off the hook, but there was a noticeable drop in their intensity. Has Pellegrini not seen *The Premiership Years 1995–96*? When the great entertainers who can't really defend are on the ropes you score as many as possible before they hit back and start scoring again themselves. For whatever reason, they chose 2–2 as the point to rest and regroup, and our players seized on this.

I could watch Coutinho's goal on repeat forever. The technique and skill required to hook that spinning ball from behind him and generate the power and direction he did – quite simply stunning. I genuinely cannot wait to see Brazil's midfield in the World Cup if this fella can't get near it.

I think I watched about 30 seconds of the next 15 minutes of football, too stressed and scatty to focus. Rudyard Kipling would have despaired at me and 44,000 others inside the ground as heads were lost all around us. I did look up just in time to see Hendo get his marching orders for an over-keen lunge on Nasri, a huge loss for the next three games, no doubt.

At the final whistle, Anfield shook once again. We had just witnessed something very special, potentially something defining. The scenes outside the ground justified this, as bear-hugs and high-fives were exchanged up and down Walton Breck Road, as jubilant fans regrouped and prepared to get blind drunk in honour of Brendan and the Boys.

I have hazy memories of many hours later, attempting a Gerrard-esque pep talk of my own, drunkenly telling my mates' back room of Pogues: 'This is what all the years of shit games and early starts is for, all that money we spend, all the sacrifices we make, all the heartache, THIS is what it is all about … THIS IS OUR TIME NOW.'

Ben McCausland

JORDAN HENDERSON

WHILE RECORDING THE RADIO SHOW that we do at the end of the season we got on to Jordan Henderson, as is often our wont. During the conversation Mike Nevin pointed out that if you Google 'Here's to You ...' it predicted you were going to type Jordan Henderson before Mrs Robinson. Thus making Farringdon's finest bigger than Simon & Garfunkel and The Graduate combined. Try it now, I hope it still works.

Up to the 93rd minute of this game Jordan Henderson had been an ever-present for Liverpool during the league campaign. His importance had grown throughout the season, almost game by game, through a combination of his own emerging talent and Liverpool not having anyone else who was remotely like him.

Henderson spent a season making life tougher for the opposition and easier for his teammates. Got yourself out of position? Jordan has you covered. Want to press an opponent? Jordan is right behind you. Looking for a pass in a tough spot? Henderson is always willing. All the time exuding the air of a man who would let you have a go instead if you asked him nicely. Even those who still had doubts about some of his qualities recognised that the team was much better with him in it than not.

I'm not going to pretend that his sending-off meant celebrations were somewhat tainted. I was just delighted to have won a top of the table clash and anyone who says differently wasn't doing it properly. Steven Gerrard certainly didn't call a huddle after the game to ask who was going to do all of Henderson's running. I think it was Tuesday before I started to wonder what the hell we were going to do without him.

He had somehow become irreplaceable, in a team where very few other players were, even those with more talent. You could bring Lucas in if Gerrard was out, change the shape if one of Suárez or Sturridge was missing and replace a centre half at the drop of a hat. You might not be quite as strong, but you'd be confident they would work it out. But any system we played seemed to necessitate Henderson being Henderson. The boy with his finger in the dyke, making everything OK.

Let's be clear, though, it was his fault he got sent off. Plenty of the blame was put onto Victor Moses afterwards, and while I can see the temptation to shift the fault from the lad who everyone likes to the lad who was on loan and didn't seem to care, it doesn't really wash. Victor Moses might have managed to turn a promising break into a loose ball with a touch so heavy a postman would have called his union in, but the ricochet was still controllable for Henderson, and even when he didn't manage it, it wasn't necessary to lunge in and win it back with so little left on the clock.

I understand why he did it. It was a tired touch and a tired tackle by a man who had given everything all game, given everything all season, and just wanted to help see us over the line. I just wished he'd have wellied it to the back of the Main Stand as soon as it came to him. But I suppose that's not really his style. Instead we'd be without him for the next three games.

Here's to you, Jordan Henderson. Liverpool will miss you more than we would know.

John Gibbons

NORWICH CITY 2 LIVERPOOL 3

20 April 2014
Goals: Hooper 54', Snodgrass 77'; Sterling 4', 62', Suárez 11'

NORWICH GET TO BE GOOD TOO

I HAVE MY DOUBTS over who it is best to play towards the end of the season. The decision seems to have been made that you want to play teams with 'nothing to play for'. They'll have just packed in, be on the beach, won't care in the slightest. This never really happens though, especially in the days of five-figure bonuses and agents always on the lookout for a player's next move. What actually often happens is that a team with nothing to play for will relax and enjoy themselves, playing football that their supporters wonder why they never bothered with earlier in the season when it actually mattered.

Conversely, a team 'fighting for their lives' are seen as a nightmare to play once you get to April or May. They'll be battling for everything, desperate not to avoid the drop. But this can bring nerves, and nerves can force mistakes and errors. How does a player react when faced with a 30 per cent pay cut when he's just bought a new house? Fear can do different things to different people. The theory also ignores the fact that they are probably 'fighting for their lives' because they're rubbish. What I would say, though, is that the team with 'nothing to play for' usually gives up when they go 2–0 down, while the team 'fighting for their lives' carries on. This turned out to be a bit of a nuisance when we went to Norwich. Earlier in the season they probably would have approached the game thinking there were other games they were more likely to get points out of, and anything against top of the table Liverpool was a bonus. Two-nil would have been the cue to batten down the hatches and embark on damage limitation. But by this point there weren't enough other games left, so they had to have a go back instead.

Plenty was made of Liverpool showing nerves during the end of the game when facing a barrage of attacks, suggesting they were showing the pressure of a title challenge. But players who are showing pressure don't go 2–0 up after ten minutes. Footballers talk about nerves going away the longer you play, not increasing. What seemed to be happening was a team with both nothing and everything to lose had a really good go at getting something out of the game. And Norwich get to be good too.

The first goal isn't a great one to concede by any stretch of the imagination. Skrtel probably clears it with his head if it's left to him, but he leaves it for Mignolet who comes and then makes a mess of it. I feel for Mignolet, in that supporters have been urging him to dominate his box more, but if you try to do that, especially if you aren't used to playing that way, sometimes things like this will happen. Saying that, it's a poor punch, but we go down the other end and score again anyway.

But much to our annoyance Norwich weren't done, their fans continued to get behind them instead of going home, and they probably had their best period of the match. If they were our team we would be praising them for showing resilience in the face of adversity, for showing fighting spirit and plenty of quality too. Although we might wonder why the players were showing it now and not an hour ago. But the point is, we can easily get into the habit of thinking that all our goals are great attacking and all the ones we concede are bad defending. We never pick apart the other team's marking when we score from a flowing move, just like we rarely praise them when they score against us. But sometimes the opposition just do good things. Why wouldn't they? They are all quite good at football after all.

Norwich's second is a good goal from concerted pressure. We could be a touch higher up the pitch, but they work it well into a dangerous position. Glen Johnson could possibly do more to close his man down, but it's a quality delivery. Jon Flanagan could do slightly better at the back post, but Snodgrass gets up early and attacks it well. The keeper has no chance. It's a good goal.

Sometimes the opposition will score a good goal – you just have to make sure you don't concede too many of them. Liverpool didn't concede another and won the game. Against a team 'fighting for their lives' they saw off the onslaught and secured the three points. Now give me a home game against a team distracted by other competitions any day...

John Gibbons

MELTING DOWN

I HAVE A ROUTINE that I follow on the morning of stupidly early and far away football games: My alarm buzzes at some ungodly hour and I slam the snooze button, then lie in the darkness as still as I possibly can so as not to wake The Kraken sleeping in the dog basket in the kitchen. Once he knows I am awake all bets are off. In this period of ten minutes before my alarm sounds again the same thoughts run through my mind: 'It's too cold … I can't be arsed with today … I wonder who's watching it in town … I could get that back fence painted instead … I'm too old to spend ten hours of today on a minibus pissing in a water bottle … I'm going to text Kev and say I'm sick…' Then the alarm sounds again and I swing my legs out of bed, listen to the dog begin howling and get the day going. Not today though, today is different. Today I wake up ten minutes before my 4 a.m. alarm and see my phone already has numerous messages all conveying similar themes ('COME ON REDMEN!!!!!' 'AAARRRRGH!!!' 'WE GO AGAIN!!!!!!' etc.) – players and managers talk about momentum, but it is equally as important for fans. In years gone by, you would not have been able to give away a ticket for a midday kick-off in deepest, darkest Norfolk on Easter Sunday, but today these are the hottest tickets in town. People are travelling to Norwich away without a ticket – this must be a title-charge season.

Norwich is fucking miles away. Norwich is fucking miles away and also nigh-on impossible to get to. No motorways go there because, with all due respect to Norwich, there is absofuckinglutely nothing to see in Norwich. I can fly to anywhere in Europe bar the furthest reaches of Eastern Russia quicker than I can get to Norwich by road. And the game is kicking off at midday. On Easter Sunday. AMF. AMFF. There is something quite surreal about watching the sunrise as you hurtle down the M6, several bottles of breakfast-beer worse off, and you get the feeling that our end is going to be decidedly wonky.

The game starts as we have become accustomed to, namely us being 2–0 up within ten minutes, that man Raheem again with the opener before supplying a delicious assist for Norwich tormentor-in-chief Luis Suárez. We are five points clear, we're going to win 10–0, it is in our hands, it is our time.

What is clear however, if it is our time, is that we are not going to do it without causing a few heart attacks along the way. Mignolet, so submissive in his own area, is beaten to a cross and Hooper taps in, deficit halved. Our end, which had been experiencing levels of delirium for the previous hour, now had some fingernails to chew. Our nervousness thankfully failed to transmit to the players, and five minutes later Sterling was slaloming his way through the entire Norwich back line, causing havoc and ultimately getting the reward his play warranted, a deflected shot looping over Ruddy. Fingernails still intact, delirium reinstated.

Unsurprisingly, we let Norwich back in, and unsurprisingly the goal came from a cross slung into the box. The next 20 minutes are horrific as the home fans smell blood and sense a comeback. As 3,000 Reds spit out fingernails and try and keep those breakfast beers from escaping, Sakho and Skrtel earn their corn by defending wave after wave of Norwich attack, and when they eventually do breach us Mignolet is there with an impressive stop from the lesser-spotted Van Wolfswinkel.

One thing that has made this season so exciting is the newness of it all – being in the title race proper is a novelty for this generation of fans and it has been fantastic going to games that actually matter this far into the season. This novelty, however, can also be our undoing, as our naivety in these situations causes tension to tumble down from the stands – a fan base with a couple of recent league titles under their belt wouldn't subject their team to this. Manchester United fans, and also I assume us in the 70s and 80s, treated these games with a laissez-faire, cocksure attitude that more often than not transmitted to the players on the pitch as they continued their procession to another league title. Not us today, though – as we watch the clock going backwards our end is not singing anymore, all guttural howls and primal screams in lieu of 'Poor Scouser Tommy' and 'We're Gonna Win the League'.

There is a man in front of me and every time Norwich lump another cross into the box I get the impression that his head is going to explode like that scene in Scanners. We are not being cool. We are not being Fonzie. When, approximately two hours later, the ref brings the game to a halt there is an outpouring of emotion and relief, which quickly manifests itself as defiance. We literally shall not be moved as we stay behind to serenade an empty Carrow Road. Again this magnificent team has put us through the wringer, and again we are leaving with three points.

Three points. Three games to glory.

I fucking love these away days.

Ben McCausland

BAYERN MUNICH 1 LIVERPOOL 2
22 APRIL 2015

I SAY WORDS SIMILAR TO THIS a lot at the minute: *'There is no footballer in the world Liverpool can plausibly buy that I'd rather see at the apex of the midfield diamond when we cut a swathe through Europe next season than Raheem Sterling.'*

That sentence, which is already beginning to bore me, would have seemed utterly outrageous six months ago. Not only am I starting Raheem Sterling but he's in the most important position in that shape.

He murdered Norwich. He marmalised them. The thunderbolt that opened the scoring was so sweetly struck and indicative of serious confidence. His lovely rolled ball across the box for Suárez's goal showed his weight of pass is sublime. And when he ran at the Norwich defence for the third the panic was palpable, acrid in Norwich mouths. You pitied them. They'd turned up worried sick about the Uruguayan international who averages a hat-trick a game against them and now there was this bloke. He can go either side. You can't knock him off it. He's quicker than you are. He can finish. He can pass. You name it, he can do it. He's 19 and he's so, so exciting.

But in three months he has redefined what I expect from that position at the apex of midfield. He makes Juan Mata look like yesterday's man. Juan, I can thread a pass as well as you can. But I can carry it quicker, beat more men and I win my battles all over the pitch. I'm probably a better cook too. David Silva had best look over his shoulder. Sterling reminds me of Laudrup, of Kaka. Of players able to carry the ball and accelerate with devastating pace in tight areas who also know how to release. Will he achieve what they did? That is now mostly down to him. But yes.

He's actually helped me redefine what I want from midfielders full stop. Much of Liverpool's success in the second half of the season has stemmed from the fact they play three or four midfielders who can all beat at least one man. Gerrard can. Henderson can. Allen can beat two. Coutinho can beat two or three. Sterling can beat three or four. These footballers can pick the ball up anywhere on the pitch and on their own open the entire game up. They can dovetail, ping their passes and do the same. Suddenly Coutinho has beaten two opposition midfielders. He has the ball at his feet, he's 60 yards from goal but all he can see is green. He has green, four opposition defenders and their holding midfielder backpedalling in panic, Suárez, Sturridge and Sterling in his sights. He's 60 yards from goal and your heart is in your mouth because *right now* you know this is a brilliant goalscoring opportunity.

Sterling epitomises all this. He wins the ball back and he is constantly moving into space when we have it. He has the tactical ability to play behind two strikers along with the blistering acceleration to play wide. He never stops working, never stops learning. If I turned up to Anfield and he was playing holding midfield, I'd think, 'Oh yeah, this could be interesting.' He's probably the best right back at the club. He's very much the player who epitomises everything Brendan Rodgers wants. He is Brendan Rodgers's Trickiest Red and on this 11-game run he has definitely been Liverpool's best attacking performer and quite possibly Liverpool's best player full stop.

So Norwich City shouldn't feel bad. Because he made a show of Manchester United in their ground. Experienced grock centre midfielders bouncing off him. United shouldn't feel bad though. Because he sent Manchester City players everywhere for his goal and made Yaya Touré's injury a blessing in disguise as it allowed them to sit Garcia on him. Manchester City shouldn't feel bad though. Because he tore strips out of Arsenal, winning it off them with ease and running directly at them. Arsenal shouldn't feel bad though. Because he embarrassed Tottenham Hotspur all over the park.

Over the course of these 11 games Raheem Sterling has had a look at the best this country has to offer and embarrassed them time and again. This isn't long-range efforts which go in, terrific as they are, this is constant, perpetual impact upon football matches in all parts of the pitch. Against Norwich he even sat in right mid for a while to help shore things up.

As a football supporter I try to live in the moment and enjoy that moment and Sterling has offered a million of them this season. And I also know the enormous margin of error for predictions. Remember, the italicised text at the top of this piece of writing would have seemed outrageous six months ago. Remember, everyone is wrong about everything to do with football. Remember all this when we get to this next bit. Here is the next bit:

In the summer of 2015 Liverpool will be building their next three seasons around this player. And hopefully the three after that.

Raheem Sterling could well be what the next ten years of watching Liverpool look like. And nothing is more exciting than that.

Neil Atkinson

LIVERPOOL 0 CHELSEA 2

27 April 2014
Goals: Demba Ba 45', Willian 90'

MOURINHO: A MATCH REVIEW

IT'S HEARTBREAKING, IT REALLY IS. Liverpool pushed all they had but sometimes you can be shut down and stopped. Football is about choices, a series of choices, made by footballers and by football managers. Football isn't moral. We get far too hung up on that. Liverpool have far more often than not made the right choice this campaign. They've made the right overarching choice. To score goals. Today they were shut down by an outfit that has made the choice that that is their thing. It worked today, it could elicit a European Cup, but they are still most likely to finish third.

This game should have been moved to Saturday. José Mourinho was right about that. It should have been moved to give Chelsea the best possible chance across these three games. Next season, when we are in the European Cup semi-final, we're all going to be furious when the Premier League don't move one of our games in order to give us the best possible chance to progress.

He's also right about the fact that Chelsea haven't been given enough credit for their performances in European competition over the last ten years. Forgetting coefficients (only because they are dull, not because they aren't important), Chelsea have been brilliant in Europe at a time when we are saturated with Europe. When Celtic won Britain's first European Cup, United won England's and when

Liverpool dominated Europe, Europe had mystique. You couldn't watch everything, you couldn't see everyone. Chelsea haven't dominated but have a terrific record over the last ten years when Britain and England have a smorgasbord of Europe proffered them and often turn their noses up. (The same thing happens with the commentators, by the way. You are sick of Tyldesley not because he isn't a good commentator; he is. It's because he's rammed down your throat weekly, locked in a past where everyone wants the English team to do well. There is no other way to commentate on those games.) There's less mystique, less romance, just tons and tons of Gazprom for you to share with your mates. Rub Gazprom on your chest. It'll get you through the winter. Who gives a shit about Chelsea?

Yet Chelsea, specifically under Mourinho, appear to have managed to do what Arsenal, City, Everton and Spurs haven't over the last 15, 20 years – create a winning mentality around a football club that sustains – see Di Matteo's European Cup win. All the above bottle that somewhere along the way. Arguably only Liverpool and Manchester United have managed that in the modern (post-Shankly/Busby) era, which is why we've actually handled this whole 'winning the league thing' pretty well even though we feel like our hearts are about to burst. It's why United will come again, why the last 24 years for us haven't been lean compared to almost everyone else, despite the lack of the title.

The problem Mourinho has is that if you complain about everything then people stop listening. Him again, with the face on. Take Garcia's goal (not a ghost goal, a goal, it says so in the record books) against them in that semi. The European Cup semi, not the FA Cup semi. Take that goal. It would have been a penalty and sending-off, instead his side which finished more than 30 points ahead of Liverpool failed to equalise. Not win. Equalise.

Complaining about not having good enough centre forwards, about refereeing conspiracies and so on and so forth. Adopting a 'no one likes us/me and we/I don't care' mentality has its plusses. But what about when you need/want people to care?

José Mourinho. The Whopper Who Cried Wolf. The massive, massive whopper who cried, 'Wolves, shitloads of wolves. Alien wolves. Wolves with antlers and glowing in the dark and nuclear teeth and three dicks and a comprehensive knowledge of Bertrand Russell's work and claws the size of radiators.' No, José. It's one wolf. And you are a really good football manager so do us a favour and put a sock in it and get on with that, will you.

All in, some things have fallen Liverpool's way this campaign. We got, with the exception of that horror show around Christmas, the fixtures we needed.

Straightforward homes in the first half of the season – Norwich City, West Ham United, Manchester United – and tougher home fixtures in the run-in. But things falling your way still need to be taken advantage of.

Here is a list of taking advantage of things:

Everton 4–0
Arsenal 5–1
Tottenham Hotspur 4–0
Manchester City 3–2

That's taking advantage of things with aplomb. Next season, we could probably do with those fixtures the other way round. But you get what you are given and you make the best of it. So we've had injuries, suspensions and so on and so forth like everyone. We were top before we played City and Chelsea away, we're the best side since playing City and Chelsea away. That's what we've done. We've addressed 36 hurdles and nothing has hurt like this. Nothing has been more heartbreaking than this result.

This football manager of ours wanted to add 20 goals this season. He didn't get a player to help with that. He got what he was given. And he made the best of it. He's worked with what he had – no public tantrums, wolf-whopper – and added more than 20 goals. He's accelerated past his own KPI – get on me, I'll be getting invited round the stats lads' houses for tea – and Liverpool have accelerated up the table. What I believe he noticed is that the side that scores the most goals has finished first or second in every season since Arsenal won the league and the Houllier/Thompson side finished second. Manchester United outscored both and came third.

This team now finishes first or second. This team still finishes first.

Brendan Rodgers got his side playing the fearless football that sees the ball go into the back of the net with astounding regularity. When we were fretting in the summer about becoming more solid, he looked at what he had and he made a choice. He made a pragmatic choice. Pragmatism isn't defensive football, too often it is used as a synonym of that. You will hear loads about pragmatism in the light of this Chelsea win. Pragmatism is deciding what is most likely to get you success. Arguably Mourinho, locked in a mire about centre forward options, has been the more idealistic, the more dogmatic manager this campaign. Today that dogma paid off in spades. It isn't that they aren't good at this. They are the best. It is, though, the value of what they are the best of. Chelsea in Mourinho's first spell were solid but they had goals in spades. They were top scorers. They finished first or second.

Chelsea were excellent today at stopping the Reds. Liverpool got anxious, fell behind. I'm heartbroken for the captain but the response of the ground was sublime.

Too many were looking to force the issue, second half. Too many looking to go alone. In a curate's egg of a cameo Aspas showed the value of collective guile. He also showed why he doesn't get on.

The most interesting chant was the one that closed the game from the Chelsea contingent. They belted it out. Now you are going to believe us. We're going to win the league. They have two points fewer than Liverpool. They are reliant on Manchester City and Liverpool dropping more points. They belted it out. They are still most likely to finish third.

That's football. That's belief. Reality is that they are most likely to finish third.

It's heartbreaking. The opening goal especially. But it isn't belief-breaking. Not from where I sit.

It is easy to sing that we are going to win the league when we win eleven consecutive games. I'll belt it out tonight. I believe it. It is here and it is now and I believe Liverpool will win the league. No backward steps. Let me ask you a question – now are YOU, YOU going to believe us?

Neil Atkinson

THE CITY

I WASN'T MEANT TO GO TO THE CHELSEA GAME. I hadn't got a ticket for that one back in November and I was very annoyed because we were going to beat them.

Of course we were going to beat them. So confident was I that we were going to beat them I put a red dress on, like a knobhead. I was going to watch it in the pub, but a spare materialised at the last minute, so me and my stupid clothes went, delighted, to Anfield. It was nice and sunny. Everyone was chipper. A bit of nerves, yes. But everyone was excited, everyone was very much alive. We'd all bought into it ages ago, the winning the league stuff. It was going to happen. We were all fully prepared for this. Energised. Ruthless.

I went in early. The Kop had already been full and going off for ages. If it had been possible it probably would have been full and going off all night, to be honest. Full of Reds trying to get their voices to carry to Formby Hall. Full of Reds absolutely made up to be alive. It was just waiting for everyone else to catch up.

There was a couple in front of me who hadn't been to Anfield before. They asked me to take their picture with the Kop in the background. They looked a bit scared. Good.

I think this full-blown mania had taken hold after Spurs. I wasn't there, but I heard about the roar on the final whistle. I heard about that roar from so many people. It sounded great.

But I went with my grandad to City the week after. My grandad, who stood on the Kop for every single game through the Shankly era. My grandad, who turned 80 this year, who I so badly wanted us to win for, said he'd not seen the ground quite like that since those days. I was made up I got to watch us continue what was very much our title procession with him.

So how could we not batter these today, after that? Unthinkable. But when we kicked off, I still felt like I was on a flight. I hate flying and I spend the entire time cold and clammy, with eyes like saucers, thinking I'm going to crash and die. But that wasn't going to happen to Brendan Rodgers' Liverpool, because we were on our way to glory and that.

And then Steven Gerrard slipped and it was half-time. Shit, everyone said. Shit. But it's OK. As long as our heads don't go now, it's OK. We'll come back from this. The Tricky Reds are coming back out and we're going to fly out of the traps again. That's what we're used to, that's how we've got here. I'd made a guess at a 2–1 win. So we were on course for that. It was fine.

Time ticked on and the collective consensus shifted. We'd have settled for a draw, just this once, just because we can afford it. Come on, Reds. This does not fucking slip now.

But before we knew it, Willian was away, and it was over. It was only in the dying seconds of injury time that I was willing to acknowledge we might have to let it go, and I don't think I was alone. But nobody was letting it go. Even on the final whistle, there was no indication that anyone was about to even consider it.

Back in town, we sat round a bit. Watched City not lose to Crystal Palace, the bastards. I said it was like being at a wake. Toyed with going home for a cup of tea and a cuddle with a cat. But then we talked ourselves round. Picked ourselves up. We were still top of the league. TOP OF THE LEAGUE.

What do you do when you're top of the league? You go to the Saddle and do karaoke and get bollocked for getting on John Gibbons' shoulders, that's what. And that's where it was confirmed that no one was letting this go for anything. Never before have I seen or been part of a group of people so joyous in defeat. But the defeat aspect was irrelevant. It wasn't about that. It was about what this season, this mad emotional roller coaster, had done for the city and for all of us.

On that evening, in that moment, we were still very much in it. We were still going to win the league. But even if, by some ridiculous turn of events, we didn't – would anyone have swapped this? Would anyone have handed back this atmosphere of pure joy, this collective happiness at being alive, just to save us from the possible pain that could potentially follow it? No, they fucking wouldn't. And if they would, then I don't want to be their friend.

Because that day and that night are what it's all about. It's why football exists. Fans had had such a fantastic time in those last weeks and months, they were not willing to let it go. And there was no reason to. Because look at us. Look at where we were. Look at what we've become. Look at what we could be.

This isn't it. I would say that I'll count 2014 among one of the best years of my life, because I can't think of a time when I've had this much fun with so many people I love. But I don't want to say that, because I want to believe this can carry on. I want to believe we can top even this.

Thinking about it afterwards, it struck me that the speed at which most people were able to dust themselves off after the Chelsea blow was astonishing, and the rate at which infectious enthusiasm has spread among everyone during the tail-end of this season overwhelming, like nothing I have ever seen before. Because it's clear none of us – not the manager, not the players, not the fans – want this to be a one-off. We want Liverpool to be all about this.

And so we go again. Next season. I want us to pick up where we left off. And we ended 2013/14 having had the best time, the most fun any of us had ever had. Because Liverpool is alive. Liverpool is off its head. Liverpool has got belief. Liverpool is dangerous, it's coming to batter the lot of you and it's going to have a great time doing it.

So let's hold on to that.

This does not fucking slip now.

Kate Forrester

THE SADDLE

SOMETIMES A CHAIN OF EVENTS leads you unknowingly into something wonderful. This was the product of an improbable number of Sunday fixtures, a great pub next door and a group of friends old and new determined to enjoy the life out of a wonderful season and everything it entailed.

A few people I know started watching Liverpool games in the Lady of Mann on Dale Street when they didn't have a ticket. For home games those of us who did would join them after. Gradually a few became more and more. It's a great place to watch the game in a city centre with surprisingly few good options. The beer is excellent, there are loads of screens and you can usually get a seat. In fact I'm not sure why I'm telling everyone about it, but anyway. Don't wreck it, will you.

Next door to that is the Saddle, an establishment a bit less loved but charming all the same. I assume someone suggested going in there after one of the wins, as we always won by that point, and properly discovered the place that became home after all our games. Jan Molby apparently once said the best thing about Liverpool is that you can go out on a Sunday night and no one is thinking about Monday. No one is thinking about Monday in the Saddle on a Sunday night.

Sunday night in the Saddle is karaoke hosted by the magnificent Candi. That is until a certain point of the night when she plays 'I Am Changing' by Jennifer Hudson over the speakers, disappears and comes back as a fella and we now know the night is beginning to draw to a close. But before that there is plenty of fun to be had, and Candi has all the hits, anything the room could want to sing.

People take turns in picking songs, but the karaoke is essentially a group activity. Singing on your own is a bad sign – you've not hit the mark with your selection. If you get it right, and most people have the canny ability of doing so to levels which stress me out, then you are essentially leading the room in a mass sing-song. Arms stretched, heads up, belt it out.

Candi says no football songs, but everything seems to be about football. Or maybe everything in the world just seems connected with football when it's all you can think of. But all the lyrics seemed to be about the title race to me.

> 'Money talks, but it don't sing and dance, and it don't walk'
> 'Yeah, set it up again, set it up again, set it up again, set it up again'
> 'I'm on my way, from misery to happiness today. I'm on my way, to what I want from this world'
> 'There's no life on earth, no other could see me through, you win

again. Some never try but if anybody can, we can, and I'll be
following you'
'Promises, promises turn to dust....'

I didn't want to go after Chelsea. We came back into town after the game and recorded a podcast and I felt deflated and done in, and I was thinking about Monday morning (sorry, Jan). Neil was adamant though: 'It's easy going out after wins,' he said. 'First defeat and everyone goes home? I'm not having that.' I considered myself told and we went the Saddle.

It was booming, of course, it was booming and arms were outstretched and everyone was funny and everyone was pretty and we made it boom even more, the centre of the city. We ended up with about 30 of ours in there and it was also full of couples who go to karaoke bars and sing at the screens instead of talking to each other. Full of groups of women who had come on shopping trips and forgot to go home. Full of lads not thinking about Monday. Full of my mates arguing over what to sing but every single one of them a group sing-along at the top of everyone's voices. I turn around and I see my friends all hanging off each other, punching the air. There were scenes. Endless scenes.

They aren't doing this in Manchester. They just aren't. This makes me happy and sad in equal measure.

It might not be the same next year but then what could be the same next year? Candi might have been poached by a cruise liner. They might realise £3.50 for a treble spirit and mixer isn't a sustainable business model. Enough of my friends might decide they should probably try and do a bit on Mondays in work after all and go home. We might even have some games on a Saturday, who knows. But the Saddle will always be connected with 2013/14 for a few of us. We just need to get Stevie down there next year. They've got all the Phil Collins you want, lad.

John Gibbons

CRYSTAL PALACE 3 LIVERPOOL 3

5 May 2014
Goals: Delaney 79', Gayle 81', 88'; Allen 18', Delaney (o.g.) 53', Suárez 55'

THE NOISE OF SELHURST PARK

MORE AND MORE PEOPLE IN THE UK have started travelling to Europe to go and watch games of football. By that I don't mean watching their teams play in Europe, I mean domestic European football, German League, Spanish League, that sort of thing. There is a whole host of reasons they do this, in fact I have done it myself. I think partly it's just because it's always nice to get out the house, but fans also go searching for a different type of football. One where the fans have a greater sense of belonging with the club, where they are seen less as customers and more as part of the family. All the things English clubs seem to play lip service to but ultimately fall down on.

But the funny thing is, while we are unlikely to see Premier League clubs becoming supporter-owned any time soon, or a return to terraces, or anything mad like being able to have a beer while you watch the game, there are other things we praise that would be easier to implement over here. The main thing is the atmosphere: everyone knows it is better in Germany, and everyone seems to complain about it, but not many seem to want to do anything significant about it. Surely if enough people genuinely want to see an improvement, then it should happen?

There are some reasons why it's tricky, of course. All-seated stadiums generally mean friends are dotted in different parts of the ground. There is also an issue at Liverpool in particular where younger fans, who historically create the atmosphere, are unable to get tickets regularly. Also at some clubs in Europe there are fans that don't even watch the game, but turn facing the supporters, almost conducting the choir. This is all well and good when you are paying £15 a ticket, but less likely to happen when someone is paying £50. Several clubs and fan groups have tried initiatives like 'singing sections', but with only limited success.

One place that it has happened almost out of nowhere is Crystal Palace. They have an 'ultras' section behind the goal to the left which is visually and acoustically brilliant. I think there are a few reasons it has worked. Going down has probably made it easier for like-minded people to get tickets together. But crucially they don't care about how 'cool' something is, so often a barrier among supporters in this country. They don't seem to care who they might have copied and how choreographed some of what they do might be. The only thing that matters is the result.

And the result is a sight and sound to behold, like nothing I have experienced in this country before. I don't know how they are not top of the league playing in front of that every week. What is great about it was the Liverpool fans on that night responded, never wanting to be shown up, creating one of the best away atmospheres of the season as well. For a while the ground was so noisy it's a wonder a football match managed to break out at all. I think I'd have just stood and watched the crowd.

I wondered what on earth would shut them up for a while. It turns out it was going 3–0 up. This was what was most frustrating about their first goal. It got everyone going again, and from then on it was much tougher for us and we weren't able to hold on. The final whistle went and the whole ground erupted in noise. They weren't shy about rubbing in too, the cheeky so-and-so's. I was too numb by that point to say anything back.

So what can we, as Liverpool fans, learn from Palace? Well, the first thing would be to accept that we can learn from others and not just put our heads in the sand and claim to be the best at everything all the time. The main thing I took from it is that they don't seem to carry any 'passengers' in that section. Don't come in to watch, you are either in or you are out. The Kop is a much bigger stand, of course, so harder to get everyone on the same page, but what annoys me are people choosing to sit there because they want to be on the Kop, without accepting any of the responsibility that comes with it. I'm not sure how you enforce it, but there should be a recognition that the Kop is there to start songs and create the atmosphere and if you choose to buy a ticket in the stand you need to get involved. If you'd rather moan and tut instead, the Main Stand isn't too far away.

It must be said that the atmosphere at home games has been much better this season, partly due to groups like Spion Kop 1906 who have added more colour, organised coach meets and encouraged people to get in earlier. But this needs to be continued even if things aren't as positive on the pitch and the feel-good factor begins to wane. Looking at what other clubs are doing and adapting it to suit our identity and culture could be the way forward, even if some don't want to admit it.

John Gibbons

VIVA, VIVA, A HOPELESS ROMANCE? MATCH REVIEW
WORSE THAN A DEFEAT. LUIS IN TEARS.

Come here, Luis. Talk to me. Listen to me. Come here. Let me tell you.

Worse than a defeat. These Red bastards. These beautiful, magnificent, crazed Red bastards.

But.

Blaming the centre halves is unnecessary. A deflection. A break. And then Skrtel pushes out because no one is holding mid. Why is no one holding mid at 2–3 when they've sat a massive lad in there?

Martin Skrtel was brilliant tonight.

But.

For their second, we should have thrown a foul out somewhere. Fucking jump on his back, Coutinho. Jump on his fucking back.

But.

We should have been 6–0 up on 55. Slaughtering the centre halves when the game shouldn't have just been put to bed, but put in the ground. Reduced to a goal-difference chase.

But.

No one has let anyone down. If anyone has let anyone down, no one has let anyone down. And no one has let anyone down. So how can anyone have let anyone down? See? I won't have a word said against anybody.

Look at those Reds. The Trickiest Reds you've seen. I won't have a word said against any of those mad, glorious bastards. This is the first time since Liverpool last won the league they go into the last day of the season with the league either won or able to be won.

Bleating about the manner of the play that brought Liverpool here is:

a) Wrong

b) Plain fucking inaccurate in this instance.

It was, till 79, a faultless second half. Johnson, Allen and Sturridge in the second 45 were terrific. The business.

If there's a criticism, a weakness, put a block in when it goes 1–3. It looked like the manager was trying to make them do it. The lads are there to do it. The lads to put that block in are there themselves. They can make this decision. They can sit or make others sit. But they are the Trickiest Reds you ever did see.

Such a shame when the performance had been what it was. Such a shame.

But put Luis Suárez in my arms. And I'll say this. At 2–3, we still need a favour from West Ham United – 12–0 wouldn't be enough. At 3–3, we need a slightly bigger favour.

Come here, Luis; 2–3 is closer to 3–3 than it was to 0–6. I promise you that. You went and caught the ball out of the net because you know that, you gorgeous, crazed bastard.

And you were all a wave, an endless wave, because you all know that.

You all know that.

This weekend at Liverpool Sound City the marvellous Married To The Sea sang a song and it made me think of all this. This isn't rare. Everything makes me think of all this. But this song, it goes:

> *Come on, I wanna dance to the music in your head*
> *Viva! Viva!*
> *A hopeless romance.*

The only issue here is we've made the music in City's head easier. Smoother.

However, there's only one romance in these parts. Perhaps hopeless, definitely brilliant. And nothing is easy. Nothing. But is it hopeless? Is it brilliant?

Come here, Luis. It hurts. Christ knows, it hurts. You think it hurts? I was nine when we last won the league. Nine. Walk around the pain. I love how much it hurts him. I love he doesn't have to. Come here, Luis.

The quantitative difference is, in real terms, this – a draw vs a defeat for City. It is minute; 2–3 vs 3–3. Minute.

This is a brilliant romance. I've seen brilliant romances. At the cinema. Some end up with the woman getting on the plane and you ending up with Claude Rains. Some end up with a Jim Carrey shrug and an acceptance of brilliant defeat.

And in some, you get the girl. You kiss her.

You kiss her.

At Sound City I told the people I left with these words:

'We meet again as Champions. We meet again as Champions.'

A kiss. A cuddle.

We meet again as Champions.

Come here, you. Come here, Luis. We meet again as Champions. Don't we?

Come and dance to the music in my head.

Viva! Viva!

Neil Atkinson

GOALS GOALS GOALS

Neil's Note – This piece comes in two parts. Liverpool, as I'm sure you remember, went into the game against Crystal Palace two points behind Manchester City with two games left to play. Manchester City also had two games left to play, against Aston Villa and West Ham United. But they had a significant advantage on goal difference. The weekend just gone they'd won at Goodison Park in a game which brought out the worst of everyone in Liverpool after a season which had to date brought out the best. It was a shame. It was a headache. It had been exhausting worrying about what other sides would do. It had been exhausting worrying about what Everton would do.

Martin wrote a piece prior to the game which we've reproduced below and he has written a coda to it which follows.

Before that, I want to say, I've never known anything like the emotional and physical carnage that greeted Luis Suárez getting the ball out of the net at 0–3. The howling. The screaming. I think of it now, days after the season has finished, and I start to well up yet again. The sheer brio of such a move defines this team and makes me inordinately proud. Liverpool didn't win the league. They didn't even win this game. But all season they told us that anything was possible. Anything at all. And that one moment when Suárez took the ball from the net, the reality Liverpool had realigned throughout the season was confirmed. I felt on fire. Thousands and thousands of people felt on fire. I've seen Liverpool score goals which have elicited trophies all my life – how lucky am I? I have never felt as on fire as I did at that moment. I've never glowed as Red.

Keep that feeling. Recall it. And next season, reality realigned, we come back together, violently ablaze.

And so, by Martin Fitzgerald, some words about goals written before Liverpool played Crystal Palace.

I'M SO BORED OF OTHER FOOTBALL TEAMS.

You wouldn't believe how bored I am, watching them, trying to work out what they're up to. What their game is. How what they will do will impact on us.

I'm so bored of other managers. I'm fed up trying to work out their motivations, what they're up to, how what goes on in their head affects us.

The season is over next week. I'm not spending any more time on them, they can do what they want. All my efforts now go into Liverpool. I'm not bored of Liverpool. How could you be bored of Liverpool?

This is in our hands, we need to take control of the situation. That's what we've been doing all season. We need to do the other thing we have been doing all season. Score. Score. Score. Score. There are 180 minutes left. We can score. We can always score.

The time for football as it usually is has gone. Football was what we did when we needed to win games.

We don't have time for football now. We only have time for goals. For all the goals.

Get the players together, sell them an idea. Show them they've scored 96 goals in the league already. Print out the table and fucking show it to them. Sit them down, make them watch every goal.

They love goals. Make them love goals more. Drill goals into them. Sell them an idea.

And then don't let them score in training. Take the goals away, starve them.

Send them out in that tunnel in south-east London absolutely starving for their goals.

And then unleash them.

The first ten minutes of that game needs to be the last ten minutes of the most important game of their lives. That's the idea.

Get an early goal. We've got loads of early goals all year. Brendan, show them the early goals.

And when you get that early goal you do this:

No one celebrates.

The team, the whole team, runs into the back of their net and picks up the ball. They're starving, they need more. They take the ball back to the centre circle and place it on the spot.

No one in the team takes up their positions. The whole team stands on the halfway line waiting for their kick-off.

The halfway line is the deepest we get. Then go again. Score again. Do it all again. Stare them down again. Take them into places football never has to go.

And this is what we do for 180 minutes. Take them into places football never has to go.

No one's ever done this. No one's ever needed to. No one's ever had to relentlessly score goals for three hours.

Suárez, Sturridge, Sterling, Gerrard, Coutinho, Allen, Johnson, Sakho, Skrtel and Flanagan.

Goals, Goals, Goals, Goals, Goals, Goals, Goals, Goals, Goals, Goals.

No one's ever done this. No one's ever needed to. No one's ever been able to. We are.

Fantasy? Deluded?

It's just a matter of how I choose to spend my time.

If you want to spend yours wondering what Fabian Delph or Stewart Downing are capable of then I guarantee you're in a worse place than me.

Sell them an idea.

The idea was sold to them. Or perhaps they came up with it on their own. But Liverpool fell short.

Martin Fitzgerald

GOALS GOALS GOALS: A CODA

TEARS.

So many tears.

Suárez.

Fans.

Friends.

South-east London awash with tears.

Shirts covering faces, hands covering faces. Sky think: Let's zoom in. Let's see these tears. Let everyone watching look at the tears.

Well, you should have zoomed in on me. You missed an opportunity with me. I've never cried so much in my life.

You were probably busy, that's why you missed me.

My tears weren't after the match. My tears weren't during that eleven minutes when Palace scored three goals.

You were probably busy, that's why you missed me.

My tears were after 18 minutes, my tears were after 53 minutes, my tears were after 55 minutes.

You were probably busy, that's why you missed me.

My tears were tears of pride.

These Reds, these Reds who I have fallen in love with, came to win. They came to score. They picked the ball out of the net and they ran back to the halfway line.

They had 26 shots, 26 shots away from home. A shot every three to four minutes. Think about that. It was, collectively, the bravest thing I've ever seen on a football field. On a more clinical evening, it would have been the most wonderful thing I've ever seen. The most wonderful thing we have ever seen.

There would have been plenty more tears.

What happened, happened. It doesn't change what I saw, what I saw this night and what I've seen all season.

How quickly some forget though. Philosophies, personnel – cast asunder. Lots of people saying what should be different before this journey has even finished. The predictors are back. The naysayers. The reasonable ones. Those who find it easier to lecture than to love. Easier to blame than show pride. Back. In their element.

Not for me though. Never name names, never ever name names.

Tears of pride for these lads.

Tears of pride running all down my face.

You were probably busy, that's why you missed me.

Martin Fitzgerald

LIVERPOOL 2 NEWCASTLE UNITED 1

11 May 2014
Goals: Agger 63', Sturridge 65'; Skrtel (o.g.) 20'

THIS WAS THE MOST FUN YOU HAVE EVER HAD IN YOUR WHOLE LIFE

I was sad going up to this game. Sad that it looked unlikely we would win the league. Sad that this wonderful season was nearly over. The players looked sad too, bless them. The Christmas Truce game of 1914 was probably played in higher spirits than this one. Usually it's up to the captain to raise morale in these cases, but he looked more depressed than anyone. He understandably wasn't over what he and his team had been through in the past week. I just hoped he'd have shrugged it off by the middle of August.

It would have been an awful way to end a wonderful season if Liverpool had lost that game. Luckily they got going second half, Coutinho in particular coming off the bench and adding impetus. For the 16th time in the league that season, Liverpool scored their opening goal from a set piece. Much has been made of Liverpool's improvement in this area, including in this book, but the fact that Liverpool opened the scoring in 42 per cent of their league games from free kicks, corners and penalties, despite not scoring at all in three of them, showed how this consistent weapon allowed Liverpool to gain an upper hand in matches and was a massive factor in them being able to play the style of football they wished. People say they worry Liverpool won't be able to carry on the same style of cavalier football in the long run. I worry we won't get the same number of goals from set pieces.

The game fizzled out once Liverpool had scored again and all the Newcastle players decided to get themselves sent off. Then came the lap of honour. Somewhat ironically titled in some seasons gone by, but not this one. For there was loads of honour that day. Honour in how many points they'd collected and the way they had done it. Honour in the remarkable run from New Year onwards that nearly, nearly clinched the title against all the odds. Honour in ignoring all the naysayers and putting up a genuine title challenge when people said it couldn't be done. Honour in giving pride to every Liverpool fan in the world, giving us all a reason to walk a bit cockier round whichever streets we call home. I clapped them all, I even clapped their kids. I felt for the captain, who looked like he would rather have been anywhere else. I hope he's fine come middle of August.

Back into town for drinks and celebrations. At first I was a bit downbeat, mainly I think because I had realised just how long it was until I got to watch this fantastic group of lads play football again. But soon we all got talking about the season, about highs and highers still. Arsenal, Spurs, Man U, Everton, Man City, picking your favourite game is almost impossible. Can I have them all? I'd like them all.

If Liverpool was meant to be mourning no one told anyone. We hosted a party of 800 at the Camp and Furnace in Liverpool, and there wasn't a glum face in there, everyone just wanted to talk about how fantastic the season had been. Round the corner people were setting pyrotechnics off in the Boss Mag party in District, and we were hearing great reports from the Spirit of Shankly party at Circo on the Albert Dock too. Elsewhere plenty more made their own fun. The police had to come and move people from North John Street where an impromptu gathering and sing-song had taken place, stopping any cars from getting through. A fire alarm in a bar on Mathew Street resulted in a street party no one wanted to leave.

I won't say we'll never have it so good again, as I genuinely believe Liverpool are on the verge of something brilliant. It might never be as fun as this season again though. For pure, unexpected, illogical, laughter-inducing brilliance it might not be beat. It was certainly my best season as a Liverpool fan, which seems strange considering I went to Istanbul and all three finals in 2001. But this was something different. Liverpool, back from obscurity and back on our perch in the most spectacular way imaginable.

My favourite Liverpool song starts with 'They all laugh at us, they all mock at us, they all say our days are numbered.' It's a song of pure Scouse defiance. They did, you know. They thought we were finished. They said we couldn't compete with the richer clubs and the ones with the bigger grounds, and we showed them when we get it right we always can and always will. At some point during the season I think we all realised that it wasn't just a mad team, but a really good one. We all realised it wasn't just going to be one crazy season, but the start of another wonderful time to be a Liverpool fan.

I hope they are all OK come August. Fans and players. I hope we're all raring to go again, and I hope whoever is unlucky enough to face us on the first day of the season doesn't know what's hit them. I can't wait. Why do I have to wait? I'm writing this in May, and August seems a life away. Bears have got the right idea, they don't put up with any of life's lulls. I'm off to hibernate. Wake me up on the first day of the season.   **John Gibbons**

THE LONG GOODBYE

I'VE HAD SIX ATTEMPTS AT WRITING THIS. There's the match review I did as the final whistle went, through bleary, teary eyes as the players did the lap of honour. I started that piece, 'Let's go and sing songs with our friends.' There was the rewrite of that I attempted a couple of days later, bold, aggressive, looking forward. God, we were going to be amazing in that rewrite. Talk of trebles and everything. Then there was something gracious about Manchester City but that got metaphorically lashed in the bin. Sell big games out and maybe we'll manage that, Sky Blues.

I tried to do something the day of the FA Cup final. About how this was the year Steve Graves got a lot right and one of those things was it would have been great to win the cup. This said when I was all about Football League championships.

But I remain all about Football League championships. So I didn't want to go down that path. There was a piece singing the unsung, those who don't get names sung or Golden Sambas handed down from the Kop, and that everyone had earned the right for their children to run around, something my curmudgeonly self doesn't normally stand for. Then something on the manager, how he's grown wonderfully enigmatic while remaining generous with himself.

My last attempt before this was the day we were flying out to Benidorm, to John Gibbons' stag weekend, and it occurred to me on the way to Pogues to meet everyone that the first time I spoke to Kev Walsh that I can remember – he of United away in the League Cup in this book, and almost every away this campaign in reality – was in Pogues. It was in late 2010, Hodgson was in charge of the team, the boardroom was all over the place and we were laughing through it. Me and Kev joked about nominating a big team to support. I chose Chelsea. You know the sort of thing: 'Well, I go and watch Liverpool but I always make an effort to see Chelsea when they are on the box.' We were joking about that. Liverpool were terrible. But I didn't feel it had legs enough. And I don't think you want to hear about that sort of thing ending this sort of thing.

However, I've got to finish this today. We need to give it to the publisher. On the plane on the way back from Benidorm I worked it out. I wrote it all out in my head and knew exactly what I wanted to say. But I'd not slept for 28 hours and had been drinking for at least 20 of them so I can't remember how it went. I can remember starting crying when it was all straight in my head and not being able to stop because everything was so beautiful. May I refer you to the start of this paragraph: not slept. Drank.

And so I've been hoping it will just hit me. I'll remember whatever it was on the flight that got me teary or something else will occur and then we'll have it. The big finish. The finale. Now, I have to finish this today. We need to give it to the publisher. I don't want to do that though.

I need this not to stop. That's what I think now when I pace the streets of Liverpool. I need this not to stop. I'm scared stiff of it stopping. I can't go back to that joke about Chelsea. I can't go back to seeing laps of honour as things to dodge. I can't even go back to plucky FA Cup final appearances, however spoiled, however 21st century that may sound. This has become my bread and butter.

I need it not to stop. I haven't written this because I don't want to write it. I don't want to stop it. I don't want to say, look, see, that's 2013/14. That's my final word on it. A final word. What on earth can any decent final word be? How do you end it? Something conclusive and pithy? How can that be? How can it be neat as a box with a lovely bow. It isn't neat. It remains around me, in bits on the floor, molecules in the air; floating, shimmering, sustaining. Just always there.

I remember Henderson leaping like a lamb filled with serotonin when one of his teammates scores a brilliant goal. Cissokho doggedly working his flank. Flanagan flashing his hips past Mata. I remember Joe Allen missing against Everton. Aspas's corners against Chelsea. Enrique and Gerrard conspiring to lose Hernandez at Old Trafford.

I barely remember a thing from the four seasons that precede this one. Barely a thing.

I'm writing this as World Cup fever builds. There are loads of people discussing nostalgia. You remember World Cups as a child and young adult in greater detail and much more fondly than you do as a grown-up. Memory fades and what you saw when you were seven and 17 becomes the answer. What you see at 27, less so. This season has made me feel seven again. Open-mouthed and moist-eyed at the genius and wonder of football and footballers. Did he really? How did? What? Dad, explain this one to me.

This season has made me feel 17 again. A big adventurous swagger of a gang of Reds clambering up hills, full of belief and the passion that comes from discovering passion. There's this thing, right, and it makes me feel like this, right, and the more I feel like this, right, I feel LIKE THIS. YEAH?

YEAH?

I never thought I'd feel like that again about football. About Liverpool.

I need it not to stop. The all-day meet-ups with five different groups. It being on everyone's lips.

The city throbbing, dancing, singing. Monday morning hangovers staved off by the wonder of what went before. Waking up and your face hurting because you were all laughing so much. It can't stop.

I need one more year. One more year of being so pleased to see everybody and yearning for those who aren't there.

I need it not to stop. I need one more year. Just one more year. One year where we go on the mad adventure and we do the crazy things and he gets the ball out the goal against Crystal Palace (HE GOT THE FUCKING BALL) and we win and we score and we win and we score and we win and we score and then they give us that big, ugly shiny thing with the daft crown on top which makes me think of the crucifixion whenever I see it and they give us that and Steven lifts it and maybe another massive one in the German capital and he lifts that as well and we all dance around and we sing songs with our friends every week and it doesn't stop.

It can't stop. It can't be allowed to stop.

Give me all that and then it can stop. Then, after my one more year, I'll take sanity. I'll settle into middle age. I will. I promise. One more year like that and I'll take FOR 76 and AGAINST 28 and its 87 ensuing inevitable points. Sense. Titles and cups and challenges and hard-fought wins and tight defeats. The way things used to be. After my one more year, I'll take it.

Before then, that one more year I need. That one more year where everybody's funny and everybody's pretty, everybody's heading towards the centre of the city. That one more year of red wave after red wave, of outrageous goals and scorelines that terrify the greybearded desperate for a reversion to the mean. That one more year that makes seven-year-olds of us in the ground and 17-year-olds of us before and after. That one more year where everything feels possible because these Reds. Because these Reds.

Just give me that one. That one more year. That one more year of feeling ablaze every weekend, unbridled, unfettered, in love. **Neil Atkinson**

ACKNOWLEDGEMENTS

SO MANY THANK YOUS ARE REQUIRED.

The footballers and the manager and his team first and foremost, we suppose. They were good.

Thanks to our families who have a lot to put up with all in. Parents and siblings who've loved the Reds with us. Look! There's a book! How did that happen? Their faith has been marvellous.

These six contributors who have come with us in putting this together very quickly. Phil Blundell, Martin Fitzgerald, Kate Forrester, Ben McCausland, Mike Nevin and Gareth Roberts. All leaped to the task magnificently and have been quicker and better than us. They've also encouraged us. Thank you so, so much.

A second thank you to Gareth as one of the larger shareholders of *The Anfield Wrap*. Jim Boardman and Ian Maloney too. Without them we wouldn't be here typing these words.

Andy Heaton gets his own paragraph. He deserves nothing less. Here's to you, handsome.

A big thank you to everyone we went the game with this year. It's a massive list as our working definition of 'went the game' is had a drink with at some point on the day of a game. This list of YOU PEOPLE starts in Australia with Timo and Albo from The Tea Street Band and a host of gloriously ACTIVE Australians, especially The General. It ends with 800 people in Camp and Furnace after Newcastle United at home. The space in between encompasses hundreds and loads of those people have been mentioned. Endless boss nights and a few *Boss* Nights. We love all these people profoundly. And of those not explicitly discussed elsewhere in these pages Neil would like to make specific mention of Marjo, and John would like to make specific mention of The Upper Solly Ultras.

We'd like to thank the Red Touch crew, especially Wayne Scholes for his ideas and constant, relentless encouragement. And if this book sells lots of copies we'll owe Jon Accarrino a thank you too. We'll just give him one anyway – we are, as you should know by now, nothing if not optimists. Cheers, Jon.

We'd like to thank our publishers. Is this the done thing? We're doing it. James Corbett has had to do a lot of work very quickly indeed and we know we are difficult to put up with. David Williams for the illustrations too. Don't even know what they look like. They'll be great.

At the time of writing I don't know what, if any, photos have been used. Thanks so much to those who sent them though. They were fantastic to see and go through.

We'd like to thank Spion Kop 1906 for giving us permission to use 'Make Us Dream' as the title.

We'd like to acknowledge the brilliant LFChistory.net website, which assisted in providing the stats at the start of each section.

We'd like to take the time to thank everyone at Radio City and Citytalk but specifically Steve Hothersall, Mick Coyle, David Downie and the marvellous Carl Woodward. They let us play at being serious radio people and only ever make us be or seem better than we are.

We'd like to thank Tony Evans, Iain MacIntosh and Rory Smith, all of whom are mentioned in the text. We'd also like to thank Kevin Sampson for similar reasons – inspirational figures, one way or another, who come and join in with us. Who chooses to be a fellow traveller is one way you know you are going in the right direction. There are many others who fall into this category and many of them take time taking to us in a room. Thank you to everyone who does that.

Third to lastly, Ben Smith's foreword nearly made us cry when we read it. His kind words even more so. He was the first grown-up we showed the rough book to and he loved it. Thanks to him for his time, energy and words.

Second to last, we want to make a fuss of Steve Graves, the sort of fuss he abhors. He gave a load of his time and energy and his guidance and advice was invaluable. He lived it with us. 'Steve Graves does a day'. It should be a banner. Write it on your hand. Tattoo it on your eyelids. There is, you should know, no higher praise. Deepest thanks.

Lastly we'd like to thank from the very bottom of our hearts Braith (Laura Braithwaite) and Brockle (Samantha Brocklehurst). Their support and belief means the world to us and their affection means much more than that. Well in them. We'll also dedicate *all* the words that precede these acknowledgements to them both. Whether they like it or not.

Neil Atkinson & John Gibbons